New Perspectives in British Literature

New Perspectives in British Literature

Volume I

Edited by
Sunita Sinha

Published by
ATLANTIC
PUBLISHERS & DISTRIBUTORS (P) LTD
7/22, Ansari Road, Darya Ganj,
New Delhi-110002
Phones : +91-11-40775252, 23273880, 23275880, 23280451
Fax : +91-11-23285873
Web : www.atlanticbooks.com
E-mail : orders@atlanticbooks.com

Branch Office
5, Nallathambi Street, Wallajah Road,
Chennai-600002
Phones : +91-44-64611085, 32413319
E-mail : chennai@atlanticbooks.com

ISBN 978-81-269-1383-1 (Vol. 1)
ISBN 978-81-269-1385-5 (Set)

Printed in India at Nice Printing Press, A-33/3A, Site-IV, Industrial Area, Sahibabad, Ghaziabad, U.P.

Contents

Preface

Running a remarkably continuous course of development and innovations through the ages, the literature of the English language is undoubtedly one of the finest and richest, incorporating creations of the human mind which are no less than rare gems. *New Perspectives in British Literature* is designed to escort the reader through some six centuries of English literature. It is a compact survey, summing up the substance and quality of the individual achievements that make up our literature. The aim is to leave the reader informed about each writer's main output, sensitive to the special character of his gifts, and aware of his place in the story of our literature as a whole. However, trying to list every important work of British literature seems as unattainable a target as keeping "a catalogued inventory of every grain of sand on the British islands' shores". From early epics about heroes and warriors to the captivating saga of a young wizard intent on defeating evil in the twenty-first century, British literature has a little something for everyone. With broad categories ranging from the romantic to the satirical, styles ranging from the sonnet to the novel to the play, and authors ranging from illiterate storytellers to Nobel Prize winners, British literature remains one of the cornerstones of literature curriculum around the world.

The anthology is designed to rethink many of the assumptions and discursive manoeuvres of British studies and embraces the extraordinary development of British literature over the century. It provides a comprehensive introduction to British literature and covers a wide range of selected authors, drawing together both established and emerging literary voices reflecting the scope of British writing. The articles included in the book display both historical depth and theoretical finesse as they attempt close and lively readings. The volume as a whole offers critical and contextual coverage of the full range of British literature.

The English literature of the Elizabethan and Jacobean Ages is one of the great phenomena of European culture and William Shakespeare, by universal consent, the greatest author of England, if not of the world, occupying chronologically a central position in the Elizabethan drama. Combining the best traits of Elizabethan drama with classical sources and enriching the admixture with his imagination and wit, Shakespeare outdid all the rest. Along with *Hamlet, King Lear, and Macbeth, Othello* is one of Shakespeare's four great tragedies and thus a pillar of what most critics take to be the apex of Shakespeare's dramatic art. Joseph Patrick and Bryan Reynolds in their groundbreaking analysis, "Venetian Ideology or Transversal Power? Iago's Motives and the Means by which Othello Falls" challenge traditional readings of Shakespeare and re-evaluate the critical methodologies that characterize them. The authors demonstrate the value of their "investigative-expansive mode", outlining a "transversal poetics" that points toward a critical future that is more aware of its subjective interconnectedness with the topics and audiences it seeks to engage than is reflected in most Shakespeare criticism and literary-cultural scholarship. In this article, they explore the social and ideological relations between Iago and Othello through the lenses of several different critical approaches, including new historicist and cultural materialist. The paper aims at emancipating "the critical history of Othello from the delimiting analytical parameters that have characterized it, and to show the transversal ways in which Iago paradoxically opposes and reifies Venetian state ideology".

In the Summer 2008 issue of the *University of Toronto Quarterly*, Paul Stevens begins his introductory essay with an epigraph from R.W. Griswold, Milton's first American editor, in 1845: "Milton is more emphatically American than any author who has lived in the United States". Prof. Bruce Boehrer, in his scholarly paper, "Milton in America: The Case of Jackson County, Florida" traces the process of imaginative filiation by which John Milton, Governor of Florida during the American Civil War, came to be regarded as a descendant of John Milton the poet. The Florida Miltons trace a mode of fantasized association with the poet that parallels both Benedict Anderson's understanding of nationalism as an "imagined political community" and Sigmund Freud's notion of individual development as elaborated through the "family romance". As a further irony, Peter Ackroyd's novel *Milton in America* offers a derogatory parallel to the same fantasy of filiation—a parallel that illustrates the pliable nature of literary history when subject to specific literary appropriations.

The Picture of Dorian Gray is considered one of the last works of classic gothic horror fiction with a strong Faustian theme. The book gained "certain notoriety for being 'mawkish and nauseous,' 'unclean,' 'effeminate,' and 'contaminating'". A large portion of the criticism was levelled at Wilde's perceived hedonism, and its distorted views of conventional morality. However, in recent times, the book has been regarded as one of the modern classics of Western literature. Esterino Adami in his explorative paper, "The Victorian and Postmodern Metamorphoses of Dorian Gray: Narrating the Body Other" remarks that *The Picture of Dorian Gray* adheres to the turn-of-the-century style of decadent fiction and its central character still occupies a dark zone of meaning...and evolving into new literary forms through the procedure of modern rewriting".

Candida, a comedy about social and sexual equality in Victorian England, sounds as if it should now be pointless. But in George Bernard Shaw's enlightened hands, it is surprisingly relevant to modern sentiments. For, despite feminism and the intervening sexual revolution, its themes of male/female relationships in friendship, marriage and temptation are timeless. Prof. Chidanand Bhattacharya's competent exploration in his scholarly paper "Shaw's *Candida*: A Double-Entendre" presents Shaw's inimitable wit, his comic spirit, his attack on the diverse sentimental illusions of his age about the male self and about women. The paper also focuses on Bernard Shaw's attitude to James Mavor Morell, "encrypted in ambiguity in terms of a double entendre. This double entendre comes to seize not only Morell but also Eugene and Candida equally with a tongue-in-cheek irreverence".

Blake's poetry, rather than specifically advocating anything, is simply a source of delight. Kenneth Usongo in his analytical paper, "The Country-City Opposition in Blake: A Study of *Songs of Innocence and Experience*" argues that in *Songs of Innocence and Experience* Blake shifts the traditional polarity between the country and the city which is often synonymous with virtue and vice by depicting both milieus as rosy and evil simultaneously. The country and the city appear to be interwoven, sharing somehow similar qualities of goodness and evil.

Baldassare Castiglione's *Book of the Courtier* was popular throughout Western Europe and was used and cited as the quintessential handbook for centuries. A glowing account of Italian chivalry, Castiglione's remembrance of things past in "*The Book of Courtier*" remains a landmark in Renaissance literature and the most definitive account of life among Renaissance nobility. The well researched paper "Baldassare Castiglione's *Book of the Courtier in Renaissance England*" by Carole Rozzonelli presents the book, not just a testimony but rather a treatise on Italian Renaissance.

Englishmen of the 16th century were profoundly interested in the history of their own nation, and this interest was ministered to, by a whole series of writings and compilations. The History plays of Shakespeare form the core of twentieth century Shakespearean studies and are being performed more in recent years than ever before, in Britain, North America and in Europe. Shakespeare's series of historical dramas, based on the English Kings from John to Henry VIII were a tremendous undertaking to dramatise the lives and rule of kings and the changing political events of his time. There is a remarkable unity in them and the ten plays look like one great work of art of which *King John* is the prologue and *Henry VIII* the epilogue. Representing a whole range of human life in its political and social relations these plays deal manifestly with the philosophy of power and politics based upon principles of kingly responsibility and authority and follow the moral-political pattern of usurpation, suffering and expiation. In his brilliant paper "Imagery in Shakespeare's Histories", Dr. Sanjay Kumar Sinha has presented a study of the significant threads and patterns of imagery—the recurrent themes through whose study and correlation—the full meaning of the work as a whole emerges.

In her scholarly paper, "Lord Byron: The Romantic Augustan" Dr. N. Sharada Iyer offers an exhaustive analysis of Byron's poetic excellence and establishes him as "The Romantic Augustan". Born in an age of Romantics, Byron composed poems which showed his sympathy and adoration for the Augustans—Dryden and Pope, much more than for Wordsworth and Coleridge.

A chronicler of contemporary Britain, Margaret Drabble will be for the late 20th century London what Dickens was for Victorian London, what Balzac was for Paris. As a novelist, she has cast her sharp and intellectual eye on life, particularly on women's lives, in seventeen novels from *A Summer Bird Cage* (1963) to the thought-provoking *The Sea Lady* (2007). Drabble's early novels describe the life of young women just out of the university, discovering sex, marriage, maternity and adultery (not necessarily in that order) with a captivating combination of insight and wide-eyed astonishment, whilst during the late 1960s and 1970s, the conflict between motherhood and intellectual challenges is brought into focus. Dr. Arpa Ghosh in her analytical paper, "Response to the Seventies: The Characterization of Rose and Frances, Heroines of Margaret Drabble's Novels *The Needle's Eye* and *The Realms of Gold*" presents Drabble as a subtle delineator of the characters and offers a thoroughgoing exposition of her heroines Rose and Frances. Beckett remains one of the giants of twentieth century literature and drama. He shares with other modernists a reputation for obscurity and difficulty, yet his work permeates our culture in unique ways. Presenting a bleak vision of life, leavened by mordant humour, his work transmits a sense of minimalism and sparseness.

Dr. Anita Myles illuminating paper, "Moral and Religious Gnosis in Plays of Samuel Beckett" brings out Beckett's concern with modern existentialist dilemma and the significance of faith and hope as the only solution for modern man to navigate through the "iron gates of life".

The most conspicuous great representative in English poetry since Chaucer, of the spirit of art for art's sake, John Keats remains one of the supreme masters of poetic expression, expressing the most beautiful, apt, vivid, condensed, and imaginatively suggestive. Keats' "Ode to a Nightingale" springs from a poet's personal life-changing, mind-wrenching experience of a timeless paradise where Keats seems to enjoy OBE by being a part of the nightingale's immortal world. Many facets of an OBE are here: drug-associated sensory deprivation, a flight upwards of a double mind through dark "ways" illuminated by a great light, the moon, a bird's-eye perspective among the tree-tops, a near-death experience, the descent of a double to its abandoned self, and a sense of having had a vivid dream. As Purnendu Chatterjee in his innovative paper, "*Ode to a Nightingale*: Keats' Clairvoyant Journey" explains and explores "an out-of-body experience (henceforth OBE), is an experience that typically involves a sensation of floating outside of one's body and, in some cases, perceiving one's physical body from a place outside one's body".

Stephen Dedalus is James Joyce's literary alter ego, as well as the protagonist and antihero of his first, semi-autobiographical novel of artistic existence *A Portrait of the Artist as a Young Man* and an important character in Joyce's monumental *Ulysses*. In his explorative paper, "Experience, Self-Realisation and Artistic Vision: Stephen Dedalus in Joyce's A Portrait", Dr. Ernest l. Veyu attempts to capture Stephen's experiences and their effect on his art as recorded in *A Portrait of the Artist as a Young Man*.

Shakespeare's Comedies are dominated by a sense of place rather than of time. The Forest of Arden ranks with the wood near Athens and Prospero island as a place set apart. Seen from the court it appears untouched by the discontents of life, a place where they "fleet the time carelessly as they did in the golden world". Dr. Manju Dutta Gupta in her well researched paper, "*As You Like It* in Amazing Location" recreates the amazing ambience of the Forest of Arden and affirms that it serves not only as a backdrop for the characters to act their roles but also as a principal subject.

Religion influenced every aspect of his life, and many considered Hopkins the priest and Hopkins the poet to be one inseparable entity. In some of his later poems, however, a dichotomy seemed to be developing between the two, with his poetry dealing with more earthly subjects than God and religion. "Gerard Manley Hopkins: The Poet and the Priest—A Study of *The Windhover*" by Dr. Nandini Sahu and Mrs. Padmini Sahu is an exhaustive analysis which presents Gerard Manley Hopkins both as a great poet and a Jesuit priest. The paper concludes with the words: "The priest Hopkins is responsible to create a sensitivity in the poet Hopkins to write poetry, nourishing his sensitive poetic imagination".

In his attempt to see the cosmos in organic rather than mechanical terms, D.H. Lawrence developed a "cosmological" myth in which living creatures replace the formulae of physics or mechanics. Philosophizing about it in Fantasia of the Unconscious in a chapter called "Cosmological", he states that "living, incorporate individuals" make up the universe, and the same tendency is evident in a number of his other works. Lawrence even comes to relate this image to the human form—a kind of rose-tree that burgeons with vitality—or else sees humans as the roses that flower on the tree of life. When proposing a cover design for the poetry volume *Birds, Beasts and Flowers*, he sketched an idiosyncratic rose-tree—or at least a tree full of diverse life-forms and crowned with roses and a later art work, *The Escaped Cock* presents a dancing woman as a kind of flowering tree in herself. The blossoming signifies a fullness of experience that rises almost to a level of divinity. "If we look for God", he states in the essay "Democracy", "let us look in the bush where he sings. That is, in living creatures". In her scholarly paper, "D.H. Lawrence: Cosmic Symbolism in

Sons and Lovers", Dr. Vinita Singh offers a competent analysis of cosmic symbolism in Lawrence's *Sons and Lovers* and remarks, "In Lawrence's novels, the symbolic aspect is more significant than the psychological".

Macbeth and *King Lear, Othello* and *Hamlet*, are usually reckoned Shakespeare's four principal tragedies. *King Lear* stands first for the profound intensity of the passion; *Othello* for the progressive interest and powerful alternations of feeling; *Hamlet* for the refined development of thought and sentiment and *Macbeth* for the wildness of the imagination and the rapidity of the action. Arindam Das in his analytical paper, "Macbeth and Lady Macbeth: A Case Study in Management" lays bare the politics of leadership, the intricacies involved in an individual pursuit and the execution of power and authority. The paper offers an able exploration of the theories of Management and Organizational Behaviour through the study of the Shakespeare's *Macbeth*.

As a poet, Coleridge's first great distinction is that he gives wonderfully subtle and appealing expression to the Romantic sense for the strange and the supernatural, and indeed for all that the word 'Romance' connotes in the present times. He accomplishes this result partly through his power of suggesting the real unity of the inner and outer worlds, partly through his skill, resting in a large degree on vivid impressionistic description, in making strange scenes appear actual, in securing from the reader what he himself called "that willing suspension of disbelief which constitutes poetic faith". Coleridge explores dreams and dreaming in his poetry to communicate the power of the imagination, as well as the inaccessible clarity of vision. He was a vivid and prolific dreamer who carefully recorded, analyzed and discussed the distinct features, possible causes and meanings of his dreams. As he himself remarks, "I have long wished to devote an entire work to the subject of dreams visions, ghosts and witchcraft...". True, Coleridge recorded and commented on his dreams throughout his life. Nishi Pulugurtha in her insightful paper, "Dreams, Nightmares and the Ancient Mariner" explores Coleridge's interest in the states of the mind—the dreams and nightmares. An awareness of his own dreams and nightmares and an interest in psychological states of the mind possibly form the core of Coleridge's poetry.

In *Sons and Lovers*, Lawrence expresses the central theme of the novel in two ways. Firstly, through various episodes—what has been referred to as 'narrative logic' of the book and secondly, by involving the use of imagery and symbolism. The use of imagery in a symbolic role often not only supplements the narrative but actually replaces it. Perhaps, the key reason why Lawrence uses symbolism so much to express his ideas is that he needs to relate not only what happens in his story but also how people feel. The symbolic image provides him with a means of doing this that allows the reader to relate the metaphor to reality. In other words, they create a bridge between the world of fiction presented by the novel and the individual world of the reader by providing him with a set of ideas that he or she can relate to. Dr Bristi Basu in her analytical paper, "The House as Sign in *Sons and Lovers*", explores the intricate pattern of images which are enmeshed with the fabric of the text, for instance, the house.

Dr. Reena Mitra in her paper, "*Of Human Bondage*: Fact-Fiction Interface" sees the novel as a work that makes the best of the interaction and reciprocity between the two genres of literature, autobiography and fiction. Autobiography here becomes a mode of literature and lends verisimilitude to the narrative which though drawing profusely from the writer's own experiences in life gains in credulity and vitality as a piece of fictional art. Maugham himself endorses this categorization of the novel in *The Summing Up* where he asserts that *Of Human Bondage* is "not an autobiography, but an autobiographical novel; fact and fiction are inextricably mingled".

When we hear the term "the Bard", our minds spring immediately to the name 'William Shakespeare'. That is because he seems to have been given the title in recognition of his stature as a great poet and the unofficial national poet of England. In her scholarly paper, "Shakespeare: The Bard Par Excellence" Dr. Vandana Datta unravels the poetic warmth in Shakespeare's creations which undeniably contain the most eloquent, evocative, and moving verse ever penned. As she rightly remarks: "He was decidedly first and foremost a poet. Not to talk of his sonnets, his plays—comedies as well as tragedies—are full of the gems of poetry. Since it is beyond the scope of this paper to analyze all of Shakespeare's plays to go into the nuances of his poetic genius, some of them have been selected here for concentrated study."

The use of symbols is one of the most striking features of Blake's poetry. There is hardly any poem written by Blake, which does not possess a symbolic meaning, besides its apparent or surface meaning. A prophetic visionary, Blake used Biblical and other imagery in his work and his poetry represents a personal idiosyncratic actualization of an ancient repertoire of magical symbols and occult visions. If one were to choose a dominant theme for Blake, it might be the imaginative vision that surpasses the common experience. He once said that "all he knew was in the Bible", and so spiritual themes and symbols are often found in his work. Sanghita Sen, in her paper, "William Blake: A Symbolist with a Prophetic Vision", discusses Blake as a master symbolist who devises and uses symbols to uphold his unique prophetic vision through his art with particular reference to his poetry.

The well-researched articles on various aspects of British literature in this book shall prove extremely useful to the students and teachers of English literature and researchers in this field.

I wish to express my gratitude to the contributors in this editorial venture, who enthusiastically contributed to this project and enriched the anthology with their perceptive papers.

I am particularly thankful to Dr. K.R. Gupta, Honorary Advisor, Atlantic Publishers and Distributors (P) Ltd. for the confidence evinced in me and for seeing the book through the press.

Sunita Sinha

1

Venetian Ideology or Transversal Power? Iago's Motives and the Means by which Othello Falls

Joseph Fitzpatrick and *Bryan Reynolds*
(with additional dialogue by Bryan Reynolds & Janna Segal)

This essay presents a new perspective on the means by which Othello falls from his position of high status both within Venetian society and in the eyes of the play's audience. By examining the pertinent critical history of Othello, especially criticism accounting for the effects on Othello of Iago's machinations, this analysis explores the social and ideological relations between Iago and Othello through the lenses of several different critical approaches, including new historicist and cultural materialist. Our aim is to reveal the contradictions and limitations in this critical history that encourage an examination of the play according to a more inclusive approach that we call "transversal theory," which will be explained as the analysis progresses.[1] In doing this, we hope to emancipate the critical history of Othello from the delimiting analytical parameters that have characterized it, and to show the transversal ways in which Iago paradoxically opposes and reifies Venetian state ideology.

Critical Traditions

In order to situate our transversal analysis in terms of the critical discourse on *Othello*, we will begin with G.K. Hunter's

"Othello and Colour Prejudice" for two important reasons: it was groundbreaking in examining how racial issues inform Othello's fall; and it was keenly aware of its own intervention in *Othello* criticism. Hunter shows "how mindlessly and how totally accepted in this period was the image of the black man as the devil" (39).[2] Yet, according to Hunter, Shakespeare's Moor defeats this prejudice of the Elizabethan audience as soon as he appears on stage in Act One, Scene Two: "This is no 'lascivious Moor,' but a great Christian gentleman, against whom Iago's insinuations break like water against granite. Not only is Othello a Christian; moreover, he is the leader of Christendom in the last and highest sense in which Christendom existed as a viable entity, crusading against the 'black pagans'"(45).

Following this passage, we may infer that the audience's acceptance of Othello, if Hunter is correct and Othello was accepted, stemmed less from his redeeming personal traits than from his association with the two dominant sociopolitical institutions of the period: Church ("Christendom") and state (the government and military).[3] Thus, the audience would have largely dismissed the paganism and demonism associated with Othello because of his race once they learned of his conversion to Christianity.[4] And much of the antipathy that the Elizabethans might still have felt toward Othello, not specifically as a black man, but more generally as an obvious non-European, is mediated by the position of authority he has earned in the Venetian military.

It is generally accepted that as the audience's potential prejudices against the black protagonist are reversed in the play's first act, when Othello is identified as worthy by both the Venetian state and by one of Venetian society's prized possessions (Desdemona), a simultaneous reversal in the opposite direction reveals the unexpected vileness of the white, Venetian antagonist.[5] Hunter describes the situation in powerful terms: "We might say that Iago is the white man with the black soul while Othello is the black man with the white soul" (46).[6] Janet Adelman advances this reading, noting, "This trope [of Iago as 'monstrous progenitor' (1.3.401–02)] makes the blackness Iago would attribute to Othello—like his monstrous generativity—something already inside Iago himself, something that he must project out into the world" (130). The "blackness" that is transferred to Iago is accompanied by the designation of "devil." Iago repeatedly refers to himself as the devil, and is joined in doing so by those who recognize his villainy in like terms. Thus a chiasmic double reversal occurs within the first act: the suspicious "outsider" Othello becomes, for the audience especially, a respected member of Venetian society, an "insider," and the outwardly "honest" Iago is unveiled as a villain. The relationship between Othello and Iago is therefore reduced by these critics, to different degrees, to symmetrical antithetism: the semblance of wholeness or totality is constructed methodologically through the binary oppositions (light/dark, white/black, insider/outsider, self/other, good/evil) either cited from or imposed onto the text to give an explanatory coherence to the characters' relationship, and to the play overall. We call this analytical strategy, which is characteristic of most dialectical argumentation, the "dissective-cohesive mode".

As an alternative, transversal theory insists on the "investigative expansive mode" of analysis.[7] Like the dissective-cohesive mode, the investigative-expansive mode requires that the subject matter of interest be divided up and partitioned into variables in accordance with the selected parameters of the investigation. But unlike the dissective cohesive mode, whose goal is to reconstruct the variables into a coherent whole, the investigative-expansive mode examines both the internal connectedness of the variables (among themselves) and the external connectedness of the variables (to other forces, such as the play's critical history) in coordination with a fluid openness to reparameterizing as the analysis progresses—in response to the emergence of unanticipated problems, information, and ideas. Thus, the purpose is not to assemble a fully accounted for whole, but to better our comprehension of the subject matter's changing relationships to its own parts, as well as to the environments of which it is a part. The subject matters of the present analysis are *Othello* and its critical history; the chosen variables include the characters Iago and Othello and various readings of the play, and the greater environment of concern is the hermeneutic space in which the play and its criticism resides, and across which they both will continue to travel.

To review, we have seen that critics who focus on the play's first act reveal the chiasmic double reversal, which is accentuated, as Adelman notes, by the act's concluding soliloquy in which Iago forms his fiendish scheme: "Hell and night," Iago exclaims, "Must bring this monstrous birth to the world's light" (1.3.402). Furthermore, we have shown how critics have found ample fodder in this act for dissective-cohesive formalizing. What happens in the following four acts, however, is an issue of much debate. Hunter and Adelman both claim that "the dark reality originating in Iago's soul spreads across the play, blackening whatever it overcomes and making the deeds of Othello at last fit in with the prejudice that his face at first excited" (Hunter 55).[8] Hunter contrasts this reading with what he calls "a powerful line of criticism on *Othello*, going back at least as far as A.W. Schlegel, that paints the Moor as a savage at heart, one whose veneer of Christianity and civilization cracks as the play proceeds, to reveal and liberate his basic savagery: Othello turns out to be in fact what barbarians *have* to be" (55).[9] This line of criticism might be best represented in the twentieth century by Bloom and Jaffa in *Shakespeare's Politics*: "Shakespeare's Moor... returns at the end to the barbarism that the audience originally expected. The first, primitive prejudice against Othello seems to find justification in the conclusion" (Bloom and Jaffa 43).[10] In terms of the earlier transfer of the role of "devil" from Othello to Iago, the two major critical traditions might be summarized thus: the Schlegel/Bloom and Jaffa line of criticism claims that Othello and Iago were *both* devils from the beginning; just as Iago hides his identity from the other characters in the play, so does Othello hide his own identity from the other characters, the audience, and himself. Hunter's and Adelman's alternative line of criticism considers the original role reversal valid, but has the devil Iago corrupting the virtuous Othello, thereby transforming him into the fiend the Elizabethans assumed him to be.

Alan Sinfield offers what amounts to a revision of Bloom and Jaffa's reading from a critical perspective that is potentially capable of avoiding the racist implications that Bloom and Jaffa see in the play. Sinfield writes, "In the last lines of the play, when he wants to reassert himself, Othello 'recognizes' himself as what Venetian culture has really believed him to be: an ignorant, barbaric outsider—like, he says, the 'base Indian' who threw away a pearl. Virtually, this is what Althusser means by 'interpellation': Venice hails Othello as a barbarian, and he acknowledges that it is he they mean" (31). Sinfield introduces the Althusserian vocabulary of ideology that informs much new historicist and cultural materialist criticism to explain Othello's transformation. Notwithstanding his high position within what Althusser would call the "Repressive State Apparatus" of the military, Othello fails to sufficiently adopt the proper Venetian ideology, falling victim instead to a contrasting "barbarian" ideology that hauntingly informs his characterization and is actualized. This reading is in effect similar to Schlegel's, but without the suggestion that Othello is somehow inherently *defective* in his otherness.[11] Yet Sinfield's approach to this line of criticism leaves us with a number of questions, including: Where and when is Othello indoctrinated with this "barbarian" ideology? Why does he recognize himself as being like the "base Indian" only long after he apparently succumbs to the "barbarian" ideology?

Even though this type of ideological interpretation jibes well with the action of the play,[12] Sinfield does not follow through with this interpretation. Instead, he leaves it stranded just a step away from the old reversion-to-savagery interpretation, separated from Bloom and Jaffa's and Schlegel's readings, one might argue, by a veneer of Althusserian jargon. It seems, though, that Sinfield has keenly pointed to the need for an understanding of how Othello's initial status in Venice and his subsequent actions throughout the play are ideologically formed.

A Transversal Disjunction

At this point, we will turn from considering an ideological reading of *Othello* to discussing these critical limitations. If the negating of one's subjectivity is a path to empowerment—even greatness (as Bradley would have it)—in the world of the play, Desdemona's final self-effacing declaration, "Nobody, I myself" (5.2.125), is a fluke: she dies powerless. If Iago does use empathy as a means of accessing Othello's psychology and thereby manipulating him, as Greenblatt persuasively argues, then Iago cannot possibly be outside of ideology, but rather is moving between ideologies and across their boundaries. It appears, then, that personal empowerment is obtained not through self-negation alone, however provisionally negated, but more effectively through imagining oneself outside of one's self, or through the active acknowledgment that one is not limited to a singular, constant self. In fact, Iago thrives within a conceptual framework of identity multiplicity. He reveals this to Roderigo: "our bodies are gardens, to the which our wills are gardeners, so that if we will plant nettles, or sow lettuce, set hyssop, and weed up thyme...why, the power, and corrigible authority of this, lies in our wills" (1.3.320–26). Iago seizes the "power" and "authority" to create and shape his own identity by placing the burden of its formation entirely upon himself, his "will". As noted previously, the language Iago uses in an earlier conversation with Roderigo anticipates this revelation: "It is as sure as you are Roderigo,/ Were I the Moor, I would not be Iago:/ In following him, I follow but myself" (1.1.56–58). "Being Iago" denotes an ability to play many different roles, rather than signifying a static identity. His statement that following Othello is equivalent to following his own desires suggests a connection and identification with Othello that would make empathy, and therefore manipulation, possible.

Put in transversal terms, empathy enables people to venture beyond their own conceptual and emotional boundaries, to think and feel as others do or might, and thus expand or transcend their own "subjective territories". We call this process "transversal movement." "Subjective territory," as

Bryan Reynolds explains, "refers to the scope of the conceptual and emotional experience of those *subjectified* by the state machinery or any hegemonic society" (146). Specifically, "subjective territory is delineated by conceptual and emotional boundaries that are normally defined by the prevailing science, morality, and ideology.... It is the existential and experiential realm in and from which a given subject of a given hierarchical society perceives and relates to the universe" (146–47). Transversal movements occur when one entertains alternative perspectives and breaches the parameters of their subjectification.

Such movements require engagement with, and, at the very least, a passing through "transversal territory", which is "the non-subjectified region of one's conceptual territory [of one's imaginative range]" (149). Thus, transversal territory is entered through the transgression of the conceptual and emotional boundaries of subjective territory.

The ease with which Iago accesses transversal territory enables him to enter freely into the subjective territories of others where he can readily comprehend their sensibilities and idiosyncrasies. He then uses this information to force them into transversal movements across the emotional and conceptual spaces of alternative ideologies. Transversal theory, however, accepts the premise that humans exist in, and are influenced by, ideology inasmuch as they are social beings. Hence, Iago can never be totally outside of ideology unless he becomes psychotic, or his consciousness is somehow shattered. Moreover, because humans are social, the "scientific objectivity" suggested by Althusser is only possible insofar as humans can experience unmediated access to social events, which is impossible.

Moving Beyond the Dissective-cohesive Mode

We have demonstrated that Othello's acceptance into Venetian society depends on his Christianity.[13] Yet, as the Schlegel line of criticism shows, Othello's jealous actions throughout the later portions of the play are antithetical to both the Christian ideology and the broader social norms enforced by the overarching Venetian state ideology. They reflect his movement, propelled by Iago, beyond the officially sanctioned parameters for living and operating in the world. Iago's subversion of Othello's Christianity is powerfully manifested in Othello's final acts. Indeed, murdering Desdemona, revenging himself upon Iago, and then taking his own life flout the most fundamental precepts of Christian ideology including "thou shalt not kill". More subtle but no less telling of his departure from Venetian state ideology is his transgression of the essential Christian imperative to "temper justice with mercy". Othello strangles Desdemona in the marriage bed, which she allegedly defiled, because, for him, "the justice of it pleases" (4.1.205). At the moment when Othello is prepared to mete out that justice, Desdemona appeals to the Christian mercy she believes is still in him:

> Oth. Thou art to die.
> Des. Then Lord have mercy on me!
> Oth. I say, amen.
> Des. And have you mercy too! (5.2.57–60)

Operating now outside of the Christian ideology, Othello can acknowledge Christian values without believing in them. He can wish the Lord to have mercy on Desdemona without feeling any imperative to grant such mercy himself. Indeed, he responds to Desdemona's plea by renewing his accusations, and finally by carrying out his threat.

Iago's method in toying with and eventually reversing Othello's Christian beliefs can best be seen by looking closely at Act Three, Scene Three, where Iago sets to work on Othello. Iago begins by playing dumb to Othello's question as to whether Cassio is "honest," causing Othello to remark, "By heaven, he echoes me,/ As if there were some monster in his thought,/ Too hideous to be shown" (3.3.110–12). Iago continues to stall, bluff, and insinuate, until finally Othello bursts out, "By heaven I'll know thy thought" (3.3.166). The phrase "by heaven" is repeated, a simple, no doubt unconscious exclamation that comes naturally to the Christian Othello. In both cases, though, it suggests that heaven alone knows what Iago is thinking. Iago picks up on this usage, and quickly twists it to his own purpose, warning Othello: "I know our country disposition well;/ In Venice they do let God see the pranks/ They dare not show their husbands" (3.3.205–07).[14] Here Iago refers explicitly to his status as an insider, as someone who understands Venice in a way that Othello never will. His claim regarding Venetian practices rouses Othello's jealousy, but also plants certain associations in his mind. It not only suggests that the man who catches his unfaithful wife has seen what was meant for God's eyes only, but it also implicates God as a silent witness to cuckoldry, telling Othello that the God in Venice is content with letting adulterers go unpunished, cuckolds unrevenged. That Othello has picked up on these meanings is clear when he says, "If she be false, O, then heaven mocks itself" (3.3.282). Othello has already made the link between Desdemona's alleged falsehood and the injustice, or even perversity, of a God that would allow this to happen. By the end of the scene, Othello has knelt down with Iago and vowed his revenge, "Now by yond marble heaven" (3.3.467).[15] Later in the play we do not see "heaven mocking itself," but rather Othello mocking heaven: he perverts the sacrament of confession first in a dialogue with Iago, in which Cassio's confession leads not to forgiveness, but to damnation—"To confess, and be hanged for his labour" (4.1.37)—and then later with Desdemona, when he tries to make her confess so that he will feel more justified in killing her.

There is evidence, then, that Othello's relationship to Christian ideology has been subverted and altered by Iago. But what about his relationship to Venetian ideology? In Act One, Scene Three, we see Venetian ideology at work in the pseudo-legal proceedings initiated by Brabantio against Othello. Implicit in this scene is the assumption that those involved are living within the same Venetian state ideology; there does not appear to be any dissent beyond Brabantio's initial vehemence and lingering bitterness. Hence, this scene revealingly contrasts Othello's shifting system of values in later acts. In the "temptation scene," for instance, as Iago is just beginning the processes of indoctrination, he offers Othello "imputation and strong circumstances,/ Which lead directly to the door of truth" (3.3.412–13). Of course, it is "imputation" and "circumstantial" evidence that Brabantio brings before the Duke to support his case against Othello. Yet, while the Duke finds this kind of evidence against Othello insufficient in court, it is here being offered by Iago as the best proof available against Desdemona, and Othello appears willing to accept it. In the next scene, Othello questions Desdemona about the handkerchief, and we find yet another inverted parallel with the earlier court scene. Othello describes the allegedly "charmed" handkerchief and its mystical history. He claims that the handkerchief was to "subdue" his father "entirely to [his mother's] love", but would have the opposite effect if lost or given away, so much so that, "To lose, or give't away, were such perdition/ As nothing else could match" (3.4.65–66). This strange fetishism recalls Brabantio's earlier argument in which he accuses Othello of witchcraft:

> I therefore vouch again,
> That with some mixtures powerful o'er the blood,
> Or with some dram conjur'd to this effect,
> He wrought upon her. (1.3.103–06)

Once again the speaker, this time Othello, masks his unreasonable expectations in a supernatural discourse, accepting this mysticism as a part of his own righteous justice. Even more blatant, however, is Othello's outright refusal to grant Desdemona the same due process that saved *him* from Brabantio's accusations. Othello was allowed to speak his case, and to send for the one witness who could resolve the problem peacefully and justly: "I do beseech you,/ Send for the lady to the Sagittar,/ And let her speak of me before her father" (1.3.114–16).

Under Iago's influence, Othello never confronts Desdemona with the actual accusation of adultery until he has already passed sentence on her. The exact point in the play when we can see Iago retraining Othello comes in Act Two, Scene Three. Pouring out liberal helpings of alcohol, Iago manages to orchestrate a brawl between Montano and Cassio. But it is only after Othello has stopped the fight and demanded an explanation that we see the wicked brilliance of Iago's plan: the two combatants, drunk and wounded, are unable to present Othello with a clear narrative of what has happened, and must defer to Iago to explain everything. Whatever his affiliation with the Venetian state, whatever his belief in civil law, Othello is operating at this point in a military capacity that allows him to make unilateral decisions based on the best information he can gather. Iago uses this situation to insinuate himself further into Othello's trust, planting in Othello's mind the idea that Iago's word should count as legal proof. This idea takes hold more and more as Iago weans Othello from Christian and Venetian state ideologies. At the end of the play, as Othello prepares to kill her, Desdemona begs him to let Cassio explain the situation: "Send for the man and ask him" (5.2.50). Othello refuses her; he has already ordered Cassio killed. Proof therefore is pursued and authorized not through justice, but through rash retribution.

Iago's motives?
I hate the Moor,
And it is thought abroad, that 'twixt my sheets
He's done my office; I know not if 't be true...
Yet I, for mere suspicion in that kind,
Will do, as if for surety. (1.3.384–88)

If we choose to take at face value, Iago's own professed motives, he himself operates according to what one might describe as a subset of Venetian ideology, that of the cuckold, a perspective that opposes cuckoldry's threat to patriarchal hierarchy. Because Iago is an organ of Venetian state power, he condemns cuckoldry; however, Iago exceeds state-prescribed subjective territory and enters transversal territory when his condemnation becomes pathological in its violation of the Venetian state's judicial process. Iago circumvents the Venetian state's legal system when he acts from a sensitivity to what is "thought abroad" about him, and dismisses the procedure, requiring burden of proof, demonstrated in the trial scene, acting "as if with surity" without searching for proof beyond "mere suspicion." As we have seen, Iago is not *trapped* within either this cuckold ideology or a particular subjective territory. The nonsubjectivity of "I am not what I am" permits him to move transversally beyond the ideology and view it as an ideology. Nevertheless, this self-negating phrase, "I am not what I am", is Iago's *modus operandi* only in the actual processes of empathizing and disseminating his ideology. But Iago's function as a representative of Venetian state power, manifest in spreading his repudiation of cuckoldry, transgresses subjective territory when he circumvents that same state ideology's legal standards. Iago's movement into transversal territory, then, challenges the Venetian state because it flouts its judicial codes. However, Iago's transversally inspired actions can be interpreted as paradoxically reinforcing Venetian state power, even while it undermines that power through the destruction of Othello.

This brings us back to Sinfield, and what he calls "the 'entrapment model' of ideology and power, whereby even, or especially, maneuvers that seem designed to challenge the system help to maintain it" (39). This model, also known as the new-historicist "subversion/containment paradigm", uses a dissective-cohesive mode of analysis in that it insists that all social phenomena work to produce a singular sociopolitical system or dominant power structure.[16] According to this model, Iago's subversion of the ideologies that have created Othello as a leader of Venice's military appears to "challenge the system" but, in actuality, would "help to maintain it." The transversal movement that Iago demonstrates by taking the Venetian state's repudiation of cuckoldry too far makes suspicion count as proof and posits the cuckold himself (and not the state) as the executioner who destroys both Iago and Othello. While the state is clearly better off without the mercilessly self-serving Iago, the benefit of destroying Othello may not be obvious until we turn to F.R. Leavis's interpretation of Othello's character.

Leavis critiques what he considers to be the sentimental idealizing of Othello's character by critics such as A.C. Bradley, arguing instead that Othello only succumbs to Iago's insinuations because his character—self-important, self-deceiving, and sentimental—is inherently prone to the jealousy that Iago suggests. For Leavis, it is "Othello in whose essential make-up the tragedy lay" (151). This reading makes Othello's downfall truly *tragic*, and not merely the lamentable result of Iago's demonic machinations. In this case, rather than undermining the order of the state's military apparatus, Iago has done the state a service, albeit inadvertently: he exposes Othello's tragic flaw in a time of peace. This is especially fortunate for the state given that the consequences of this flaw surfacing while at war would be unpredictable and potentially disastrous. Hence, Iago's vindictive measures play directly into Sinfield's entrapment model.

Yet this reading supposes that Iago really acts from the motives he cites in his concluding monologue of Act One. What are we to make, then, of the fact that Iago himself lays out a completely different set of motivations in his Act One, Scene One, dialogue with Roderigo? In lines 8–33, Iago explains that he was passed over for promotion by Othello, and that his job was instead given to Cassio, who, unlike Iago, "never set a squadron in the field,/ Nor the devision of a battle knows,/ More than a spinster" (1.1.22). Iago's motive is therefore revenge: revenge against the military general who did not promote him, against the captain who, lacking his qualifications, got his place, and against the system that permitted it. Put differently, Iago seeks revenge against an unjust and capricious hierarchical institution of the state by causing the destruction of the institutor of hierarchical order (symbolized by Othello) and its nepotistic beneficiary (Cassio). More than in the jealousy scenario in which Iago indirectly challenges the Venetian state, Iago is here seen as directly attacking it. But it is still easy to see the entrapment model at work. By directing his revenge primarily against the representative of state hierarchy (Othello), Iago not only causes the elimination of himself and Othello, but he also carelessly allows Cassio to live. Since Iago's machinations necessarily brought out the flaws in Othello's character, it is reasonable to assume that at the end of the play Cassio stands an excellent chance of being restored to the official position he held before he was cashiered by the Othello that Venice now sees was deluded by jealousy. Iago's attempts at revenge, it seems, have in the end done no substantial harm to his hated rival Cassio, and have even potentially *helped* him by creating an open position further up in the military hierarchy.

The problem with the subversion/containment paradigm in both cases, however, is that it does not account for the complexity of the situation. As Reynolds argues, "It is especially significant that this paradigm, as it is often applied, precludes or ignores micro-subversions, or small revolutionary changes" (148). In the two scenarios discussed here, the immediate impact on the morale and organization of the state is not considered. For instance, Iago can be seen as scoring a small victory against state order in that his vigilantism challenges the ability of the military leader to make unilateral decisions regarding his inferiors without fear of violent retribution. It is also entirely likely that Iago's subversive activity will affect how the state is likely to treat converted Moors in the future. Moreover, the parameterization behind these entrapment scenarios is dissective-cohesive and state-centred; as a result, the analysis does not consider questions such as: What happens to Iago, Cassio, and the state at the play's conclusion? Where did Othello and Iago come from in the first place? What impact will Desdemona's murder have on her family and friends, and therefore the state? And how might the audience respond to the play's action?

In order to foreground this transversal analysis, it is helpful to go beyond Althusser, and look instead to Gilles Deleuze and Félix Guattari.[17] They accept an essentially Althusserian model of the state, dividing the state apparatus into "two heads: the magician-king and the jurist-priest" (Deleuze and Guattari 351). These "heads" of the state "are the principal elements of a State apparatus that proceeds by a One-Two, distributes binary distinctions, and forms a milieu of interiority" (352). In this "milieu of interiority," the state apparatus creates an ordered, "striated," hierarchical society, organized by the state-imposed system based on supposedly absolute categories and binary oppositions. Opposed to this state apparatus is the "war machine," a "pure form of exteriority" (354) that operates outside of the state apparatus. The war machine opposes the state's rigid hierarchy, its order, its "striation," its binary oppositions, its stasis: "the war machine's form of exteriority is such that it exists only in its own metamorphoses" (360). Yet, while the war machine is defined in opposition to the state, as "a form of pure exteriority," it can become involved in the state system when it is "appropriate[d]...in the form of a military institution" (355), and in the relation between the two "heads" of the state apparatus: "One would have to say that it is located between the two heads of the State, between the two articulations, and that it is necessary in order to pass from one to the other. But 'between' the two, in that instant, even ephemeral, if only a flash, it proclaims its own irreducibility" (355). While the war machine can surface within the state apparatus, its presence is problematic because by its nature it lies outside of the state's control.

If Iago is attacking the military order that passed him over for promotion, then he can be seen as a manifestation of Deleuze and Guattari's war machine. Iago originates in the state's military institution, appropriates the war machine, and moves insidiously into the state apparatus. He subverts in Othello both Christian ideology and Venetian state ideology as they are manifested in judicial codes; these two ideologies are aligned with the "jurist-priest" head of the state, characterized as "the clear," "the calm," "the weighty," and "the regulated" (Deleuze and Guattari 351). What Iago turns Othello into resembles more closely the "magician-king" head of the state as described by Deleuze and Guattari: "the obscure," "the violent," "the quick," and "the fearsome" (351). Thus, "Between the magical-despotic State and the juridical State containing a military institution, we see the flash of the war machine, arriving from without" (353). From here we can understand Iago's relationship to the Venetian state's ideological machinery as an almost ironic reversal of Deleuze and Guattari's statement that the state supporter "can only appropriate [a war machine] in the form of a military institution, one that will continually cause it problems". Iago, the "problematic" part of the military war machine that the Venetian state has appropriated, attacks the state hierarchy by appropriating and transversalizing the methods of Venetian state ideology.

In order to further reveal Iago's transversal relationship to Venetian state ideology—that is, his movements in and out of subjective and transversal territories—it is necessary to review the two motivations that Iago gives for his actions, either as a cuckold or as an undervalued military official. Turning to the play, we see that the latter explanation is highly dubious. Bradley cautions us against believing Iago too readily: "One must constantly remember not to believe a syllable that Iago utters on any subject, including himself, until one has tested his statement by comparing it with known facts and with other statements of his own or of other people, and by considering whether he had in the particular circumstances any reason for telling a lie or for telling the truth" (198). By these well-justified standards, Iago's conversation with Roderigo must be considered suspect. The only statement he makes in that dialogue, which can be verified by recourse to facts within the play, is that Cassio is Othello's lieutenant. There is no evidence that Othello passed Iago over for the promotion, or that Iago was ever even considered for it. Iago's own statements do not support this motivation anywhere else in the play, and his subsequent monologue at the end of Act One, Scene Three, offers a completely different motivation without mention of Cassio's promotion. Iago would certainly benefit from lying to Roderigo: he has to offer some sort of motivation, and this is one that Roderigo would easily understand and believe, without the condescension he might feel toward a cuckold.

Perhaps, then, Iago really does believe he has been cuckolded. There does not seem to be any reason for him to tell lies in a monologue directed to the audience; moreover, there appears to be support for this motive in Emilia's lines, "Some such squire he was,/ That turn'd your wit, the seamy side without,/ And made you to suspect me with the Moor" (4.2.147–49). This support, Ridley says, "disposes of any idea that Iago's suspicions of Othello (1.3.385; 2.1.290) were figments, invented during momentary 'motive-hunting' and dismissed. They have been real, and lasting, enough for him to challenge Emilia" (159). Even if Iago's suspicions were real and lasting, however, this does not prove that they are in fact the motivating force behind his actions, a fact that becomes clear upon closer examination of Iago's language in the Act One, Scene Three, monologue. In this speech, Iago first states his motivation of cuckoldry in the following words: "I hate the Moor,/ And it is thought abroad, that 'twixt my sheets/ He's done my office" (1.3.384–86). This is supposedly a statement of motivation, of cause and effect. Yet the sentence is not constructed on the logical model of "A then B," but rather on the model of a different Boolean operator, on "A *and* B": "I hate the Moor,/ *And* it is thought abroad"... (our emphasis). On the most basic level of language and of symbolic logic, Iago is not stating a motive; he is merely listing two separate facts that are simultaneously true. Here we can see why Coleridge labeled this monologue "the motive-hunting of motiveless malignity" (49). Iago knows only that he "hates the Moor"; he puts this together with his belief that "it is thought abroad...," and realizes that this is sufficient motive to act on his preexisting, "motiveless" hatred of Othello.

If Iago does represent this "motiveless malignity," where does that leave him in relation to Venetian state ideology? If he does not work as a normal agent of the state, fully inculcated in one of its minor ideologies (that of the cuckold), and does not work against the state, as a war machine that appropriates the methods of state ideology, then how *does* he work? In Act Three, Scene Three (right before the temptation scene in which Iago interpellates Othello as cuckold), Othello makes the prophetic statement in his apostrophe to Desdemona: "Excellent wretch, perdition catch my soul,/ But I do love thee, and when I love thee not,/ Chaos is come again" (3.3.91–93). Even proponents of the entrapment model would have to admit that Iago brings some degree of "chaos" into the functioning of the state; and those, like us, who dismiss the idea that he is a true mechanism of the state may see this as the primary result of his actions. Without ascribing to the Iago-as-war machine model, then, we may still believe that his effects are very much like those of a war machine, breaking down the hierarchical order of the state apparatus, turning the violence inherent in a military man such as Othello against the state's ordered society. What is needed, however, once we have dismissed his Act One, Scene One, motive of revenge against the military system, is a model that does not rely on the aggression toward the state that Iago does not seem to possess.

Such a model can be found in our concept of "transversal power." Transversal power is any force (physical or metaphysical) that causes movements in or through transversal territory. As Reynolds puts it, "transversal power induces people to transversally cut across the striated, organized space of subjectivity—of all subjective territory—and enter the disorganized yet smoothly infinite space of transversal territory" (150). Like the war machine of Deleuze and Guattari, "Transversal territory invites people to escape or deviate from the vertical, hierarchicalizing and horizontal, homogenizing assemblages of any organizational social structure" (149). Iago enters the "nonsubjectified" (once again, "I am not what I am") transversal territory outside of the conceptual boundaries set on him by the state. Without just cause, and separate from any existing suspicion of cuckoldry, Iago hates his commanding officer and desires the "chaos" of Othello's downfall. As would the war machine, Iago appropriates the form of the Venetian state official, and recreates Othello's subjective territory in a manner that reveals—relative to the subjective territories created by the state—transversal movement; Othello's conceptual and emotional boundaries are reconfigured under the influence of Iago's transversal power. Thus, from the "motiveless" irruption of transversal power into Iago's subjective territory we see a chain of events that lead inexorably to "chaos."

There may be some danger of implying with this interpretation that *Othello* should be read as a reactionary text, condemning all subversive action because of the results of Iago's deeds. Of course, this reactionary conclusion could never actually be reached from the evidence given in the analysis: the power that Iago wields over Othello demonstrates the frightening power that the state itself can wield if its ideological mechanisms and institutions are not constantly questioned and challenged. Yet this raises an important point, which is the inadequacy of all interpretations that attribute a didactic moral to Shakespeare's works, whether reactionary or "progressive." Bloom and Jaffa summarize the moral of *Othello* with the following formula: "*Othello* appears...to leave us with this choice—a mean life based on a clear perception of reality or a noble life based on falsehood and ending in tragedy" (66). An Althusserian reading of the play, if it accomplishes nothing else, at least shows the error of Bloom and Jaffa's moralizing oversimplification. Othello's downfall is not simply a matter of being mistaken about the facts; it is rather a result of an entirely different way of relating to the world around him that is developed in him by Iago. Othello is indoctrinated with an ideology that does not require the same degree of proof of wrongdoing as does Venetian state ideology, and which is harsher in its punishment than the Christian faction of that ideology. Both the old ideology of the Venetian state and the new, minor ideology of the cuckold are "based on falsehood" in the sense that they are "imaginary" (in Althusser's definition), and mutually contradictory. Othello's tragedy comes from his indoctrination into an ideology that encourages him to ignore (or at least distort) the facts and act swiftly, "justly," and without mercy.

And Now for Something Completely Different[18]

In keeping with the analytical strategy of transversal theory, Bryan Reynolds and Janna Segal here expand upon Fitzpatrick and Reynolds' investigation by introducing a new variable into the discussion: Deleuze's deconstruction in "Coldness and Cruelty" of "the spurious sadomasochistic unity" (40). Looking at the relationships among Iago, Othello, and Desdemona in light of Deleuze's pedagogical distinctions between "the sadistic 'instructor'" and "the masochistic 'educator'" (19), Reynolds and Segal will offer another parameter of exploration that will further elaborate upon Iago's transversal power, and reassess the submissive status of the martyr Desdemona.

Criticism analyzing sexual and marital relations, and, in particular, male desire in *Othello* has generally ignored sadism (named after the Marquis de Sade), masochism (named after Leopold von Sacher-Masoch), and the sadomasochistic model, preferring instead to see the relationships among the characters through the lens of normalized notions of what constitutes a healthy relationship between the sexes, and then to criticize Shakespeare's characters for breaching those constructs in their behavior.[19] For example, owing to the "abnormal" violent relationship between Iago and Emilia, their marriage has been negatively described as a "part-time job" (Kállay 42), and "a weary stale alliance, entrenched in the reactionary rut of dominance/subordination and routine abuse" (Deats 248). Iago himself has been chastised for his supposed inability to love (Gronbeck-Tedesco 261–62; Kállay 42), and has been cast as "the most abysmal sexual villain in all literature" (Cummings 80). Desdemona has also suffered at the hands of critics who have dismissed her as a passive female character, frequently pointing to her final words ("Nobody. I myself./ Farewell. Commend me to my kind lord—O, farewell" [5.2.122–23])[20]—which are delivered in response to Emilia's request for the name of her murderer—as proof of her unflinching obedience to Othello and the patriarchal order.[21] While critics have shown how Iago, Desdemona, and Othello do not conform to dominant Renaissance and modern codes of "proper" behavior, we want to explore how the characters function in their "perverse" relations with one another.

In "Coldness and Cruelty," Deleuze defines sadism and masochism as two separate "perversions"[22] that operate through different means to achieve a shared, subversive end. According to Deleuze, "nothing is in fact more alien to the sadist than the wish to convince, to persuade, in short to educate" (18), while the masochist "needs to educate, persuade and conclude an alliance with the torturer in order to realize the strangest of schemes" (20). Although each uses a different pedagogical approach, both the sadist and masochist function to subvert the law: the sadist transcends the law by creating "anarchic institutions of perpetual motion and permanent revolution" (87), and the masochist demonstrates its absurdity by converting "the very law which forbids the satisfaction of a desire under threat of subsequent punishment...into one which demands the punishment first and then orders that the satisfaction of the desire should necessarily follow upon the punishment" (88–89). Deleuze further distinguishes these two forms of perversion/subversion by their relationship to the law: the sadist creates an institution of anarchy that seeks "the degradation of all laws" and establishes itself as "a superior power" to accepted authority (77), and the masochist draws a contract that "generates a law," rather than negating all laws (77).

In transversal terms, by degrading the law and thereby the official culture from which it was drafted and that reinforces it, the sadist can be said to be creating an institution that moves beyond subjective territory into a transversal terrain that threatens the foundations upon which subjective territory is constructed and maintained. The masochist's contract also similarly challenges official territory; however, the masochist does not seek to overturn the law and official culture, but to perpetuate their capacity as punishment in a different pursuit: pleasure. With the masochist, the function of the law is subverted into a means of obtaining pleasure while at the same time working to maintain, at least ostensibly, the law's structure and power of authority over individuals. With the sadist, the law is destroyed and replaced with an institution that resists maintenance and, because it remains in "perpetual motion and permanent revolution" (87), denies itself the ability to become a new form of official territory.

Based on Deleuze's division, it could be argued that Iago is a masochist: he succeeds in manipulating others into participating in his plots, and forms alliances with his enemies in order to realize his "schemes". Yet, in his attempts to orchestrate the events that lead to Othello's destruction, Iago does not so much persuade as "instruct" his victims as to how to carry out his revenge.[23] For instance, when Iago suggests to Roderigo that he kill Cassio, he does not persuade Roderigo to do it, but rather outlines how it will be done: "He sups tonight with a harlotry, and thither will I go to him. ...if you will watch his going thence—which I will fashion to fall out between twelve and one—you may take him at your pleasure. I will be near to second your attempt, and he shall fall between us" (4.2.235–40). Following his lecture on the details of the murder, Iago offers to "show" Roderigo "a necessity in his death" (4.2.242). While "show" suggests that Roderigo needs to be persuaded, the scene ends before Iago "educates" Roderigo as to why Cassio must die. In Act Five, Scene One, when the deadly duo next appears, Iago is again issuing instructions to Roderigo: "Here, stand behind this bulk, straight will he come./ Wear thy good rapier bare, and put it home" (5.1.1–2). Iago's commands aside, Roderigo suggests that in the interim of the planning and the execution of the scheme he has been persuaded by Iago to kill Cassio: "I have no devotion to the deed/ And yet he hath given me satisfying reasons:/ 'Tis but a man gone. Forth, my sword: he dies" (5.1.8–10). The "satisfying reasons" given, however, are less than compelling, which suggests that little convincing was needed to spur Roderigo on. After repeating the reason Iago gave, Roderigo simply follows Iago's orders, which further establishes Iago as more the "instructor" than "educator" of his revenge schemes.

Iago can be described as persuading Othello to believe that Desdemona has been false by spurring suspicious thoughts and images of her sexual impropriety, indirectly leading his superior officer on a self-destructive path. But the seeds of suspicion planted by Iago are generally coupled with instructions for how Othello should proceed in light of Iago's insinuations. For example, in the first temptation scene, after acknowledging his lack of "proof," Iago tells Othello, "Look to your wife, observe her well with Cassio./ Wear your eyes thus, not jealous nor secure;/ I would not have your free and noble nature/ Out of self-bounty be abused: look to 't" (3.3.199–204). Specifically, Iago instructs Othello not only to "look to 't", but also where to cast his gaze (on Desdemona "*with* Cassio," which implies that she has been "with" him before) and how to perceive what he then sees (to be "not jealous nor secure"). In effect, Iago is able to insure that Othello sees not what is before him, but what Iago desires him to see. Iago uses a similar tactic when he instructs Othello as to how to punish his wife: "Do it not with poison, strangle her in her bed—even the bed she hath contaminated" (4.1.204–05). Again, Iago blends images of sexual misconduct—here asserting that Desdemona has been unfaithful in the bed she shares with Othello—with commands for precisely how Othello should respond to her adultery. Of course, Iago's influence is confirmed by the fact that Othello follows Iago's orders, suffocating Desdemona in "her bed."

In the final scene of the play, when the roles are reversed and Iago becomes the captive facing punishment, Iago is still able to maintain his position as the "instructor." Asked by Othello to explain, "Why he hath thus ensnared my soul and body?" (5.2.299), the imprisoned Iago flatly refuses to cooperate: "Demand me nothing. What you know, you know./ From this time forth I never will speak a word" (5.2.300–01). By taking a vow of silence, Iago retains his dominance over Othello, further torturing him by withholding the knowledge Othello so desperately seeks. Iago's refusal to "educate" his captor is also issued with an order, "Demand me nothing," which Othello obeys. With their positions switched, Iago the "instructor" preserves his authority.

While Iago is, according to Deleuze's distinctions, the sadist in Shakespeare's story, Desdemona is the masochist whose ability to derive pleasure from pain is presented as the facilitator of her love for Othello. Prior to her arrival in the story, Desdemona's fascination with cruelty is introduced by her husband, who describes how he was able to woo his wife by telling her violent stories, which she would "with a greedy ear/ Devour" (1.3.150–51). According to Othello, Desdemona, upon hearing of his painful youth, often cried and "wished she had not heard it, yet she wished / That heaven had made her such a man" (1.3.163–64).[24] Due to her capacity to simultaneously feel what are typically seen as opposing emotions—pain and pleasure—Desdemona was able to relish the cruel content of Othello's stories and achieve love, being the climax of the sorrow she experienced upon hearing Othello's autobiographical narratives.

Equally engaged in his role in Desdemona's masochistic scenario, Othello admits that he was able to enjoy the suffering his stories caused her. According to Othello, he fell in love with her precisely because "she did pity" him upon hearing his tales of woe (1.3.169). The "pity" that he found so attractive in Desdemona not only signals the pleasure he derives from her pain, but the dialectical nature of their relationship. Since her pity was issued from a position of privilege—she pitied that which she did not experience as a white woman—her sympathy served to validate the pain of his enslaved youth.[25] Having decided that Othello's pain was worthy of her tears, Othello deemed her worthy of his love. Likewise, although Othello is Desdemona's torturer and she his victim, he is controlled by her, which he is keenly aware of. So afraid of her ability to sway him, Othello vows to forbid her to speak at the time of her murder: "I'll not expostulate with her, lest her body and beauty/ unprovide my mind again" (4.1.201–03). Desdemona also identifies her husband as both her servant and her master. Confident in her influence over him, she promises Cassio that she will "tame" her husband and restore their friendship (3.3.23). However, wary of angering her husband, Desdemona dismisses Emilia at Othello's "bidding," answering Emilia's protests with, "We must not now displease him" (4.3.13–15). Both husband and wife share a revolving status in their marriage as the dominator and the dominated, and both are equally capable of inflicting pain on, and receiving it from, each other.

Although Desdemona and Othello both love and fear each other, it is Desdemona who can be more appropriately described as the "masochistic 'educator'." Unlike Iago, who issues orders to enact his schemes, or Othello, who so willingly follows Iago's commands, Desdemona tries to persuade her husband to do as she pleases. In describing to Cassio how she will convince Othello to renew their friendship, Desdemona reveals her role as the persistent teacher in their marriage: "My lord shall never rest,/ I'll watch him tame and talk him out of patience,/ His bed shall seem a school, his board a shrift,/ I'll intermingle everything he does/ With Cassio's suit" (3.3.22–26). Deats's argument that in this passage Desdemona "promises to play the shrew if her husband does not heed her suit" (242) implies that Desdemona intends to conform to a constructed notion of "negative" feminine behavior if her husband does not agree to her demands, and dismisses the possibility that Desdemona plans to use language to her advantage, empowering herself with her persuasive "talk". Desdemona's verbalized intentions reveal that she is not merely a passive voice in the play, but rather that she invokes her power through discourse, not commands, and believes that through discussion she can convince, not order, her husband to reconcile with Cassio, who, recognizing Desdemona's influence over Othello, vows to be her "true servant" (3.3.9).

As noted, critics have chastised Desdemona for embracing victimization at the end of the play as she submissively waits for her husband to kill her in her bedroom, and, with her last breath, insists that Othello is blameless for her demise. Deats (241; 243), Orlin (181–83), and Rose (221) all comment on the "contradictions" of Desdemona's character, whose final role as the martyr for her husband's jealousy and honor is incongruous to the young wife defying what we would identify as her subjective territory at the beginning of the play. Deats accounts for the disjuncture in her character by arguing that "Desdemona is never as unconventional as she first appears" (243), and that from her first appearance, she "accepts her subordinate role in society and defines herself in relation to men, as either a wife or daughter, but not as an independent individual" (244). Bevington's assessment of Desdemona is in accordance with Deats's: "The play as a whole confirms this wish in her to obey" (227), and, like Deats, Bevington refers to Desdemona's willingness to lie in wait for her wrathful husband as evidence for his argument (227).

Unlike Deats, Orlin, and Rose, however, Bevington does not refer to Desdemona's final line as a "lie" reflective of her willingness to accept a subordinate position as a woman in a patriarchal society,[26] but rather as one of the two instances of "disobedience, prevarication, or managerial assertion of control of which she is 'guilty' in the play" (227). Bevington's reading acknowledges Desdemona's agency, but he still identifies her last words as an act of self-betrayal and self-sacrifice, as her "attempt to take the blame for her own death" (227). We suggest instead that Desdemona's final words can be interpreted as more than a false statement issued from the mouth of a martyr in order to exonerate a guilty husband. As is evidenced by her behavior prior to her murder, Desdemona's last line implies that she recognizes herself as an active agent, not a passive victim, in what could be described as a masochistic scenario in which she has agreed to participate.

Prior to her death, Desdemona's behavior implies that she is keenly aware of the danger awaiting her, and her various attempts to orchestrate the scene of her own demise are suggestive of her masochistic role in her marriage. Although aware of her husband's murderous intentions, she obeys his order to dismiss Emilia, thereby allowing herself to be vulnerable to his attack. Having previously requested that her bed be adorned with her wedding sheets (4.2.107), she now asks Emilia to, following her death, "shroud me/ In one of these same sheets" (4.3.22–23). Since she has created the opportunity for her husband to assault her unguarded, and purposefully decorated her deathbed in her nuptial garments, Desdemona's destruction at her husband's hands can be described as a suicidal scenario of which she is a willing participant. However, her actions during the attack suggest that Desdemona found the threat of death, or rather, the fantasy of punishment, more enticing than its actuality.

As noted, Deleuze identifies the contract as a specific feature of the masochist fantasy, as opposed to the anarchic institutional tendency of the sadistic scenario. According to Deleuze, "The masochistic contract implies not only the necessity of the victim's consent, but his ability to persuade, and his pedagogical and judicial efforts to train his torturer" (75). In *Othello*, the victim's failure to draw a contract with her torturer signals her demise, as well as the deconstruction of the notion of "divine justice." During her death scene, after she unsuccessfully tries to convince Othello of her innocence, she pleads for her life by offering him four alternatives: "O, banish me, my lord, but kill me not!" (5.2.77); "Kill me tomorrow, let me live tonight!" (5.2.79); "But half and hour!" (5.2.81); "But while I say one prayer!" (5.2.82). Othello rejects her attempts at negotiation, and her last appeal, "O Lord! Lord! Lord!" (5.2.83), is not answered by God, but by the pillow that her husband uses to smother her. Desdemona's failure to adequately "train" her torturer prior to the moment of her death leads ultimately to her destruction, and demonstrates, within the context of the play, the absurdity of the concept of a "higher" court of law that protects the innocent.

Desdemona's actions prior to Othello's final entrance—her adornment of her bedchamber, her specificity regarding her death shroud, her dismissal of her waiting-maid—are evidence that Desdemona was aware of the possibility that Othello intended to harm her, and that she took active and purposeful steps to facilitate his desire. While this can be read as an affirmation of Bevington's reading of the "wish in [Desdemona] to obey" (227), it also suggests that she had more than a "wish," but rather a desire "to obey." If we accept the possibility that the manifestation of Desdemona's desires were outside official culture's codes of "proper" sexual practice, we can reassess her supposedly "contradictory" character without reducing her to a submissive woman who martyrs herself in her unyielding devotion to a man. Rather, we can read her final words as an acknowledgment of her responsibility in a masochistic scenario gone awry. This reading does not imply that Desdemona asked for what she got; on the contrary, our reading of Desdemona's final line and actions reclaim Desdemona's agency, empowering her with the possibility that her passivity in the final act was only seemingly so, and that her death was not merely the result of her retreat into a submissive, "female" role. As evidenced by her attempts to invoke the power of discourse within an official culture that privileges the male voice to negotiate a masochistic contract with her torturer in the final moments of her life, Desdemona did not go quietly or submissively to her grave.

Although Desdemona, as well as Othello and Iago, can be cast according to Deleuze's distinction between the pedagogical style and subversive intent of the sadist and the masochist, the play as a whole calls into question the stability of his definitions. According to Deleuze:

> In the contractual relation, the woman typically figures as an object in the patriarchal system. The contract in masochism reverses this state of affairs by making the woman into the party with whom the contract is entered into. Its paradoxical intention extends even further in that it involves a master-slave relationship, and one furthermore in which the woman is the master and torturer. The contractual basis is thereby implicitly challenged, by excess of zeal, a humorous acceleration of the clauses and a complete reversal of the respective contractual status of man and woman. (92)

Deleuze's account of the masochistic contract's capacity to overturn patriarchal law implies that the masochist moves transversally by disrupting official culture; however, this can only occur within the distinctly heterosexual and patriarchal framework within which Deleuze has constructed the masochist: the woman is always the torturer and the man the victim who, despite surface appearances, remains in control. In *Othello*, the Shakespearean heroine reverses the assumed gender of Deleuze's masochist by becoming a female "masochistic 'educator'," who attempts to "train" her male abuser. In her masochistic role, Desdemona appears to reverse the patriarchal order of things: contrary to conventional gender constructs, she is the "captain's captain" (2.1.74). While her failure to generate a contract with her male torturer, along with Othello's rejection of her denials in favor of Iago's hearsay, reveal the cruel injustice of an official culture that privileges the male voice, they do not cause the overturning of the dominant, patriarchal judicial structures within the world of the play. On the contrary, the conclusion reaffirms those very structures, embodied in the forms of the Venetian noblemen, Lodovico and Gratiano, and the newly appointed governor of Cyprus, Cassio, all of whom are brought in at the end of the play to restore order and ensure that Iago receives his just desserts.

Othello further calls into question Deleuze's deconstruction of the "sadomasochistic unity" by suggesting that the role of the torturer and the tortured is subjective, and dependent upon the individual perspectives of those engaged in the fantasy. While Desdemona is the martyred victim in her own scenario, Othello identifies her as the torturer, "the cause" (5.2.1), in his. What is revealed by the relationship between Shakespeare's newlyweds are not affirmations of the "sadomasochistic unity," but an awareness of the subjective perspectives of the participants in either a masochistic or a sadistic scenario, and the subjective framework within which Deleuze has constructed his distinctions between sadism and masochism.

By comparing Iago's sadistic tendencies to Othello and Desdemona's masochist style, we have further elucidated differences among forms of subversion and transversal movement in *Othello*. Iago's successful destruction of Othello highlights the difference: more than just questioning the subjectivity of Venetian state ideology, Iago undermines it, asserting himself transversally. While we question Deleuze's construction of the masochist within a framework of gender roles and "norms" perpetuated by the sociopolitical conductors of various official cultures, we recognize the usefulness of his analysis to transversal theory, and apply it in this section not only to expand Fitzpatrick and Reynolds's exploration, but to exemplify the benefits of the investigative-expansive mode of analysis, which has allowed Reynolds and Segal to reparameterize the proceeding inquiry in response to new ideas that challenge common interpretations of Iago's intentions, Othello's odious cruelty toward his wife, and Desdemona's docile devotion to her husband.

Toward Investigative-expansiveness

Having moved from critical history to ideological indoctrination, from Schlegel and Hunter to Althusser and Iago to Guattari and Deleuze to Reynolds and Segal, Fitzpatrick and

Reynolds's transversal analysis defies the sort of holistic conclusion that is characteristic of the dissective cohesive mode of analysis. More importantly, though, our view of the role that transversal power plays in Iago's machinations leads us to believe that a dissective-cohesive conclusion, one that seeks to explain Iago or to explain *Othello* itself, would necessarily misrepresent the play. *Othello*, as we have noted, breaks the world into binary oppositions, and encourages us to use these oppositions to categorize its characters, its plots, and its themes: thus, as Hunter tells us, the black foreigner turns out to be a good Christian, while the white Venetian is quickly seen to be an evil man who masks his true self with a veneer of honesty. Nevertheless, when we use these oppositions to assemble a holistic view of the play, we arrive at contradictions. Where Hunter sees the black man with a white soul being corrupted by the white man with a black soul, Schlegel sees a black foreigner who masquerades unsuccessfully as a Venetian before reverting to his original barbaric state. These readings use the binary oppositions found in *Othello* to describe each character at each point in the play (and beyond the play, during events we may assume took place before the beginning of the play); and then they use these definitions to determine how the characters move from point to point. By contrast, our analysis is concerned primarily with this movement, the process of change, rather than the initial and final states. Iago is postulated as an Althusserian state supporter only because the action of the play suggests ideological indoctrination; we accept Althusser's designation of objectivity as the opposite of ideology only because Iago's transversal movement out of his own subjective territory, symptomatically revealed when he exceeds the state-prescribed position on cuckoldry, requires some concept of exteriority. While *Othello* lays out a system of interrelated binary oppositions, it exists neither in nor between them, but in its own movement through them. To use an example from Hunter's essay, the play is not built on categorizations such as that of Othello as the black man with the white soul and Iago as the white man with the black soul; nor is *Othello* built on black and white distinctions between sadism and masochism.

Rather, it is built on such actions as the audience's realization that their expectations have been contradicted. It is a play neither of seeming nor of being, but of becoming. And the character that best represents *Othello* is Iago, who shows us "motive hunting" rather than a motive, and whose transversal movements constitute the action of the play.

Notes

1. For more on "transversal theory," beyond the introduction to this book, see Bryan Reynolds, "The Devil's House, 'or worse': Transversal Power and Antitheatrical Discourse in Early Modern England," *Theatre Journal* 49.2 (1997): 143-67, and "Becoming Criminal: Transversal Performance and Cultural Dissidence in Early Modern England" (Baltimore: Johns Hopkins University Press, 2002); and Bryan Reynolds and Joseph Fitzpatrick, "The Transversality of Michel de Certeau: Foucault's Panoptic Discourse and the Cartographic Impulse," *Diacritics* 29.3 (1999): 63-80.
2. See also Karen Newman, "'And wash the Ethiop White': Femininity and the Monstrous in *Othello*," *Fashioning Femininity and English Renaissance Drama* (Chicago: Chicago University Press, 1991).
3. Of course, Othello's relationships with these two institutions are themselves both interdependent and intertwined, leading, for example, Allan Bloom and Harry Jaffa to comment: "How is he able to make himself so Venetian? It is surely, in part, his Christianity that is responsible" (48).
4. Though the first conclusive textual evidence for his conversion comes at 2.3.161-63 ("Are we turn'd Turks, and to ourselves do that/ Which heaven has forbid the Ottomites?/ For Christian shame, put by this barbarous brawl"), Othello's Christianity is implied both by his references to heaven during the trial scene (1.3.163; 266), and in his initial dialogue with Iago, in which Iago implies that the supposed theft of Desdemona was a legal marriage (1.2.11).
5. Here we side with A.C. Bradley in calling Iago a Venetian. Bradley cites 3.3.201 and 5.1.89 f. as evidence, and reads Cassio's comment, "I never knew a Florentine more kind and honest" (3.1.42-43) to mean, "not that Iago is a Florentine, but that he could not be kinder and honester if he were one" (200). M.R. Ridley appears to agree with Bradley in his 1958 edition of

the text, in which his annotation of this line clarifies it as "i.e. *even* a Florentine (Cassio being from Florence)" (Ridley, ed., *Othello* 92).

6. Hunter may be paraphrasing A.W. Schlegel here, who writes in an essay later alluded to by Hunter, "While the Moor bears only the nightly colour of suspicion and deceit on his visage, Iago is black within" (Schlegel 196).
7. Bryan Reynolds and James Intriligator introduced this methodology in a paper entitled "Transversal Power," given at the Manifesto Conference at Harvard University on May 9, 1998. For a detailed analysis of transversal methodology, see Zooz's "Transversal Poetics: I.E. Mode" in the appendix of this book.
8. In Adelman, see especially pages 129-31 and 137-44.
9. Schlegel writes: "What a fortunate mistake that the Moor, under which name a baptized Saracen of the Northern coast of Africa was unquestionably meant in the novel, has been made by Shakespeare in every respect a negro! We recognize in *Othello* the wild nature of that glowing zone which generates the most raging beasts of prey and the most deadly poisons, tamed only in appearance by the desire of fame, by foreign laws of honour, and by nobler and milder manners" (195).
10. An even more recent example would be Walter S.H. Lim's comment: "That Iago finds it easy to undermine the Moor's emotional stability reveals that Othello can never fully obliterate his African self when he fabricates his Venetian/white identity" (62).
11. Julie Hankey has mentioned Marowitz's 1972 adaptation *An Othello* as an example of how a radically conceived reworking of the play, which Hankey herself labels "propaganda," demonstrates the deep-rooted investment of Shakespeare's original in problems of ideology (Hankey 113-14).
12. For an in-depth analysis of the power of storytelling in the play, see Stephen Greenblatt, "The Improvisation of Power", *Renaissance Self-Fashioning: From More to Shakespeare* (Chicago: University of Chicago Press, 1980), 222-54; especially pages 237-47.
13. Here we can explain in Althusserian terms Bloom and Jaffa's assertion quoted in note 4: it is because Othello has been inculcated in the state ideology through the "Ideological State

Apparatuses" of religion (Christianity) that he is able to assimilate, to whatever extent, into Venetian society.

14. The explicit connection of the term heaven to Christian thought is even more clear in the folio and second quarto texts, where "God" is replaced by "Heaven".
15. Oliver Parker's film version presents an interesting interpretation of this scene, breaking Iago and Othello's discussion into segments that occur in different settings at different times of the day, suggesting that the conversation is either repeated almost verbatim a number of times, or dragged out for much longer than the audience is shown.
16. While Sinfield does not apply his "entrapment model" specifically to the type of interpretation given in this essay, he does note that, "entrapment...arises generally in functionalism, structuralism, and Althusserian Marxism" (39). For discussion of this subversion/containment paradigm, see, among other sources, Bryan Reynolds, "The Devil's House, 'or worse': Transversal Power and Antitheatrical Discourse in Early Modern England," *Theatre Journal* 49.2 (1997): 143-67, 148-49; Jonathan Dollimore, *Sexual Dissidence: Augustine to Wilde, Freud to Foucault* (Oxford: Clarendon Press, 1991), 81-91; Michael Bristol, *Shakespeare's America, America's Shakespeare* (London: Routledge, 1990), 189-211; and Louis Montrose, "Professing the Renaissance: The Poetics and Politics of Culture," *The New Historicism*, ed. Aram H. Veeser (New York: Routledge, 1989), 15-36, 20-24.
17. In fact, Althusser's system does not allow for such a creature as Iago, an ideologue who *opposes* the state, whose indoctrination of state citizens constitutes his own private *war* against the state.
18. Bryan Reynolds and Janna Segal have purposefully appropriated for their title of this coauthored section the phrase commonly used in *Monty Python's Flying Circus* to introduce a new skit that is supposedly a non sequitur, yet fits within the theme and contributes to the whole of a single episode. Borrowing Monty Python's framing technique, Reynolds and Segal offer this section as "something different," a new variable found through the process of the proceeding investigation that is not "completely" unrelated to the previous argument.
19. For an examination of desire and the role of marriage in *Othello*, see, among others: Catherine Belsey's "Desire's excess and the English Renaissance theatre: *Edward II, Trolius and Cressida,*

Othello," *Erotic Politics: Desire on the Renaissance Stage*, ed. Susan Zimmerman (New York: Routledge, 1992), 84-102; David Bevington's "*Othello*: Portrait of a Marriage," *Othello: New Critical Essays*, ed. Philip C. Kolin (New York: Routledge, 2002), 221-31; Lawrence Danson's "'The Catastrophe is a Nuptial': The Space of Masculine Desire in *Othello, Cymbeline*, and *The Winter's Tale*," *Shakespeare Survey* 46, ed. Stanley Wells (Cambridge: Cambridge University Press, 1994), 69-79; Sara Munson Deats's "'Truly, an obedient lady': Desdemona, Emilia, and the Doctrine of Obedience in *Othello*," *Othello: New Critical Essays*, ed. Philip C. Kolin (New York: Routledge, 2002), 233-54; Géza Kállay's "'To Die Upon a Kiss': Love and Death as Metaphors in *Othello*," *HJEAS* 3.2 (1997): 25-58; Lean Cowen Orlin's "Desdemona's Disposition," *Shakespearean Tragedy and Gender*, ed. Shirley Nelson Garner and Madelon Sprengnether (Bloomington: Indiana University Press, 1996), 171-92; Edward Pechter's "'Have You Not Read of Some Such Thing?': Sex and Sexual Stories in *Othello*," *Shakespeare Survey* 49, ed. Stanley Wells (Cambridge: Cambridge University Press, 1996), 201-16; Mary Beth Rose, "The Heroics of Marriage in *Othello* and *The Duchess of Malfi*," *Shakespearean Tragedy and Gender*, ed. Shirley Nelson Garner and Madelon Sprengnether (Bloomington: Indiana University Press, 1996), 210-38; and Yoko Takakuwa's, "Diagnosing Male Jealousy: Woman as Man's Symptom in *The Merry Wives of Windsor, Othello, The Winter's Tale* and *Cymbeline*," *Hot Questrists After the English Renaissance: Essays on Shakespeare and His Contemporaries*, ed. Yasunari Takahashi (New York: AMS Press, 2000), 19-36. For an examination of masculine desire in *Othello*, see in particular Bevington, Danson, and Takakuwa. For a discussion of Desdemona's obedient devotion to Othello, refer especially to Bevington, Deats, Orlin, and Rose.

20. In this section, all citations from the play will be taken from *Othello*, ed. E.A.J. Honigmann (London: Arden Shakespeare, 2001).

21. Bevington (227), Deats (246-48), Orlin (181-83), and Rose (221-23) refer to Desdemona's passivity in the final moments of her life as a reflection of a patriarchal order. Deats (247), Orlin (181), and Rose (221-22) specifically refer to the line we have cited as a "lie" told by Desdemona in order to exonerate Othello. Only Orlin identifies a possible subversive effect arising from Desdemona's death: "Her innocence exposes the predictive

incapacity of patriarchalism and is in this respect subversive of its conceptual power" (187).

22. Reynolds and Segal disagree with the labeling of either masochism or sadism as a "perversion". It is their contention that "perversion" carries a negative connotation, and implies that there is a sex standard or norm against which a particular practice can be deemed "perverse." (Fitzpatrick was unavailable for comment on this issue.)
23. In "Morality, Ethics and the Failure of Love in Shakespeare's *Othello*," John Gronbeck-Tedesco recognizes Iago's instructive style, and attributes it to his military background: "No one understands the military ways better than Iago. He relies on the direct relationship between words uttered in the chain of command and the actions of authority" (*Othello: New Critical Essays*, ed. Philip C. Kolin [New York: Routledge, 2002], 255-70, 264). Gronbeck-Tedesco does not account for why Othello, who is as equally aware of "the military ways" as his ensign is, does not relate to others with the same commanding force.
24. In "*Othello*: Portrait of a Marriage," Bevington notes that Desdemona "gives us no reinforcement of what Othello has presumed to say about her motives, about her pitying him and loving him for the dangers he had passed" (225). However, asking the Duke for the right to accompany Othello to Cyprus, Desdemona states, "I saw Othello's visage in his mind,/ And to his honours and his valiant parts/ Did I my soul and fortunes consecrate" (1.3.253-55). Her insistence that she saw Othello as he perceived himself implies that she knows Othello from his vantage point, from how he presented himself to her during their courtship. Furthermore, the "honours and valiant parts" of Othello to which Desdemona has "consecrate[d]" herself can be read as a reference to the stories of "his honours and valiant parts" that Othello has admitted to wooing Desdemona with.
25. In "*Othello:* Portrait of a Marriage," Bevington agrees with our observation that Desdemona's admiration validates Othello, making him feel better about his own person (224-25). Unlike us, Bevington insists that Desdemona's love is able to affirm Othello's ego precisely because it comes from one who, as a woman, is in a lowly social position that is beneath Othello's: Desdemona's "admiration [is] made all the more keen by the great distance between her uneventful and constricted domestic life and the unlimited opportunity for adventure that he has

enjoyed as a man. He finds her pity so gratifying because it dramatizes him as the protective male" (224-25). Of course, Othello, as a former slave, has not enjoyed an "unlimited opportunity for adventure," even though he is a man. By situating Desdemona as disadvantaged by her gender, Bevington disempowers her, ignoring her rebellion against the racist ideology of the play's official culture. Although his analysis of Desdemona and Othello's relationship neglects the role of race in their marriage or in their society, the play, with its constant allusions to Othello's "blackness" issuing from, among others, Othello himself, refuses to let the theater audience or reader disregard the social codes that have been breached by Othello and Desdemona's interracial marriage.

26. Refer to note 21.

Works Cited

Adelman, Janet. "Iago's Alter Ego: Race as Projection in *Othello*". *Shakespeare Quarterly* 48.2 (1997): 125-44.

Althusser, Louis. "Ideology and Ideological State Apparatuses (Notes towards an Investigation)". *Lenin and Philosophy*. Trans. Ben Brewster. New York: Monthly Review Press, 1972. 127-86.

Bartels, Emily C. "Making More of the Moor: Aaron, Othello, and Renaissance Refashionings of Race." *Shakespeare Quarterly* 41.4 (1990): 433-54.

Belsey, Catherine. "Desire's Excess and the English Renaissance Theatre: *Edward II, Troilus and Cressida, Othello.*" *Erotic Politics: Desire on the Renaissance Stage*. Ed. Susan Zimmerman. New York: Routledge, 1992. 84-102.

Bevington, David. "*Othello:* Portrait of a Marriage." *Othello: New Critical Essays*. Ed. Philip C. Kolin. New York: Routledge, 2002. 221-31.

Bloom, Allan, with Harry V. Jaffa. *Shakespeare's Politics*. Chicago: University of Chicago Press, 1964.

Bradley, A.C. *Shakespearean Tragedy: Lectures on Hamlet, Othello, King Lear and Macbeth*. New York: Penguin, 1991.

Cavell, Stanley. *Disowning Knowledge in Six Plays of Shakespeare.* Cambridge: Cambridge University Press, 1987.

Coleridge, Samuel Taylor. *Coleridge's Shakespearean Criticism.* Vol. 1. Ed. Thomas Middleton Raysor. Cambridge: Harvard University Press, 1930.

Cummings, Peter. "The Making of Meaning: Sex Words and Sex Acts in Shakespeare's *Othello.*" *Gettysburg Review* 3.1 (1990): 75-80.

Danson, Lawrence. "'The Catastrophe is a Nuptial': The Space of Masculine Desire in *Othello, Cymbeline,* and *The Winter's Tale.*" *Shakespeare Survey* 46. Ed. Stanley Wells. Cambridge: Cambridge University Press, 1994. 69-79.

Deats, Sara Munson. "'Truly, an obedient lady': Desdemona, Emilia, and the Doctrine of Obedience of *Othello.*" *Othello: New Critical Essays*. Ed. Philip C. Kolin. New York: Routledge, 2002. 233-54.

Deleuze, Gilles. "Coldness and Cruelty." *Masochism*. New York: Zone, 1991. 9-138.

Deleuze, Gilles and Félix Guattari. *A Thousand Plateaus: Capitalism and Schizophrenia*. Trans. Brian Massumi. Minneapolis: University of Minnesota Press, 1987.

Dollimore, Jonathan. *Sexual Dissidence: Augustine to Wilde, Freud to Foucault*. Oxford: Clarendon Press, 1991.

Greenblatt, Stephen. "The Improvisation of Power." *Renaissance Self-Fashioning: From More to Shakespeare*. Chicago: The University of Chicago Press, 1980. 222–54.

Gronbeck-Tedesco, John. "Morality, Ethics and the Failure of Love in Shakespeare's *Othello.*" *Othello: New Critical Essays*. Ed. Philip C. Kolin. New York: Routledge, 2002. 255-70.

Hankey, Julie. "Introduction." *Othello*. By William Shakespeare. Ed. Julie.

Hankey. *Plays in Performance Series*. Bristol: Bristol Classics Press, 1987. 1-147.

Hedrick, Donald and Bryan Reynolds. "Shakespace and Transversal Power." *Shakespeare Without Class: Misappropriations of Cultural Capital*. Ed. Donald Hedrick and Bryan Reynolds. New York: St. Martin's Press, 2000. 3-47.

Hunter, G.K. "Othello and Colour Prejudice." Dramatic Identities and Cultural Tradition: Studies in Shakespeare and his Contemporaries. New York: Barnes and Noble, 1978. 139-63.

Kállay, Géza. "'To Die Upon a Kiss': Love and Death as Metaphors in *Othello.*" *HJEAS* 3.2 (1997): 25-58.

Knight, G. Wilson. "The Othello Music." The Wheel of Fire: Interpretations of Shakespearian Tragedy with Three New Essays. London: Methuen, 1949. 97-119.

Leavis, F.R. "Diabolic Intellect and the Noble Hero: or The Sentimentalist's Othello." 1937; rpt. in *The Common Pursuit.* Harmondsworth: Peregrine, 1952.

Lim, Walter S.H. "Representing the Other: *Othello*, Colonialism, Discourse." *The Upstart Crow 8* (1993): 57-78.

Little Jr., Arthur L. "'An essence that's not seen': The Primal Scene of Racism in *Othello*." *Shakespeare Quarterly* 44.3 (1993): 304-24.

Montrose, Louis. "Professing the Renaissance: The Poetics and Politics of Culture." *The New Historicism*. Ed. Aram H. Veeser. New York: Routledge, 1989. 15-36.

Newman, Karen. "'And wash the Ethiop White': Femininity and the Monstrous in Othello." *Fashioning Femininity and English Renaissance Drama*. Chicago: Chicago University Press, 1991.

Orlin, Lena Cowen. "Desdemona's Disposition." *Shakespearean Tragedy and Gender*. Ed. Shirley Nelson Garner and Madelon Sprengnether. Bloommington: Indiana University Press, 1996. 171-92.

Pechter, Edward. "'Have You Not Read of Some Such Thing?' Sex and Sexual Stories in *Othello*." *Shakespeare Survey* 49. Ed. Stanley Wells. Cambridge: Cambridge University Press, 1996. 201-16.

Reynolds, Bryan. Becoming Criminal: Transversal Performance and Cultural Dissidence in Early Modern England. Baltimore: Johns Hopkins University Press, 2002.

——. "The Devil's House, 'or worse': Transversal Power and Antitheatrical Discourse in Early Modern England." *Theatre Journal* 49.2 (1997): 143-67.

Reynolds, Bryan, and Joseph Fitzpatrick. "The Transversality of Michel de Certeau: Foucault's Panoptic Discourse and the Cartographic Impulse." *Diacritics* 29.3 (2000): 63-80.

Ridley, M.R. Introduction. *Othello*. By William Shakespeare. Ed. M.R. Ridley. London: Methuen, 1958. xv-lxx.

Rose, Mary Beth. "The Heroics of Marriage in *Othello* and *The Duchess of Malfi*." *Shakespearean Tragedy and Gender*. Ed. Shirley Nelson Garner and Madelon Sprengnether. Bloomington: Indiana University Press, 1996. 208-38.

Schlegel, Augustus William. *A Course of Lectures on Dramatic Art and Literature*. Vol. 2. Trans. John Black. London: J. Templeman and J.R. Smith, 1840.

Shakespeare, William. Othello. Ed. E.A.J. Honigmann. London: Arden Shakespeare, 2001.

——. Othello. Ed. M.R. Ridley. London: Routledge, 1958.

Sinfield, Alan. Faultlines: Cultural Materialism and the Politics of Dissident Reading. Berkeley: University of California Press, 1992.

Stallybrass, Peter. "Patriarchal Territories: The Body Enclosed." *Rewriting the Renaissance: The Discourse of Sexual Difference in Early Modern Europe*. Ed. Margaret W. Ferguson, Margaret Quilligan, and Nancy J. Vickers. Chicago: Chicago University Press, 1986. 123-42.

Takakuwa, Yoko. "Diagnosing Male Jealousy: Woman as Man's Symptom in The Merry Wives of Windsor, Othello, The Winter's Tale and Cymbeline." *Hot Questrists After the English Renaissance: Essays on Shakespeare and His Contemporaries*. Ed. Yasunari Takahashi. New York: AMS Press, 2000. 19-36.

2

Milton in America: The Case of Jackson County, Florida

Bruce Boehrer

> I shall be Milton among the Americans! And you shall write it down.
>
> Peter Ackroyd, *Milton in America*

1. Imaginary Ancestors

John Milton was elected Governor of Florida in November, 1860. Given the state's more recent electoral history, one might wonder if voters understood, that year, just who was running for office. And who knows? Perhaps, even the governor-to-be was a bit confused as to his identity. In its more speculative dimension, the present essay explores this possibility. On a more prosaic level, it integrates the history of Florida's Civil War governor into the current scholarly archive on Milton reception in America and the poet's family legacy.

Governor John Milton was not, of course, the first bearer of his name, but then neither was the author of *Paradise Lost*. The poet's father is famously eponymous; as for the governor in question, he was the grandson of yet another John Milton, this last (or, chronologically—if we overlook additional preceding and intervening John Miltons, of whom there is no shortage[1]—third). John Milton being a lieutenant-colonel in the Continental Army during the American Revolution, Secretary of State for Georgia from 1777 to 1799, the recipient of two electoral votes during the presidential election of 1789, and the figure for whom Milton County, Georgia was christened in 1857. The county in question no longer exists; it was absorbed into Fulton County in 1932. Likewise, the Milton who lent it his name rests in an unknown grave.[2]

This John Milton's grandson, in turn, was born in Jefferson County, Georgia, on April 20, 1807, read law at the University of Georgia, was admitted to the Georgia bar, and first ran for office, unsuccessfully, as a Georgia congressional candidate on the Nullification ticket of 1833. After a stint practicing law in Mobile, Alabama, Milton commanded a company of Alabama militia in the Seminole War of 1836-37, then moved his law practice to New Orleans, remaining there (apart from a brief spell in Texas) until 1846, when he settled into presumptive retirement on a plantation called Sylvania in Jackson County, Florida.[3]

At the start of the twenty-first century, Florida affords no better approximation to the locus amoenus of Miltonic pastoral than Jackson County. It is an area rich in bovinity. But in the years before secession, when most of the state remained a sweltering, malarial marsh, its white population lay concentrated along the border with Alabama and Georgia, between Pensacola in the west and Jacksonville in the east. As a result, Jackson County occupied an important position in the state, seventy miles west of the capital in Tallahassee and astride the Apalachicola River, which afforded Florida its best water route to Georgia and Alabama in the north and one of its better harbors on the Apalachicola Bay to the south. Here Milton became a prominent cotton planter; by 1859 his landholdings extended to 7326 acres, and he is listed in 1861 as owning fifty-two slaves.[4] In 1850 he entered Florida politics by securing election to the lower house of the state's General Assembly, from which he retired after a single term.

Of course, none of this would be of much interest to anyone now if the John Milton in question had not reentered politics in time to serve as Governor of Florida during the Civil War. And even so, nothing here would interest literary historians at all if not for a curious, but understandable, genealogical error: the Miltons of Jackson County, Florida, consider themselves relations of the poet.

I take it for granted that this misapprehension will intrigue scholars in Milton studies and nineteenth-century American history. But beyond this specialized appeal, the tale of Florida's Miltons offers an edifying theoretical spectacle as well, a spectacle that involves the convergence of two parallel but distinct narratives of origin operating at the levels of family history and national identity.

As regards the latter, one might recall Benedict Anderson's influential account of the origins of nationalism, if only because the story of Governor John Milton illustrates its dominant concerns so well. Famously describing the nation as "an imagined political community", Anderson derives the imagined character of such communities from their lack of personal cohesion—from the fact that "the members of even the smallest nation will never know most of their fellow members, meet them, or even hear of them, yet in the minds of each lives the image of their communion".[5] This imagined communion, in turn, is enabled by a repertoire of historical factors including the development of print culture; its relation to a prior culture of religious experience formulated through the medium of a dead language ("in fact, the deader...the better");[6] the concomitant rise of colonialism and creole colonial elites who experience their bond to the metropole through the paradigm of pilgrimage; and the development of a sense of community rooted in language—"above all in the form of poetry and songs"—and defined against notions of race, with their emphasis upon the "biological physiognomy" of individuals and groups.[7] For Anderson, the resulting social formation exerts a unique form of emotional authority; it can demand the ultimate sacrifice of individuals precisely because of its imaginary character.

For the slave-owning secessionist Governor John Milton, these elements of nationalist fervor all loom large, and the ensuing discussion will aim in part to account for their presence in Milton's gubernatorial career. But if Governor Milton thus exemplifies the psychic formations of an incipient nationalism, he also suggests the degree to which family, like the nation, can operate as an imagined unit. Freud notably proposed that "the liberation of the individual...from the authority of his parents" could entail a neurotic revision of the circumstances of one's own birth, such that "the child's imagination becomes engaged in the task of getting free from [his biological] parents...and of replacing them by others, who, as a rule, are of higher social standing."[8] By this logic, Governor John Milton's imaginary reconfiguration of his ancestry enacts a form of personal neurosis that parallels, in turn, the collective neurosis of the Civil War South in which he played a leading political role.

The result, when taken in conjunction with Anderson's model of imagined communities, is a fantasy of social and cultural affiliations acted out on the levels both of national and personal destiny. Performative in nature but also collective and subliminal, this fantasy may perhaps best be understood as a particular manifestation of the political unconscious. As Judith Butler has suggested, it should "be construed not as a set of projections on an internal screen but as part of human relationality itself," a drive that is "neither exclusively biological nor cultural, but always the site of their dense convergence".[9] It is also, in the case of Governor Milton and his family, a deeply personal matter.

2. Meet the Miltons

Governor Milton's erroneous lineage is a matter of public record, and one can trace it back to within at least a generation of the governor himself. In a typically reassuring instance of taxpayer funds at work, the Florida State Office of Cultural and Historical Programs begins its online biography of Governor Milton by claiming that he was "a descendant of the English poet John Milton".[10] J. Randall Stanley's *History of Jackson County* derives the Florida Miltons from the family of "John Milton, the poet, who wrote the immortal epic, *Paradise Lost*".[11] In his biography of Governor John Milton's youngest son, Jeff Davis Milton, J. Evetts Haley declares "the great blind poet of England" to be a "distinguished and distant relative" of the Florida Miltons.[12] But the most detailed version of this story appears in an article in the Tallahassee Historical Society Annual for 1937 by Daisy Parker entitled "Governor John Milton".

Coincidentally, Daisy Parker would go on to a noteworthy academic career under the married name of Daisy Parker Flory. Her 1937 article on Governor John Milton was condensed from the undergraduate honors thesis she presented that same year to the History Department of Florida State College for Women (now Florida State University). After receiving her doctorate from the University of Virginia she took a faculty appointment at her undergraduate alma mater, where she rose to be Dean of the Faculties in 1973. In 1940 she revisited the subject of Governor Milton in her M.A. thesis for the University of Virginia, and in 1942 she reworked this into an article in the *Florida Historical Quarterly* that remains a basic source for biographical information on the governor.[13] But in 1937 she made her most detailed statement regarding the hereditary background of the Florida Miltons, a statement she began by declaring "John Milton, the poet," to be the governor's "thrice-great uncle":

> [Governor John Milton's] great-great-great-grandfather, Sir Christopher Milton, brother of John Milton [the poet], had four daughters and two sons, one of the sons being Thomas Milton who had two sons, Richard and John, both of whom came to America about 1720. This John Milton lived in Virginia and was a vestryman in Virginia on the same vestry with George Washington and Lord Fairfax. His son, likewise named John Milton, moved to Burke County, Georgia, and was a captain in the regular army during the Revolution, serving on the Committee of Georgia Affairs.[14]

This particular John Milton, Parker continues, was the governor's grandfather, Secretary of State for Georgia, whose career I have already described in brief.

Sadly, this tale cannot be correct as it stands, for several reasons. To begin with, the poet John Milton's younger brother, the royalist Sir Christopher, of course had a son named Thomas (born in 1647); for the record, Christopher also begot another John Milton, an obscure nephew of the poet. But Sir Christopher did not have "four daughters and two sons". In fact, apart from two offspring who died in early childhood, he appears to have had four sons—Christopher, John, Thomas, and Richard—and four daughters—Anne, Thomasin, Mary, and Catherine.[15] Beyond this, while it is true that Thomas appears to have married and had children (indeed, he seems to have been the only son of Sir Christopher Milton to do so), there is no record of him producing a son named John. On the contrary, I suspect the genealogy reported by Daisy Parker has confused generations so as to translate Thomas Milton's brother John into his son. This error is made more plausible, in turn, by the fact that Thomas also had no son named Richard, although, as pointed out above, he did have a brother of that name; again, the name seems to have shifted down a generation in Daisy Parker's account.

In any event, although the surviving records of Thomas Milton's children are sketchy, they offer no confirmation of the tale reported by Daisy Parker. Instead they suggest that Thomas Milton left two daughters[16] and, more importantly for the Milton family name, two sons: one named Thomas, who was baptized on June 26, 1679, and buried on "either July 1, 1680 or 30 December 1683";[17] and one named Charles, who was baptized on January 20, 1684, and of whom nothing further is known.[18] William Riley Parker has surmised that this son "may have lived on to perpetuate the family name",[19] but if so his offspring, like Milton's angels, must rest "contented with thir fame in Heav'n".[20] On earth, nothing is known of them.

Joseph M. French claims in his Life Records of John Milton that the families of the poet's "sister Anne and his brother Christopher have continued into the twentieth century",[21] but French offers no explanation of his remark and no evidence to support it. In the case of the sister, Anne, he must have been referring to the line of descent created through her second marriage, to Thomas Agar, in January of 1631/32.[22] But as for French's remark about the line of Sir Christopher Milton, its meaning remains uncertain. All one knows is that the most plausible male line of descent to be traced from the family of John Milton the poet into the twentieth century would have to run through Milton's grandnephew Charles, yet for whatever reason, Daisy Parker's genealogy of the Florida Miltons mentions no such worthy.

Then there is this to consider as well. When she returns to the subject of Governor John Milton in her 1942 *Florida Historical Quarterly* article on the subject, while in general giving less genealogy than in her article and honors thesis of five years earlier, Daisy Parker does add the following new information. Having noted in 1937 that the forebear of Governor John Milton "who came to America about 1720" was "a vestryman in Virginia on the same vestry with George Washington and Lord Fairfax," she goes on in her later article to declare that "The author [i.e., Daisy Parker herself] found a John Milton on the vestry of Christ Church, Alexandria, [Virginia,] in 1783.... If this Milton were the John who came over in 1730 [sic], he would have been about seventy-three years of age at the time of his vestry service."[23] This is the same John Milton whom Parker regards as being "the son of Thomas,...son of Sir Christopher Milton, brother of John Milton, the poet".[24] But Sir Christopher's son Thomas was born in 1647, which means that if he were to beget a son named John who was about seventy-three in 1783, he would have had to do so in 1710 or thereabouts, at the advanced age of approximately sixty-three. Never mind that there's no record of him doing so; in itself this priapic feat seems most unlikely, given that the Thomas Milton in question departed this world on October 17, 1694.[25]

So what, in turn, is the source of Daisy Parker's own misinformation, and why is it worth considering at such length? First, Daisy Parker got her tale from the obvious place; as she remarks in the endnotes of her honors thesis, "All of the Milton family history has been very kindly furnished me by Mr. William Hall Milton of Marianna, grandson of John Milton" the governor.[26] In her *Florida Historical Quarterly* article, Parker goes a bit further, attributing her information to "the late William Hall Milton of Marianna,...as told to him by his father, William Henry Milton".[27] If we can rely on this attribution, then we can trace the Florida Miltons' putative association with the poet at least to the generation following Governor Milton himself. As it happens, J. Evetts Haley's historical research on Jeff Davis Milton offers independent support of this hypothesis, since Haley ascribes his own parallel family history of the Florida Miltons to personal testimony drawn both from Governor Milton's youngest son and from "Mrs. Elise Gamble, Jeff Milton's oldest sister".[28] To this extent, Parker's and Haley's research becomes an exercise in the promulgation of personal mythologies and in their relation to the historical record, an exercise that happens to affect the reputations both of England's most famous epic poet and of a distinguished southern American political family. This exercise is worth revisiting, in turn, partly because of the intrinsic interest of the principals involved in it, but also because of what it might suggest, at least in this specific case, about the relation between personal identity and historical formations.

On this latter level, the case of Governor John Milton engages the venerable, precarious anthropological distinction between achieved and ascribed status.[29] It is an opposition with which early versions of New Historicism and Cultural Studies were deeply preoccupied because it proves both essential to traditional European social structure and yet always in some sense compromised. On one hand, the Miltons of Florida exemplify the fictive character of genealogically-ascribed identity; in their fantasized descent from England's epic poet, they perform a mode of relation that acquires a measure of historical authority simply by virtue of the performance itself. And yet the terms of the performance are also in a way constrained by the very relation they enact; to situate oneself within this lineage is to assume a burden of historical responsibility—an intellectual and cultural legacy—that may be adapted to individual circumstances but cannot be wholly abandoned. In this sense, while the ascription of identity is achievable, the achievement in question entails a complex assignment of allegiances and expectations. In illustrating this dynamic, Governor John Milton also affords a rare instance of the intersection of family history with literary appropriation.

3. My Father Was a Paiute Indian Chief

In embodying this peculiar conjunction of family history and literary assimilation, Governor John Milton himself arguably acquires the character of a literary artifact. This aspect of his identity is only enhanced by the governor's own apparent lack of insight into it. He seems to have inherited the fiction of his illustrious ancestry as received truth. To this extent, one might think of him not as a figure for Coleridge's willing suspension of disbelief, nor even for the unwilling suspension of disbelief, but for a suspension of disbelief that is in some sense anterior to—perhaps even constitutive of—the will itself.

One must be somewhat cautious on this score, because the record is not confirmed by Governor Milton's own testimony. Almost all his surviving writing lies in his gubernatorial letter-books?—hardly a compendium of musings on family history. When the main house of Sylvania Plantation burned down in the 1920s, whatever personal papers it might have contained were lost. Yet even so, it seems clear from the testimony of Daisy Parker and J. Evetts Haley that the governor's children grew up believing themselves descendants of Milton the poet. The family genealogy given by Parker shows signs of transmission over time. And then there is the governor's grandfather.

In a family given to recycling the Christian names of its male children, the onomastic preferences of Governor John Milton's grandfather John Milton prove hard to ignore. Eschewing the more sober practice of his own father (another John), this John Milton endowed his sons with a series of flamboyant names that seem to operate as a calculated mode of personal expression. As for the personality thus expressed, its dominant features include a self-conscious classicism, a fixation upon martial heroics, an apparent fondness for the radical Protestant leaders of seventeenth-century Europe, and—for want of a better phrase—a certain epic frame of mind. Consider, for instance, the unfortunate case of Augustus

Caesar Gustavus Adolphus Milton,[30] whose name is a virtual haiku of historical aspirations and phantasmatic relationships. Twenty-first century parents might shrink from afflicting their offspring with such a title, but Colonel John Milton, Georgia's first Secretary of State, was made of sterner stuff. Nor should we overlook the redoubtable Lucius Quintus Cincinnatus Milton,[31] whose name not only evokes the highest standards of Roman virtus but also celebrates Colonel Milton's own personal history by recalling the fact of his admission into the Society of the Cincinnati, founded in May, 1783, as the oldest military hereditary society in the United States, with George Washington elected as its first President General and its initial membership limited to officers of the Continental Army (and their foreign allies) who fought in the American Revolution.[32]

Against the backdrop of such sibling competition, the name Colonel Milton chose for the father-to-be of Governor Milton—Homer Virgil Milton—may seem an exercise in refined understatement. But in some ways it is the most ambitious of the lot. Certainly its classicism is not to be outdone, and the subject-matter of Homer's and Virgil's poetry keeps our focus squarely upon the field of martial endeavor. But the turn toward Homer and Virgil is specifically a turn toward the literary—a unique move for Colonel Milton. If to this we add the Colonel's demonstrated tendency to use his sons' names as a register of family history, we are left with an overdetermined epic progression, from the Greek to the Latin to the English, all culminating and in a sense present within the identity of Colonel John Milton's son. Taken with the other evidence we have, this naming practice would seem to point toward the existence of a long-standing family mythology, probably originating sometime in the early to middle eighteenth century, in which the Miltons of Florida figure as descendants of John Milton the poet.

So what might it mean to inherit such a mythology? In his recent book-length study of the poet Milton's relations with his family, John Shawcross argues "that family makes a difference in one's life. Family is significant in one's life, but it also establishes 'signifiers' that tell us about the person, that may lead us to awarenesses that we otherwise may miss."[33] As Nancy Armstrong and Leonard Tennenhouse have remarked in their own study of Milton and his times, "even the most sophisticated scholars and critics tend to assume that consciousness enters history and takes up a definitive relationship with the world by means of the family."[34] But if this is so, what about imaginary family? Surely, in a case like this of the Florida Miltons, imaginary relations have acquired something like the force of the real thing.

And if so, what might it mean to be John Milton, son of Homer Virgil Milton, son of John Milton, son of Thomas Milton, son of Christopher Milton, brother of John Milton? What might it mean to be known—to know oneself—through the name and prevenient reputation of England's preeminent epic poet? In Joseph Heller's *Catch-22*, the similarly-challenged Major Major Major Major collapses under the psychological demands imposed by his name: "[T]he effects were disastrous.... Nobody would have anything to do with him.... He grew awkwardly into a tall, strange, dreamy boy with fragile eyes and a very delicate mouth whose tentative, groping smile collapsed instantly into hurt disorder at every fresh rebuff."[35] But to their credit, the Miltons of Jackson County proved a hardier breed of plant; again and again, from one generation to the next, they rose to meet the demands of their imaginary history, and they did so again and again in the same way. They became soldiers.

Colonel John Milton of Georgia is only the first good example of this tendency, which in his case led to his being taken prisoner by the British at the siege of Fort Howe in 1777.[36] Homer Virgil, in turn, earned an officer's commission in the U.S. army and participated in the Canadian campaign of the War of 1812, in which he lost an arm and gained promotion to the rank of colonel.[37] Later, when Homer Virgil's son campaigned for Governor of Florida, it was largely on the basis of his own military reputation. He is referred to in contemporary newspapers as "General Milton" (a rank he received, like his father before him, in his state militia), and an anonymous "Soldier" contributes a column to The East

Floridian attesting that during "the creek war [sic] of 1836" then-captain Milton "was always at every post to brave all the dangers that might surround him."[38] All things being equal, this experience served "General Milton" well; his gubernatorial term was consumed by military matters and he "more than once hinted to [Jefferson] Davis that he would rather be a Confederate brigadier-general than a civilian governor."[39] After the Civil War, Governor Milton's son Jeff Davis joined the Texas Rangers and earned a lasting reputation as a gunfighter; as his biographer declares, the Miltons of Florida "were more than men of policy; they were men of action."[40] The record on this score is impressive, bespeaking a masculine ethic of military rather than literary orientation.

But it is no light task to assimilate John Milton the poet to a family mythology so heavily invested in the ethos of martial heroism. To do so is to perform a decisive, if implicit, misreading of *Paradise Lost* whereby the poem extends rather than contests the military thematics of its classical predecessors. On the whole, contemporary scholars don't like to understand Milton's epic this way. They prefer to see in it a "rejection of the conventional heroic argument of warfare and its displacement...by the ordeal of spiritual combat";[41] they tend to view Milton as "educating...his...audiences about the failures of conventional heroism";[42] they like to take seriously the poet's own claim that he is "Not sedulous by Nature to indite/Warrs" (9.27-28), opting instead to celebrate "the better fortitude/ Of Patience and Heroic Martyrdom" (9.29-30). This view of *Paradise Lost* has been patiently elaborated by scholars and critics over the past two centuries, largely in response to Voltaire's and Johnson's famous complaints about the absurdity of Milton's war in heaven, with its artillery and general "confusion of spirit and matter".[43] The result, in its most fully-developed versions, has been an approach to *Paradise Lost* that regards Milton's battle-scenes as "ridiculous," culminating in Book 6 in a "grand finale of physical ridicule" and fueled by the conviction that "all wars are games of the most infantile kind".[44]

Hardly fertile ground, this, in which to root a family of career soldiers. But then again, the anti-war view of *Paradise Lost* is a fairly recent one. If, as the foregoing evidence seems to suggest, the Florida Miltons began tracing their lineage back to the poet sometime in the early to mid 1700s, we should recall that earlier readers of Milton tended to take his epic on different terms. As Merritt Hughes pointed out some time ago, the critical response to *Paradise Lost* from its first appearance until the late eighteenth century was marked by a general "enthusiasm for Milton's battle scenes", with the heavenly war of Book 6 often regarded as "the most moving part of the whole work" and taken as evidence "that Milton's style was worthy of its classical models".[45] Here, in the celebratory conjunction of martial subject-matter and classical influence, we may perhaps encounter the literary paradigm from which the Miltons of Jackson County, Florida drew their imagined ancestry. In this respect, one might venture to say, the family's spurious genealogy is subtended by an equally spurious literary criticism. Surely this is reconnaissance writ large.

Not that one should be surprised to find Milton's work and influence subject to such misconstruction: Milton appropriation is often about just this sort of thing. In his own recent contribution to the field, Richard Rambuss has studied the antebellum roots of New Orleans'secret-society Carnival clubs, in particular the great original of them all, the Mistick Krewe of Comus, which enlivened the Mardi Gras of 1857 with a nocturnal procession entitled The Demon Actors in *Paradise Lost*. For Rambuss, this choice of subject-matter was right in its very wrongness. Rather than embodying the "Riot, and ill manag'd Merriment" of Comus' followers in A Mask Presented at Ludlow-Castle (172), the Krewe of Comus represented "an inversion of carnivalesque inversion" whereby a "distinctly Anglo-American social and cultural order" sought to assert its dominance over New Orleans' "proud antecedent francophone culture" by remaking Mardi Gras as "elevated and dignified...in a word, Miltonic".[46] Of course, it takes a certain squint to regard Milton's Comus as "elevated and dignified"; likewise, anybody who has ever read the Defenses of the English People, or Eikonoklastes, or the Pro Se Defensio may have trouble accepting these adjectives as a full characterization of the Miltonic temper. But for the gentlemen in the Mistick Krewe of Comus, such objections would have been beside the point.

Curiously, there exists at least the possibility of a material connection between the Krewe of Comus and the Miltons of Jackson County, Florida. As Samuel Kinser has pointed out, the Mistick Krewe was originally founded by a group of six young men from Mobile, Alabama, who had participated, during their time in that city, in the New Year's pageants organized by the Cowbellion de Rakin Society from 1831 forward.[47] The Cowbellions of Mobile had begun to infiltrate New Orleans Mardi Gras in 1837, prior to establishing the Mistick Crewe some twenty years later;[48] as for John Milton the governor-to-be of Florida, he practiced law in Mobile during the 1830s before moving in turn to New Orleans, where he continued at the bar from 1837 to 1846. White Mobile in the 1830s was a decidedly compact community; the US census of 1840 lists the county's total free white population at 11,763, and its free white male population (of all ages) at 7,597.[49] Given Milton's residence there, his standing as an attorney, and his subsequent command of an Alabama volunteer company during the Seminole War, it seems plausible that he might have been known to the group of Mobilians who, like him, emigrated to New Orleans between 1837 and 1857, when the Krewe of Comus performed its first Mardi Gras parade.

In any case, the Miltons of Jackson County seem to share with the Mistick Krewe of Comus a marked impulse toward the creative misreading of England's greatest epic poet, a misreading that in both cases enables some form of strategic appropriation. But if anything, the Miltons seem to have gone the Krewe of Comus one better in this regard by admitting the poet not only into their cultural and intellectual but indeed into their biological ancestry. Given the enduring American penchant for self-fashioning and self-reinvention, this fantasy may seem like an early expression of national character; then again, some American writers elevate it to the status of a transcendent principle. In Don DeLillo, for instance, such historical error emerges as a necessary defensive construct–almost a kind of evolutionary adaptation:

> The family is the cradle of the world's-misinformation. There must be something in family life that generates factual error. Overcloseness, the noise and heat of being. Perhaps something even deeper, like the need to survive.... [W]e are fragile creatures surrounded by a world of hostile facts. Facts threaten our happiness and security. The deeper we delve into the nature of things, the looser our structure may seem to become. The family process works toward sealing off the world.... Magic and superstition become entrenched as the powerful orthodoxy of the clan.[50]

Given the fluid interplay of literary and historical experience exemplified by this essay's subject-matter, it seems right that DeLillo's view of the family as a "cradle of... misinformation" should itself take shape within a fictive context. Nor is it unique in this respect. Nathan Weinstein, who knew enough about American self-reinvention to write under the name of Nathanael West, pursued a similar vision:

> Parents are also part of the great business of dreams. My father was a Russian prince, my father was a Paiute Indian chief, my father was an Australian sheep baron, my father lost all his money on Wall Street, my father was a portrait painter. People... were unable to do without such tales. They told them because they wanted to talk about something besides clothing or business or the movies, because they wanted to talk about something poetic.[51]

"Something poetic": when Colonel John Milton named his third son Homer Virgil, this is just what he was reaching for. A man whose own classicism, flamboyant as it was, seems never to have reached *Cedant arma togae* nonetheless felt the need to install a poet—indeed, three of them—at the heart of his family history.

4. Milton's Paradise Found!

In the meantime, however, one person's liberating self-reinvention may become another's purgatorial confinement. This principle looms large in the American Civil War, which from a certain angle looks distressingly like a big-budget American remake of its English predecessor, done with more extras and bigger explosions. Both cases present a superannuated agrarian cultural order surviving on a diet of gross social injustice and self-indulgent chivalric fantasy but yielding at last to an unlikely urban alliance of beady-eyed commerce and psalm-singing self-righteousness. In both cases the humanitarian benefits conferred by the crisis—whether through Diggers and Levellers or through Abolitionists—appear almost by accident, to the great displeasure of almost everyone with a say in the matter. In both cases, bad hair prevails. (Roundheads, sideburns.)

For Governor John Milton of Florida, this is unhappy news, to the extent that one can call it news at all. In America's remake of the English Civil Wars, it is clear whose side John Milton the poet must be on. His conscription to the literary lineage of New England Puritanism remains the best-documented aspect of Milton' appropriation in the United States, so much so that one has trouble compiling an exhaustive list of pronouncements on the subject. From F.O. Matthiessen's description of Milton as "the archetype of the poet of New England"; through G.F. Sensabaugh's claim that "Milton made his first imprint on America in the liberal settlement of Rhode Island"; to Keith Stavely's account of Milton as "the most distinctly Puritan literary figure"—and New England, "the most distinctly Puritan society"—in America; to Kevin Van Anglen's placement of him "among the New England elite's pantheon"; the "American cultural cathexis onto Milton" has been "nearly always treated in northern, usually New England, contexts".[52] Moreover, this is clearly how many contemporary Americans, both in the north and the south, saw things during the Civil War itself. As Alice Fahs has pointed out, "Southern poets characterized their countrymen as 'cavaliers'," while their Union counterparts "instead called on the strengths of Northern 'Puritans'."[53] Nor were the strengths in question limited to the masculine sphere; a Union poet like Caroline A. Mason could present Milton's counsel that "They also serve who only stand and waite" as a model for the comportment of Northern women in wartime.[54] All in all, the Union won the battle for control of Milton's American influence, and won it early.

Yet Southerners could, and did, assimilate Milton to their own sectional agendas, and not just in the relatively benign case of Mardi Gras. John Wilkes Booth, it is worth recalling, was named after one of eighteenth-century England's greatest Whig dissidents, a man who could trace his political lineage to Milton, and in his recent biography of Booth, Michael Kaufmann sees this fact as no coincidence. Noting that Booth attended preparatory school at the Milton Academy north of Baltimore (named for the poet), Kaufmann surveys the school's curriculum as follows:

> Academy students were expected to read and recite from the works of Herodotus, Cicero, Tacitus, Horace, and Livy. Though not specifically mentioned in their literature, one other writer must have figured largely in the curriculum as well: John Milton, the poet. Milton was an ardent opponent of tyranny, and...argued that tyrannical leaders might justly be put to death.... It would be surprising, indeed, if Headmaster [John Emerson] Lamb had left him out of the program.[55]

For a figure like Booth, as much as for Governor John Milton, the Miltonic heritage of political dissent and insurrection could be coupled with classical models of civic activism to license the Confederate cause.

If this mode of appropriation offers any broad moral for literary historians, it is that the act of appropriation itself need not be constrained by inconvenient facts. Booth may draw upon Miltonic precedent for his assassination of Lincoln notwithstanding the very different legal form adopted by Parliament in its execution of Charles I, to say nothing of the obvious problems associated with adducing Milton as an intellectual precursor of the Confederate polity. The Mistick Crewe of Comus affiliates itself with a Milton who has been almost completely divested of literary and ideological content. It is enough that he stand as a convenient signifier for Anglo-Saxon Culture, and to that end it is in fact best if he be purged of any disagreeable associations that might derive from serious intellectual contact with his life and work. As for Governor Milton, his surviving political pronouncements can be said to rehearse the grand themes of his notional forebear's work—liberty and its demands, the duty of resistance to tyranny, the paramount importance of free speech and free press—but only because the mental universe of Milton the poet is so expansive as to admit connections with almost any conceivable topic.

When Milton the governor writes Jefferson Davis that Florida's "gallant sons and daughters would rather perish bravely, sword in hand, vindicating their rights, than yield submissively to or entertain a moment's thought of ever living under the same Government with the people of the North,"[56] his rhetoric may recall Satan's refusal "To bow and sue for grace" to the victorious Son (1.111). When he denounces the "sinuosities of policy" of Lincoln's Republicans and accuses them of "a flagrant invasion and usurpation" of constitutional power,[57] one may be reminded of the "usurpation" that Satan claims God to have effected upon the realm of Chaos and Night through the act of creation (*Paradise Lost* 2.983); or the "sensual Appetite" that governs Adam and Eve after the fall, "Usurping over sovran Reason" (9.1129); or the "female usurpation" with which Dalila threatens Milton's Samson (Samson Agonistes 1060). Samson's claim that "Nations grown corrupt/... love Bondage more than Liberty,/ Bondage with ease then strenuous liberty" (267, 269-70) may parallel Governor Milton's assessment of "the people of the United States":

> Once, who more firm in the maintenance of chartered guarantees than they? Who more watchful of their rights or more quick to resist aggression than they?... And yet where are they now? Their Constitution openly violated; their laws trampled under foot; their

press muzzled; the freedom of speech a thing of the past and they applauding.[58]

But in the end, these connections, such as they are, seem coincidental. For the most part, Milton the governor seems unconcerned about the substantive intellectual heritage of Milton the poet, as if this were of no real consequence for the process of appropriation itself.

Not so the governor's detractors. For them, at least, the putative genealogical connection to Milton the poet seems to have entailed certain ideological obligations as well. Thus, within months of Governor Milton's assumption of office, his political enemies reconvened the state's secession convention with the aim of assailing the governor's executive authority. The reassembled convention at once embarked on an aggressive plan to restrict the powers of the governorship, first by repealing an act Milton had proposed against monopolies, then by accusing him of mismanaging state funds, then by creating a three-man executive council to share his powers, and finally by dissolving the state militia.[59] As Governor Milton's opponents readied this political offensive, they sought to influence public opinion as well. One result of these efforts was an editorial column appearing in the Florida Sentinel for January 21, 1862, written by one J.E.F. of Ocala and gaily entitled "Health of Florida, and Gov. Milton as Physician of the State". The title's medical metaphor does not survive long at J.E.F.'s hands, but it hangs around sufficiently for him to exclaim in grief, "Alas, poor Florida! It is hard, indeed, to be made a victim of misplaced confidence; but harder still, when it results in being purged, vomited, bled, blistered to death! Thy paradise lost and never to be regained, by Milton!"[60]

The piece then launches into a florid ad hominem diatribe, replete with references to Lycophron, Tacitus, and La Rochefoucauld, and as it progresses one begins to realize that J.E.F. is drawing an unspoken contrast between Governor Milton and John Milton the poet, presenting the former as a kind of anti-Milton, as it were. Echoing Samuel Johnson's censure of "Lycidas" as "easy, vulgar, and therefore disgusting,"[61] J.E.F. declares that the governor's "manners...

would be polite, graceful, and attractive, were it not for that affectation, bombast, and vulgar leer, that make them disgusting". Recalling the poet's Accedence Commenc't Grammar as well as his general scholarly reputation, J.E.F. goes on to sneer at Governor Milton's "productions in bad grammar" while insisting that the governor "would arraign before the Miltonian bar all who should dare to say that he is not a scholar or a statesman". He attaches to Milton a damning phrase from Tacitus, who first applied it to the Emperor Galba; then, "Desiring to accommodate Governor Milton, and knowing that he knows nothing about Latin", he appends an English version of the line. (It is a common schoolboy text that illustrates certain cheerful things about the ablative.) Setting Governor Milton in implicit opposition to the principles of free printing advanced in the Areopagitica, J.E.F. charges that he "would make the existence of the press dependent upon its zealous advocation of the Miltonian practice; appointing as editors those who are prepared naturally to endorse his purposes, and expelling those whom independence and pride, positively forbid it". As a result, J.E.F. concludes, the reconvened secession convention should "find a true bill against John Milton for mala praxia". Never mind that neither vulgar leering, bad grammar, nor ignorance of Latin is or ever was an indictable offense in the state of Florida. The point is a deeper one; the governor has betrayed his responsibilities to the state, J.E.F. implies, because he has betrayed the principles of his ancestry.

This abuse was inspired most particularly by Governor Milton's removal of one Colonel Edward Hopkins, a political opponent, from command of the Confederate garrison at Apalachicola. As historians have observed more than once, the Apalachicola River basin formed the linchpin of Milton's defense plan for the state.[62] On one level, this was clearly for sound strategic reasons; it encompassed the administrative and economic center of mid-nineteenth-century Florida. But one cannot shake the thought that Governor Milton felt an additional, personal commitment to preserving this part of the state. After all, it was his home; his own plantation, Sylvania, lay just to the west of the Apalachicola River, and it was there that he returned in early April, 1865, as Jefferson Davis abandoned Richmond and Robert E. Lee prepared to surrender the Army of Northern Virginia. If, as J.E.F. suggested, Florida was Paradise, north central Florida was Governor Milton's personal corner of it. If Paradise were to be lost, other parts of it would have to go first.

The identification of Florida with Paradise was not, of course, an invention of J.E.F. or of Governor Milton. The place has held such associations at least from the time of Ponce de Leon; by 1860 these were conventional enough for the St. Augustine Examiner to describe "the neighborhood of Indian River in South Florida" as "Eden,"[63] and by 1885 a real-estate ad could appear in *The Gainesville News* under the single-word heading "Paradise!"[64] "Four and a half miles north of Gainesville," the ad continues, "on the S.F.&W. Railroad, is a Beautiful Location for a Town IN THE PINE WOODS"! Nor are such effusions confined to Florida. "Milton's Paradise Found!" crows an advertising brochure from the late 1980s: "When Milton wrote his famous novels, he could hardly have guessed that one day there would be a Milton, Washington, and available nearby, the incomparable lifestyle offered by Surprise Lake Village."[65]

But the inhabitants of north central Florida—quite apart from the fact that they nurture a violent prejudice against Gainesville and its environs, which they view as anything but Edenic—have given such language a striking turn toward the literal. This is recorded in a classic work of Florida travel literature, Gloria Jahoda's *The Other Florida*. Here, amidst an affectionate tour of the north Florida countryside, one encounters Jahoda's fourth chapter, entitled simply "The Garden of Eden," which documents the local belief that before the fall, God had placed Paradise on the banks of the Apalachicola.

The chief of Jahoda's witnesses to this belief is Elvy E. Callaway, ordained Baptist minister, NAACP lawyer, great-nephew of Confederate General John Bell Hood, and unsuccessful Republican candidate, in 1936, for the governorship once held by John Milton. According to Callaway, "The original Garden of Eden was here on the banks of the Apalachicola. God created the Adamic man one mile east of Bristol[, Florida,] and breathed into his nostrils the breath of life and then gave him a soul. Then he created the Garden of Eden just north of town."[66] Callaway's views derive from close, if eccentric, reading of Genesis 2:

> "First, the Bible tells us that 'a river went out of Eden to water the Garden and parted and became four heads.' It's all in Genesis 2. Well, the Apalachicola is the only four-head river system in the world. The US Army Engineers' map shows you that. Second, the Bible says there were onyx and bdellium, or pitch, and good gold in the land. Now, the best gold in the world is found in north Georgia, where the Chattahoochee has its source before it flows into the Apalachicola.... Four rivers—the Chattahoochee, the Fish Pond Creek, the Spring Creek, and the Flint—they all flow into the Apalachicola on the Georgia-Florida border, in Liberty and Jackson counties. You can see it at the Jim Woodruff Dam."[67]

These arguments reappear, along with others, in the testimony of "A.R. Jones, Ph.D., of Eclectic, Alabama, author of *Man Before the Flood*," who maintains that

> The Garden's location along the east bank of the Apalachicola River between Bristol and Chattahoochee, Florida, is now definite.... These facts NAIL DOWN BEYOND INTELLIGENT CONTRADICTION [the capitals are his] that this is the exact location of the original Garden of Eden, and the birthplace of our first parents.[68]

Truly a Miltonic setting, this: one might call it the Miltonic setting. But even more than the Civil War, the Garden of Eden returns us to a tale we have heard before, and this tale, like that of the Civil War, also ends in death. In *Paradise Lost*, as in Genesis, this is a penalty deferred—specifically, in the case of Paradise Lost, by the Son: "So judg'd he Man, both Judge and Saviour sent,/ And th'instant stroke of Death denounc't that day/ Remov'd farr off" (10.209-211). But this postponement itself may strike one as a refinement of cruelty, pointing the way toward a less timely end. As Eve exhorts Adam after the fall,

> Then both our selves and Seed at once to free
> From what we fear for both, let us make short,
> Let us seek Death, or he not found, supply
> With our own hands his Office on ourselves.
>
> (10.999-1002)

And so it was that on April 1, 1865, Governor John Milton returned from Tallahassee to his plantation in Jackson County, where he took his own life. The circumstances surrounding this event remain unclear, so much so that twentieth-century accounts differ as to the precise cause of his death.[69] However, the most common version holds that Milton was exhausted and depressed by his administrative labors. Less than a month earlier, when Confederate forces had headed off a Union effort to capture Tallahassee, he had seen off the troops at the Tallahassee rail depot platform, where he was noticed "walking up and down...with the air of the most profound abstraction and depression", as if he were "suffering from some disease of the brain".[70] The governor's son William Henry, commander of Florida cavalry at the ensuing Battle of Natural Bridge, persuaded his father to return to Sylvania later that month, and they arrived home on April 1. Governor Milton then retired to an upstairs bedroom. Shortly thereafter the household heard a gunshot and found him lying on the bedroom floor with a shotgun resting on his outstretched foot.

5. Perpetual Civil War

My thesis here is that Governor Milton's life may be understood in part as a reaction to literature—as, in fact, a particularly earnest, if bizarre, kind of reader-response. Insofar as this is so, it gives the lie to conventional bourgeois complaints about the irrelevance of literature to life, while simultaneously complementing that body of literary theory that derives from or agrees with Wilde's old claim that life imitates art.

But if Governor John Milton is in some sense a function of reader-response, the question remains: who is the responding reader? The governor himself? His father or his father's father? Some of the above? All of the above? All and more? Is Governor Milton himself a pre-scripted textual event, devoid of agency even when he chooses to take his own life?

Such questions are perhaps more important to raise than to answer. But it is also perhaps worth noting that the literary resonances do not end with Governor Milton's death. For some, the self-inflicted demise of such a determined wartime leader proves hard to accept, and so one can trace a series of efforts, beginning almost at once, to rehabilitate the governor by casting doubt upon the circumstances of his death. In April of 1865, the Lake City Columbian reports the suicide while expressing disbelief in it: "It has been known for some weeks past that [Governor Milton] had been suffering from mental disease, but we had not supposed it to be serious, and certainly not such an attack as could hurry him to the dread resort by which he ended his life while still in the discharge of his duties as Executive of the State."[71] By 1937, Daisy Parker can insist that

> Milton's action in taking his own life was prompted by anything but heart-break, disillusionment, and patriotism, emphasized wrongly, perhaps. Any charges that fear of coming punishment or disgrace because he had dared to fight for what he believed prompted his action are absurd. With better foundation is the contention that he could not live to see himself subject to a "damn Yankee."[72]

By 1950, Stanley's *History of Jackson County* can claim that while "contemporary newspapers reported [Governor Milton] had committed suicide, ...no one actually knows, and there is strong circumstantial evidence that the gun was discharged accidentally."[73]

Stanley makes no effort to review the evidence in question, and I, for one, have encountered none of it in my study of the subject. But precedent for Stanley's argument is easy to find in the works of John Milton the poet, whose Samson lies dead in the ruined temple of Dagon, "self-kill'd/ Not willingly, but tangl'd in the fold,/ Of dire necessity" (Samson Agonistes 1664-66). To this extent, one could say that the Milton effect has survived Milton himself, in at least two of his potentially innumerable manifestations.

Yet again, perhaps as proof of its irrepressible nature, the Milton effect returns to forge improbable connections between the history of Florida's Civil War governor and Peter Ackroyd's recent novel Milton in America (1996). Ackroyd's book participates in a venerable tradition of Milton-baiting that one can trace back through Eliot and Graves in the early twentieth century to Johnson and Lauder in the eighteenth. The novel's conceit—that at the Restoration Milton emigrates to the New World, where he abandons writing for civic leadership, establishes a Puritan community as "an Eden in the wilderness,"[74] grows increasingly intolerant, and wages "perpetual civil war"[75] on a neighboring Catholic settlement—parallels the story of the Florida Miltons in ways too obvious to enumerate. Rather than rehearsing the apparent correspondences, we might more profitably note the following. First, Ackroyd's Milton-bashing, like that of Graves and, in a cruder way, Lauder before him, seeks to modify the poet's historical reception by elaborating a fiction that might retroactively color the biographical record. Second, this fictional revision of Milton's reputation, as derogatory as it is, nonetheless parallels in various ways the more honorific but equally factitious appropriations enacted by the Miltons of Florida. Third, in pursuing their separate but parallel agendas, Ackroyd and the Florida Miltons oddly and unintentionally end up replicating each other, so that a self-acknowledged fiction that aspires to the status of literary history repeats the contours of an unself-consciously fabricated genealogy.

And finally, in this coincidental self-replication, both Ackroyd and Governor John Milton end up appropriating England's epic poet to political purposes that the poet himself never endorsed, and that serve him ill in the present historical moment. This observation is important enough to provide an end-point for the present essay. Whatever else one may recall about Governor John Milton—as soldier, as administrator, as textual effect, as dedicated adherent to a lost cause—one should remember the nature of the cause to which he adhered. As he stumped for governor in 1860, the Cedar Keys Telegraph ran an editorial approving his candidacy in part because "Gen. MILTON is like a brave southern man should be—not willing to take a big 'buck-nigger' to his bosom as the Black Republicans would have us do."[76]

This is a history not to live up to, or to live over, but to live down.[77]

Notes

1. For some additional John Miltons, see the genealogical discussion to follow; for more detail, see William Riley Parker, *Milton: A Biography* 2 vols. (Oxford: Clarendon, 1968) *passim*, who discusses a dozen different individuals with the names of John Milton or Melton. Needless to say, this is not an exhaustive list.
2. See William J. Northen, ed., *Men of Mark in Georgia* 6 vols. (Atlanta: A.B. Caldwell, 1910), 2:181-82 for further biographical information relative to this John Milton.
3. For a brief summary of Governor John Milton's background, see John E. Johns, *Florida During the Civil War* (Gainesville, U of Florida P, 1963), 82-83; W. Buck Yearns, "Florida," in W. Buck Yearns, ed., *The Confederate Governors* (Athens: U of Georgia P, 1985), 61-62.
4. Johns 83.
5. Benedict Anderson, *Imagined Communities: Reflections on the Origin and Spread of Nationalism* (London: Verso, 1983), 6.
6. Anderson 13.
7. Anderson 145, 148.
8. Sigmund Freud, "Family Romances," in ***The Standard** Edition of the Complete Psychological **Works** of Sigmund Freud*, ed. and trans. James Strachey et al., 21 vols. (London: Hogarth P, 1959), 9:238-39.
9. Judith Butler, *Undoing Gender* (New York: Routledge, 2004), 15.
10. See the Florida Office of Cultural and Historical Programs, "Florida Governors' Portraits," http://dhr.dos.state.fl.us/museum/collections/governors/ about.cfm?id=12.

11. J. Randall Stanley, *History of Jackson County* (Marianna, FL: Jackson County Historical Society, 1950), 183.
12. J. Evetts Haley, *Jeff Milton: A Good Man with a Gun* (Norman: Oklahoma UP, 1948), 4.
13. Daisy Parker, "John Milton, Governor of Florida," *Florida Historical Quarterly* (April, 1942), 346-61.
14. Daisy Parker, "Governor John Milton," *Tallahassee Historical Society Annual 3* (1937), 14. This genealogy is also reproduced almost verbatim in Parker's honors thesis, n.p. [but: 2].
15. For the number and identities of Sir Christopher's children, see Perceval Lucas, "The Family of Sir Christopher Milton," *Notes and Queries* ser. 11, v. 7 (1913), 21-22, and John Shawcross, *The Arms of the Family: The Significance of John Milton's Relatives and Associates* (Lexington: UP of Kentucky, 2004), 24-30. Shawcross's more recent findings correct Lucas's on some points, particularly the latter's listing of two daughters named Anne.
16. For the daughters in question—a "Mrs. Milton of Grosvenor Street, a housekeeper to Dr. [Thomas] Secker, [Archbishop of Canterbury],...who died 26 July 1769," and a daughter Margaret, "baptized on 7 March 1681 at St. Dunstan's in the West and...buried on 25 June 1685"—see Shawcross 31, 33.
17. See William Riley Parker 2.1176, n. 138, who observes that two Thomas Miltons were listed for burial in the registers of St. Dunstan's in the West on July 1, 1680, and December 30, 1683, respectively. Also see Shawcross 32.
18. William Riley Parker 2.1176-77, n. 138; Shawcross 33.
19. William Riley Parker 2.1177, n. 138.
20. John Milton, *Paradise Lost* 6.375, in *The Riverside Milton*, ed. Roy Flannagan (Boston: Houghton Mifflin, 1997). Further references to Milton's verse are to this edition.
21. Joseph Milton French, *The Life Records of John Milton*, 5 vols. (New Brunswick: Rutgers UP, 1949-58), 5.352.
22. This union in turn produced a daughter named Anne, a niece to the poet, who in turn received a license to wed one David Moore of Richmond, Surrey, on December 29, 1662.

    For the wedding of Thomas Agar and Anne Milton Phillips, see A.W. Hughes Clark, ed., *The Register of St. Dunstan in the East, 1558-1664* (London: Harleian Society Publications, 1939), 115. For Anne Agar's wedding to David Moore, see George J. Armytage, ed., *Allegations for Marriage Licenses issued from the*

Faculty Office of the Archbishop of Canterbury, London (London: Harleian Society Publications, 1886), 67.

23. Daisy Parker, *Florida Historical Quarterly*, 347, n. 2.
24. Daisy Parker, *Florida Historical Quarterly*, 347.
25. Shawcross 30.
26. Daisy Parker, honors thesis, n.p., n. 3. In this case the honors thesis is more useful than the *Florida Historical Society Annual* piece, which includes no endnotes or source documentation of any kind.
27. Daisy Parker, *Florida Historical Quarterly*, 348, n. 7.
28. Haley, 3, n. 1. Haley does not claim either Jeff Davis Milton or Elise Gamble as the specific source for his remark that the Florida Miltons descend from "the great blind poet of England"; in fact, he cites no source for this remark at all. But given Haley's extensive contact with this generation of the family and his identification of them as the source for his general family history, it seems unlikely that his information would have come from elsewhere.
29. For a conventional summary of the distinction between ascribed statuses as, "those which are assigned to individuals without reference to their innate differences or abilities" and achieved statuses as "those requiring special qualities" and "not assigned to individuals from birth," see Ralph Linton, *The Study of Man: An Introduction* (New York: Appleton-Century-Crofts, 1936), 115.
30. Daisy Parker, honors thesis, n.p. [but: 3]. Parker's genealogy, as reported here throughout, has been confirmed by my own correspondence with John Milton of Marianna, Florida, the great-great-great grandson of Governor John Milton.
31. Daisy Parker, honors thesis, n.p. [but: 3].
32. Northen 2.182. For a general history of the Society, see Minor Myers, *Liberty Without Anarchy: A History of the Society of the Cincinnati* (Charlottesville: U of Virginia P, 1983), *passim.* Milton was charter secretary of the Society's Georgia branch.
33. Shawcross 2-3.
34. Nancy Armstrong and Leonard Tennenhouse, *The Imaginary Puritan: Literature, Intellectual Labor, and the Origins of Personal Life* (Berkeley: U of California P, 1992), 70.

35. Joseph Heller, *Catch-22* (New York: Simon and Schuster, 1955), 83.
36. Northen 2.181.
37. He also earned the rank of brigadier-general in the Second Brigade, First Division of the Georgia Militia. See Daisy Parker, honors thesis, n.p. [but: 3]; Northen 2.182.
38. A Soldier, "Gen. Milton as a Soldier," *The East Floridian*, Thursday, September 27, 1860.
39. R[obert] S[pencer] C[otterill], "Milton, John," *Dictionary of American Biography*, 22 vols. (New York: Charles Scribner's Sons, 1934), 13:21.
40. Haley 5.
41. John Steadman, *Milton and the Paradoxes of Renaissance Heroism* (Baton Rouge; Louisiana State UP, 1987), 173; also see Steadman, *Milton and the Renaissance Hero* (Oxford: Clarendon, 1967), for the argument that Milton sought "to spiritualize the heroic poem" by "retaining such conventional motifs as kingship and warfare" while "alter[ing] their traditional character by stressing their internal rather than external significance" (193).
42. Catherine Gimelli Martin, *The Ruins of Allegory: "Paradise Lost" and the Metamorphosis of Epic Convention* (Durham: Duke UP, 1998), 203.
43. For Voltaire's characterization of Milton as a "barbarian...who, imitating in all seriousness the comic invention of firearms in Ariosto, has the devils fire cannon in Heaven," see *Voltaire's Candide, Zadig and Selected Stories*, trans. Donald M. Frame (Bloomington: Indiana UP, 1961), 84; for Johnson's complaints about "the confusion of spirit and matter which pervades the whole narrative of the war in heaven," see the *Lives of the Poets*, 439-40, in *Samuel Johnson: Selected Poetry and Prose*, ed. Frank Brady and W.K. Wimsatt (Berkeley: U of California P, 1977), 337-642.
44. Stanley Fish, *Surprised By Sin: The Reader in "Paradise Lost"* (Berkeley: U of California P, 1971), 179; Arnold Stein, *Answerable Style: Essays on "Paradise Lost"* (Minneapolis: U of Minnesota P, 1953), 25; Fish 171.
45. Merritt Hughes, *Ten Perspectives on Milton* (New Haven: Yale UP, 1965), 201-02.

46. Richard Rambuss, "Spenser and Milton at Mardi Gras: English Literature, American Cultural Capital, and the Reformation of New Orleans Carnival," boundary 2 27.2 (Summer, 2000), 50, 55, 50.
47. Samuel Kinser, *Carnival, American Style: Mardi Gras at New Orleans and Mobile* (Chicago: U of Chicago P, 1990), 88-89.
48. Kinser 88.
49. I draw these figures from the University of Virginia's *Historical Census Browser* (http://fisher.lib.virginia.edu/census).
50. Don DeLillo, *White Noise* (Harmondsworth: Penguin, 1985), 81-82.
51. Nathanael West, *Miss Lonelyhearts and The Day of the Locust* (New York: New Directions, 1962), 23.
52. F.O. Matthiessen, *American Renaissance: Art and Expression in the Age of Emerson and Whitman* (London: Oxford UP, 1941), 103; G.F. Sensabaugh, *Milton in Early America* (Princeton: Princeton UP, 1964), 37; Keith Stavely, *Puritan Legacies: "Paradise Lost" and the New England Tradition* (Ithaca: Cornell UP, 1987), 2; Kevin Van Anglen, *The New England Milton* (University Park: Pennsylvania SUP, 1993), 41; Rambuss 55.
53. Alice Fahs, *The Imagined Civil War: Popular Literature of the North and South, 1861-1865* (Chapel Hill: U of North Carolina P, 2001), 66.
54. Fahs 67.
55. Michael W. Kaufmann, *American Brutus: John Wilkes Booth and the Lincoln Conspiracies* (New York: Random House, 2004), 87.
56. *The War of the Rebellion: A Compilation of the Official Records of the Union and Confederate Armies*, 70 vols. in 128 (Washington, DC: Government Printing Office, 1880-1901), series 1, 6.325.
57. *War of the Rebellion*, series 1, 6.342.
58. *War of the Rebellion,* series 1, 6.343.
59. For a summary of these events and Milton's response to them, see Yearns 62-63, Johns 84-96.
60. J.E.F., "Health of Florida, and Gov. Milton as Physician of the State," *Florida Sentinel*, Tuesday, January 21, 1861.
61. Johnson, *Lives of the Poets*, 426.

62. See Johns 84; Yearns 62; William H. Nulty, *Confederate Florida: The Road to Olustee* (Tuscaloosa: U of Alabama P, 1990), 28-29.
63. "Tropical Fruits," *The St. Augustine Examiner*, Saturday, July 4, 1860.
64. *The Gainesville News*, April 31, 1885.
65. Qtd. in *The New Yorker* 63.39 (November 16, 1987), 148.
66. Gloria Jahoda, *The Other Florida* (New York: Charles Scribner's Sons, 1967; rpt., Port Salerno, FL: Florida Classics Library, 1984), 68-69.
67. Jahoda 69-70.
68. Qtd. in Jahoda 70.
69. Daisy Parker's honors thesis claims that the Governor "hanged himself in his barn" (n.p.). However, most accounts agree that he in fact killed himself with a shotgun while alone in an upstairs bedroom of the plantation house. See, for instance, Clifton Paisley, *The Red Hills of Florida, 1528-1865* (Tuscaloosa, U of Alabama P, 1989), 209; Stanley, 181.
70. Dr. Charles Hentz, "My Autobiography." MS #332 in the Hentz Family Papers, Southern Historical Collection, Library of the University of North Carolina, Chapel Hill. 1:361-62.
71. "Death of Governor Milton," *Lake City Columbian*, Wednesday, April 5, 1865.
72. Daisy Parker, honors thesis, n.p.
73. Stanley 181.
74. Peter Ackroyd, *Milton in America* (London: Sinclair-Stevenson, 1996), 8, 74.
75. Ackroyd 214.
76. "Gen. Milton", *The Cedar Keys Telegraph*, Saturday, July 28, 1860.
77. I would like to thank Peter Nicholls, Leigh Edwards, the two anonymous readers for *Textual Practice*, and the Florida State University English Department Faculty Works-in-Progress Seminar for helpful guidance in revising this essay. Likewise, I am deeply grateful to Diane Roberts, Jerry Singerman, Mark Hinson, Linda Hall, and John Milton for their kind assistance with my early research and writing.

3

The Victorian and Postmodern Metamorphoses of Dorian Gray: Narrating the Body Other

Esterino Adami

> Perhaps a new kind of thinking began like everything else when the Monsters started being born. I am sorry, you keep saying the truth, you want the truth, and that is how we saw you, all of you, at first. Monsters. The deformed ones, the freaks, the cripples.
>
> Doris Lessing, *The Clefts*

Published in 1891, *The Picture of Dorian Gray*[1] has entered the canon of British literature and yet its central character still occupies a dark zone of meaning, questioning the reader and evolving into new literary forms through the procedure of modern rewriting. Not only a Victorian flamboyant dandy, imbued in decadent symbolism, Dorian Gray surfaces again in contemporary fiction. Within such intertextual perspective, the essence of the Wildean protagonist is updated and recreated so that the question of the translatability and writing of narrative and cultural bodies problematically arises. The thorny issue of moral corruption, which metaphorically devastates the human body and transforms it into a kind of monster, represents a constant preoccupation in the modern world too.

When it first appeared, the ground-breaking novel had a shocking effect upon English society: although it had been constructed as a sort of *fin de siècle* fairy tale, it subtly aimed at challenging ethics and codes of behaviour by questioning the strict norms of the Victorian world in a daringly ambitious style. Built upon a complex intertextual net of references, the novel adheres to the turn-of-the-century style of decadent fiction, by establishing connections with the work of authors as diverse as Poe, Maturin, Rossetti and Stevenson. Probably the most important literary source of inspiration for Wilde lies in Joris-Karl Huysmans' *À rebous* (1884), a novel known in English as *Against Nature* or *Against the Grain*, which reverberates with suggestive intimations of hedonism bound to the disintegration of the body and the soul. The exoticism that emerges from the French novel spreads to the English text and, similar to a poisonous orchid, inebriates the reader with its polluting power. Intertextually, the innermost flavour of that decadent narrative is interwoven in Wilde's novel so as to depict a web of references, of fanciful echoes and dreams:

> It was the strangest book that he had ever read.... It was a novel without a plot, and with only one character being, indeed, simply a psychological study of a certain young Parisian, who spent his life trying to realize in the nineteenth century all the passions and modes of thought that belonged to every century except his own, and to sum up, as it were, in himself the various moods through which the world-spirit had ever passed, loving for their mere artificiality those renunciations that men have unwisely called virtue, as much as those natural rebellions that wise men still call sin. (*PDG*, 109)

In particular, I would like to underscore a strategy that Wilde seems to adopt regularly, which is the focus on the visibility of characters and objects in his storyline. Dorian Gray, Henry Wotton, Basil Hallward, Sybil Vane, Alan Campbell and the others that constitute the intricate narrative tapestry are represented in pictorial terms, so that they are able to foreground their personalities and bodies. As Mario Praz points out, "Wilde's point of view, in fact, is always scenic: he sees things as in stage-perspective; he is all the time arranging his characters, his landscapes, his events, and making them pose".[2] However, in Wilde, the emphasis of showing and displaying ought to be interpreted as an oscillating movement between meanings and their opposites, such as the presence of beauty and corruption, or the absence of the passing of time and the dissolution of bodies. Such twofold opposition primarily marks Dorian and his evil double: committing sins and indulging in evil twists the feature of the young dandy only on his portrait, while his physical body remains untouched, crystallised in an ephemeral exquisiteness. Ultimately, the two Dorians become the double representation of human perversity and malady: we are here presented with the birth of a monster.

Dorian's obsession with aestheticism and the search for fine craftworks function as a mask hiding the dark sides of his personality: by filling his rooms and apartments with splendid flowers, embroidered cloths, leather-bound books, jewels and other fabulous items, he desperately seeks to soothe the bareness that dominates the devastating landscape of his soul: "Dorian's delight in his own beauty and youth (symbolically shown to be transient through the portrait which ages while he remains untouched by time) leads him to place the stimulation of the senses through exotic beauty above other value".[3] The price to pay for his debauched conduct brands the young aristocrat with the token of otherness and monstrosity, progressively disfiguring the features of the portrait. When Dorian observes the painting carefully after having badly treated Sybil Vane, he cannot avoid noticing some slight forms of magical metamorphosis:

> The bright dawn flooded the room, and swept the fantastic shadows into dusky corners, where they lay shuddering. But the strange expression that he had noticed in the face of the portrait seemed to linger there, to be more intensified ever. The quivering, ardent sunlight showed him the lines of cruelty round the mouth as clearly as if he had been looking into a mirror after he had done some dreadful thing.... He

> rubbed his eyes, and came close to the picture, and examined it again. There were no signs of any change when he looked into the actual painting, and yet there was no doubt that the whole expression had altered. It was not a mere fancy of his own. The thing was horribly apparent. (*PDG*, 80)

Unlike other writers of his age, Wilde decides not to represent monstrosity mixed and juxtaposed with the other characters of the plot, but segregates it to the limits of the canvas: paradoxically the flashy visibility of the protagonists seems to hide the threat of otherness, which looms within the intertextual interstices. Other authors of the Victorian time, Charles Dickens *in primis*, exploit to the full the uncanny and sometimes macabre appealing of the broad category of monsters: in his works, indeed, we can find "misshapen bodies that belong to the category of 'freaks' or to the area of the grotesque; characters who are the illustration of particular vices or transgressions; hybrid creatures that occupy the uncertain boundaries between the animate and the inanimate worlds; incorporeal constructs that signal themselves through such uncanny figures as ghosts or appearances".[4] The monstrous portrait of Dorian subtly betrays his kinship with such horde of liminal creatures, and we should interpret the imprecise and vague description of his painting as a textual site of alterity and meaning, albeit, in retrospect, we also observe a return to the myth of Narcissus, which in Gray Kochhnar-Lindgren's words "is a poetic narrative that depicts a way of being that wants to destroy the surface of things, the appearances, in order to plunge into the depths and shatter the reflecting mirror so that the other of love—which is only apparently other—might be possessed".[5]

Such making up of monsters—viz. the textual construction of "bodies other"—works also with opposite forces, namely with the disintegration of structured wholes, bodies that are shattered, torn into pieces and dismembered into segments, or spurious parts. Upturning the archetypal image of monster-making, popularised by Mary Shelley with *Frankenstein* (1818), the author here grafts this theme on his exploration of human vices, their apotheosis and their unspeakable consequences: the annihilation of bodies violates the sacrality of the person, and the episode of the removal of Basil's body, darkened by a gothic atmosphere, bespeaks of underground horrors, granting Dorian with the aura of evil. Dorian compels his friend Alan Campbell to get rid of the body of the dead painter, by now a heavy burden to be disposed of in order to conceal the appalling secret: "'You must have something to do with it.... All I ask you of you is to perform a certain scientific experiment. You go to hospitals and deadhouses, and the horrors that you do there, don't affect you.... Indeed, to destroy a body must be far less horrible than what you are accustomed to work at.'" (*PDG*, 146-47). When the tone of dreadfulness climaxes as in such episode, Dorian the dandy and Dorian the painted monster are matched together and evolve into the same Janus-like corrupted soul perpetrating evil. Thus, we need to highlight the double operation of amalgamation and dissection at both thematic and textual levels, bearing in mind that, according to what Jeffrey Cohen underscores, "monstrous interpretation is as much process as epiphany, a work that must content itself with fragments".[6] The accumulation of narrative layers and the construction of beautiful/monstrous bodies undermine the positive sense of integrity in Victorian fiction, and such loaded paradigmatic framework will also mark the maelstrom of postmodernism.

Indeed, I would now like to focus upon Will Self's scandalous rewriting of the novel by Wilde, published in 2002 under the apparently plain title *Dorian*[7]. Here the author updates the moral and physical make-up of the Wildean landscape through a plethora of gnarled and twisted stories, so as to create powerful metaphors about the notion of the body, sickness, decay and human complexity. The novel spans over two decades, starting from the troublesome 1980s up to the void of the present era, and, although it follows the main storyline of the 19th century novel, which becomes a sort of hypotext if we are to use Genette's terminology, it is grounded upon a postmodernist vision, with its persistent questioning. The eclectic style of Self transforms the mysterious portrait into a magical video installation called "Cathode Narcissus" created by the artist Baz Hallward (the alter ego of Basil Hallward), and then it generates a series of episodes polluted by domestic corruption, abuse of drugs, and spread of diseases. The amazing work of art crystallises the beauty of Dorian's body through the continuous repetition of taped images that acquire his sins and signs of decay: "Then Dorian saw it: the faces on the screen had all changed—and for the worse. An exaggerated moue twisted his formerly flawless mouth. A distortion of a perfect symmetry such as his was far worse than a harelip on an ordinary face. He grimaced and drew closer—surely there must be some grease or fluid on the screens? But no. Closer and closer he drew, until all he could see were lines of dots leading into the future. His temples rang like a bell as his conscience clapped at their insides" (*D*, 70).

Self's operation is double inasmuch as it is structured as an interlingual and cultural translation. In his dense discourse on the obsession of contemporary society with the perfection of bodies and reproducibility of art, the writer explores the metamorphosis of his characters, who undergo the hellish experience of dope and illness and obscenely destroy their own bodies. Once again, it is Dorian who takes up the monstrous and cruel role in this textual web: by discarding the burden of his sins and bad behaviour onto the Cathode Narcissus, he feels free to indulge in his own unbridled ambitions and wild passions. However, his rotten and virulent soul is always mirrored on the screens as an immortal warning to human futility:

> The monitors whined and zigged and zagged and sprang jaggedly to life. But was it life? In place of the unchanged Dorian who stood before Baz, as fresh and youthful as the first evening he'd met him at Phyllis Hawtree's, was the Dorian Baz had for years now suspected he ought to be—an anguished figure, his face, neck and hands covered with Kaposi's, his mouth wet with bile, his eyes tortured by death and madness, his bald pate erupting with some vile fungus. And there were nine of these animated

> pathology plates, nine of them, halting disporting themselves. Concentration-camp victims forced by an insane Nazi doctor to dance. (*D*, 162-63)

The shocking revelation of the sick body constitutes an indictment of the protagonist's fall into the wasteland of ethical devastation, lost in the postmodern quest for meaning.

Daftly, the novelist extends his experiments with the composition, fragmentation and transformation of bodies to the concept of writing: the textual body is thus manipulated and structured as a collection of self-contained Chinese boxes that enchant, frighten and puzzle the reader. When, at the end of the novel, the levels of fiction fray in a metanarrative chaos via rhizomatic extensions and restrictions, an aphorism of re-born Henry Wotton ("'We're all inventions of one sort or another'", *D*, 276) puts in a nutshell the ebullient category of intertextuality. Echoing Barthes' approach, Graham Allen reminds us that "the theory of the text, therefore, involves a theory of intertextuality, since the text not only sets going a plurality of meanings but is also woven out of numerous discourses and spun from already existent meaning".[8] As a consequence, the plurality of the bodies in *Dorian* emerges not only in the frequent cultural references and popular icons that appear throughout the story but also in the open ending that challenges the reader.

It is a reversing process aimed at weakening the monolithic role of the author by introducing multiple, metafictional perspectives with writer and character swapping their functions in the literary wood. The gift of creativity is further challenged and multiplied because in the Internet-dominated era Dorian, who turns out to be a philanthropist and benefactor dealing with several international charities, decides to digitalise Baz's work in order to make it accessible to the world all over: "there was a true niceness to this marriage between form and content that made the transfer of Cathode Narcissus from leaky videotape vessel to unsinkable digital virtuality seem an inevitable aspect of the life of the piece itself" (*D*, 264). Reproducibility and interchangeability of bodies and texts become the key concepts that seem to haunt the entire narrative structure, so that eventually the reader wonders which Dorian should be trusted. The video installation represents a kind of grotesque parody of the body on the interdisciplinary agenda of Self, and is close to the threatening weight of reduplication of which Jean Baudrillard too speaks. We could find in Self's radical treatment of the body/text the goal to free inner, indecipherable forces that postmodernism tries to investigate. To a certain extent, the distorted and monstrous body, a direct legacy from Wilde's hypotext, surfaces as the token of the impossibility of meanings in a superficial and valueless world, and, as the sociologists Sue Scott and David Morgan sustain, "there is, indeed, something fluid and indeterminate in the interplay between individual and societal representations and concerns with bodies".[9]

I would like to expand the scope of my analysis by focusing upon Hanif Kureishi's *The Body*[10], a story which is grounded on a highly suggestive intertextuality that pays an oblique homage to works as diverse as Wilde's *The Picture of Dorian Gray* and Mary Shelley's *Frankenstein*, or Dostoevsky's *The Double*. However, the author's choice should not be interpreted as a re-writing of classic models: on the contrary, the first-person narration is imbued with the modern and postmodern anxieties of the contemporary age. As the title suggests, it coldly depicts a conflict between materialism and thought, between the idea of being and that of appearing, in a Faustus-like manner. Adam, a senior versatile writer and playwright, is given the chance to have his brain and mind transplanted into a new, young and handsome body. The absurd proposal, which seems to have been borrowed from a science fiction romance, turns the protagonist, whose name is highly symbolic, into a wandering Dorian Gray. However, it is not just the wish for eternal youth that motivates Adam to opt for this miraculous operation, but rather the possibility of experimenting an alternative existence and scanning the meaningful interstices of life.

In the aseptic atmosphere of the mysterious hospital, where a sort of Orwell's Newspeak identifies the categories of "Newbodies" and "Oldbodies", Adam faces up to the doctor, a futurist wizard who deals with both organic material and mental essence. Their encounter is worth citing at full length:

> 'Words are your living' he said. 'Bodies are mine. But I would imagine so'. 'The existence of Newbodies, as you call them, will create considerable confusion, won't it? How will we know who is new and who old?' 'The thinking in this area is yet to be done', he said. 'Just as there has been argument over abortion, genetic engineering, cloning and organ transplants, or any other medical advances, so there will be over this'. 'Surely this is of a different order', I said. 'Parents the same age as their children, or even younger, for instance. What will that mean?' 'That is for the philosophers, priests, poets and television pundits to say. My work is only to extend life.' (*B*, 22)

The surgeon's explanation dilates the narrative scope and conveys a philosophical enquiry, one in which postmodernity highlights the insistence on the centrality of the body, imagined through discursive practices and visual or textual performances. As the new Millennium age brings the double technique of staging the body, in a bulimic assimilation, or devouring, of images and simulacra on the one hand, and anorexic refusal to conformity, as generational conflicts and crumbling traditions show on the other, the body affirms anew a pivotal role in current thinking and perception. Considered as a laboratory item, the body dramatises a growing angst: like the monster of Frankenstein, it too is a chimera, a fictional object. To misquote the French philosopher Jean-Jacques Lecercle,[11] the body of the monster gives voice to the others and illuminates their discursive contradictions. The body in Kureishi's story and the monster in Shelley's text bind together the different frayed narrative levels; and they operate as a kind of *tabula rasa*, a site of cathartic transformations that may absorb or imitate an external agency. It is an organic metaphor which requires a new taxonomy in order to describe both the components of the body and the textual structures. The holders of Newbodies, nearly endowed with the boon of immortality, make up a new hybrid category, albeit they are paradoxically marginalised in their own higher ranks; arguing with a friend who shares the same status, Adam affirms that "Matt and I were both mutants, freaks, human unhumans—a fact I could at least forget when I was with real people, those with death in them" (*B*, 102).

In postmodern literature, the motif of the double body/soul originally employed by Oscar Wilde is revitalised in a phenomenology of transgression in the case of Self, with teratological implications, or through the anatomy of otherness as a metaphor for the schizophrenic unhappiness of undecipherable contemporaneousness. Therefore, we should construe the narrative body as a dynamic code, a cultural machine that may generate monstrous forms and correspond to the regression and oblivion of the mind and the conscience, stemming from the Victorian age and leaping into the present time: not incidentally, "sin in all its aspects became a preoccupation with Wilde amounting almost to an obsession".[12] The final outcome in such daring literary experiments lies in the impossibility of wholeness, with the subject either split or made grotesque: the postmodern writers deconstruct the text through the strategy of canonical rewriting but it is with Wilde that we encounter the aporia haunting the western vision of life, opposing materialism with spirituality, so that the concluding paragraph of the novel by Wilde reads: "lying on the floor was a dead man, in evening dress, with a knife in his heart. He was withered, wrinkled, and loathsome of visage. It was not till they examined the rings that they recognized who it was" (*PDG*, 193). If we try to apply this modality to postmodern fiction, we realize that the death of the protagonists predicts the death of the author whereas the text and the body eventually become the means to express the impossibility of leading a life on hedonistic terms.

Notes & Reference

1. Oscar Wilde, *The Picture of Dorian Gray* (1891) in *The Picture of Dorian Gray and Other Writings*, New York, Bantam Books, 1982. All quotations refer to this edition and are parenthetically inserted in the text with abbreviation *PDG* and page reference.

2. Mario Praz, *La carne, la morte, il diavolo nella letteratura romantica*, 1932, English translation: *The Romantic Agony*, London, Fontana Books, 1962, 378.
3. Martin Fido, *Oscar Wilde*, London, Cardinal, 1976, 88.
4. Maria Teresa Chialant "Charles Dickens and the Declension of Monstrosity" in Carlo Pagetti and Oriana Palusci, edited by, *Delicate Monsters. Literary Creatures of Wonder*, Milan, Cisalpino, 2007, 151.
5. Gray Kochhar-Lindgren, *Narcissus Transformed*, University Park, The Pennsylvania State University Press, 1993, 9.
6. *Ibidem*, 6.
7. Will Self, *Dorian*, London, Viking, 2000; all quotations refer to this edition and are parenthetically inserted in the text with abbreviation *D* and page reference.
8. Graham Allen, *Intertextuality*, London, Routledge, 2000, 67.
9. Sue Scott and David Morgan, "Bodies in a Social Landscape", in Sue Scott and David Morgan, edited by, *Body Matters*, London, The Falmer Press, 1993, 15.
10. Hanif Kureishi, "The Body" in *The Body and Other Stories*, London, Faber and Faber, 2003 (2002); all quotations refer to this edition and are parenthetically inserted in the text with abbreviation *B* and page reference.
11. See Jean-Jacques Lecercle, *Frankenstein: mythe et philosophie*, Paris, Presses Universitaires de France, 1988.
12. H. Montgomery Hyde, *Oscar Wilde*, London, Mandarin, 1991 (1976), 237.

4

Shaw's *Candida*: A Double-Entendre

Chidananda Bhattacharya

Shaw's *Candida* is a universally popular play which refuses to date, no matter how greatly our tastes may have changed or how radically newer times may have inducted newer socio-ontologies. Yet, while the play remains so enjoyable reading or watching on stage, it offers almost insurmountable difficulties to drama-producers and actors who must produce it on stage. Critics also have split upon the rocks of Shaw's intended meanings behind the textation. "What did he exactly mean—' to communicate by his pageant? The whole play foxes the best overtures of the critic who with dismay discovers that as 'at the end of a most laborious bid for coming to terms with 'meaning' he thinks he may have just got hold of one that dearly attained meaning seems to flit and fade into another meaning which seems set all over against the former one. *Candida* literally hauls the critic over a seesawing terrain and the critic finds the meaning-mirage constantly receding—from domestic comedy to realistic comedy, then on to Morality, and then again to, Mystery. All the while the critic has a hunch that Shaw has something very definite to tell us, but that 'something' never settles down into a solid more and Shaw seems to shroud it all over with his puzzlesome wit!

It is indeed Shaw's inimitable wit and penchant for paradoxism that queers the pitch for the critic and scholar of Shaw. He loves to look a dabbler in never-to-be-resolved dichotomies and antinomies in a hopelessly oxymoronic way where every new position, dearly gained, is aborted, at the very next swath and laughed at as a conceit or folly. In his egoism and intelligence, in his offering his art in the vein of jigsaw puzzles Shaw reminds one of a fallow-traveller of his, though this man was pre-eminently a novelist—George Meredith. The kinship between these two egotistical talents is very palpable after all, since both use the 'comic spirit' (Meredith's term)[1] wittily 'to prick pins into pigs' (the unmistakably Shavian phrase); both burn with a reformist's ardour; and both seem to speak things which, they allege, sprang from "the first-born of common-sense, the vigilant comic, which is the genius of thoughtful laughter," but, alas; their age understood not their epiphany.[2] Shaw's *Candida* is at heart a 'serious comedy,' like Meredith's *The Egoist* (a novel though), but whereas Meredith digs into the sphere of nice and refined intellectual irony and shears up the lack of critical intelligence on the part of the Victorian readership through the sword of common-sense and comic wit, Shaw is too Irish for this typically British disposition—a strictly academic, high-toned irony with its patrician nudges and winks.[3] The Shavian brand of comic wit in Candida runs off a series of apparent paradoxes to expose the reader/auditor in her/his undermature sensibility. Both Meredith and Bernard Shaw look upon themselves as teachers of their fellow-beings and both conscientiously hit out at the diverse sentimental illusions of their age about the male self and about women. However, there is one important difference between these two iconoclasts—that while Sir Willoughby (who is the Egoist) is clearly discovered as the ugly, possessive Victorian male, so odious in his sentimental bourgeois illusion about lording it over women, and while Meredith has been seriously deliberating on the Woman Question and the concept of New Woman with all the professed gravity of a sociologist, Bernard Shaw's attitude to James Mavor Morell is encrypted in ambiguity in terms of a *double entendre*. This *double entendre* comes to seize not only Morell but also Eugene and Candida equally with a tongue-in-cheek irreverence. Shaw's mock-heroic enthusiasm extends as much over the Woman and the Poet, for just as at the end of the play we cannot assert with definiteness as to who has won and who has lost—Morell or Marchbanks?—so also we find that while Candida behaves very candidly at the auction her heart remains opaque to us.

For one thing, Candida is not the New Woman of the lately emerging sociological discourse. Candida does not queue up for entry into the 'feminine-feminist-female' format expounded (much later, through) by Ms Ellen Showalter and Shaw determinedly makes the socio-political construct of the New Woman irrelevant by deriving the brain and the brawn of his Woman from the domestic and religious spheres.[4] Candida is the eternal Woman, as old as the Virgin, as all-powerful as Shaw's own mother, and as enduring and sagacious as the Wife in almost every household. She is a New Woman not because women have all on a sudden, in the wake of the modern era, reassessed their role all anew, but because—and here lies exactly Shaw's literary wit and humour—men are dumbstruck after a chilling discovery: The discovery is, that 'Woman' far from being a domesticated article under male possession and supervision is actually the sustainer of men. Woman understands Man as a mother understands her child; this discovery made for men by Shaw is an unnerving revelation, enough to get the priggish and complacent male off his feet. Both: Eugene and Morell receive this 'revelation' at the close of play, and Shaw works this out with constant gyres and counter-gyres throughout the dramatic action.

To find out the direction through indirections had hitherto remained the sole privilege of the master—Mister Shakespeare. But Shaw now sets up for a title clash: The royal challenger: Take for instance the Question of the New Woman. It became customary at one time to imagine Shaw to have followed Ibsen in his toes in the matter of presenting Candida as a somewhat softer variation on the Nora theme. Yet, nothing seems farther from the truth than fancying Candida as being of Nora's ilk. The *primum mobile* is different in Shaw's *Candida*: Ibsen framed and executed the theme basically from a socio-economic angle; sex in its implication of androcentric politics formed the ballast there, and not sex in its biological context so much.[5] In *Candida*, it ought not to evade one's scrutiny, pressure builds up at the base at least not because of the economics but rather owing to a psycho-sexual tension amassed around an inscrutable woman whose unstinted grace to both of the hapless co-runners for her kind condescension and refuge creates an awful situation through its quibbling ambiguity which no New Woman from the regular sociological purlieus should find honourable at all to entertain. In *The Egoist* of Meredith Clara flays Willoughby, and flies out at a post-haste speed; Nora in Ibsen also calls it the quits and walks off into the night in a mix of disdain, despair and determination. Neither of the two does so because there has been a third person—the other or the outsider—who has engendered the crisis for them sexually. Krogstad, in Ibsen does never really stay in the running for Nora from the sexual point of view. The Sqwaks and the squirms which Candida at once arouses in Morell and Marchbanks, together with the long speechifications of Morell and the romantic moonshines of panegyrics from Marchbanks—why, all rather go to show how the lady at their midst has been sitting on with plump satisfaction and enjoying althrough (without the least moral compunctions or vestiges of shame) her fatal hold on these two pitiable victims. Nora danced her tarantella in a mad orgy because it appeared to nerve her up for earning freedom from anxiety as well as from the deadlock her wedlock had produced for her. But what do we descry in Candida, instead? Well, by an ironic contrast, it is Eugene Marchbanks and James Mavor Morell, the two pets of Candida, that are driven to dance attendance on her by turns and then, later, together in their frantic bid to retain their grounds and yet feeling no, better off either because of those exertions. For Nora's getting out into the night. Shaw gives us his counterpart through a quirk—it is Eugene retiring hurt into the night. The poet is at once the hero and the Quixotic fool in one pack: the double bind with its *double entente*.

Indeed, in Candida Shaw is passing off a 'serious comedy' under the specious cover of a 'pleasant play'. Apparently he is writing another of those 'domestic comedies' then in vogue which thrived on its formulaic 'love triangle': husband—wife—

the philandering outsider. Shaw does this to entice his reader/auditor into watching or listening to the Shavian drama of ideas as it unfolds before her/him with all the due surprises. Levity has been a serious tool in Shaw's hands in communicating the Shavian message that is pretty heavy stuff in reality. And it is impossible to, predicate this deeper and nobler Shavian vision of life unless the existing, and severely crippling stereotypes are busted—stereo-types of ideas within the stereotyped drama-forms which have been traditionally holding lay men's wits to tyranny by preempting their minds and stunting their aesthetic and intellectual appreciation of the true situation, the in-thing that is, of life. The different (though related) genres of comedy in England and France towards the close of the nineteenth century were, according to Shaw, artificial and distorted forms of comedy and their different paradigms of the love-triangle were all without exception distorted and sentimental, at times even perverse. It will be my effort here to explicate how, backed up by his serious purpose, Shaw picks up the 'triangle' of the tradition only to abrogate the validities given to it by such genres as the Domestic Drama, Domestic Comedy, Palais Royal of the French stage, and transcend the pedestrian notions about love, marriage and conjugality, only to found it on the mysterious but manent operation of the Life Force. The mouldy, puritanic conception of morality is the main target of Shaw, since this stale, unfeeling Victorian moral complacence simplifies issues by turning them into stereotypes and thus raising conceited falsifications.

On the surface, with reference to the genre foundation, *Candida* is analogous to Domestic Comedy although it also resembles the Farce. Domestic Comedy and Farce in the nineteenth century theatre were twin-born; only, Domestic Comedy took good care of its moral tone and ambience while the Farce unleashed a gay abandon of indecorous irresponsibility. Conjugality and romantic longings formed the staple of the 'moral' in Domestic Comedy while extra-marital adventure with all its pricks of sex and adultery was the share of the Farce. Candida remains littered all over in elements of 'bedroom farce' as the lady's affair with Marchbanks produces squirms in Morell. Also, the Curate's irrepressible urge for nicknaming Proserpina as Prossy does underscore this 'light' element. In his preface to his own farcial comedy *Overruled*, Shaw gives his own observation on the farcical comedies of his day:

> "The stage has been preoccupied by such affairs ('the gallantries of married people') for centuries, not only in the jesting vein of Restoration Comedy and Palais Royal, Farce, but in the more tragically turned adulteries of the Parisian School which dominated the stage until Ibsen put them out of countenance and relegated them to their proper place as articles of commerce. Their continued vogue in that department maintains the tradition that adultery is the dramatic subject *par excellence*, and indeed that a play that is not about adultery is not a play at all."[6]

Interestingly, even the so-called Domestic Tragedies used this adultery as the staple, only to cover it up with the piety and morality of the seduced household angels. They were extensions of the stereotype of 'despairing magdalens' of Melodrama. Palais Royal farce made it a point to uphold the view that the act of adultery was less immoral than the prude and maudlin exhibitionism of sexual morality by the magdalens of Domestic drama. Candida's utter indifference to whatever moral question over adultery looks back archly to this ethos of the Palais Royal farce. In Domestic magdalen plays (tragedies and melodramas) adultery had a sure consummation while Domestic comedy was a compromise, stopping as it did at the very brink of a moral lapse. It was a halfway-house between the violently amoral Sex Farce and the tragically tuned magdalen plays in which sex takes place but is morally denounced and condemned. The connexion between *Candida* and this whole range of comedies, from the tragic to the farcical extremes of sexual misadventure, is pretty obvious. Shaw uses them to caricature them and then get past them. As Martin Meisel points out, "Shaw uses the conventions of Domestic Comedy to say something not only about domesticity but also about the relation of the artist to modern life."[7] Meisel's observation arises strictly out of the dramatic context of the play, and yet it assumes an altogether different significance, exceeding its ostensible dramatic perspective, once the biographical facts of Shaw's life are taken into account. Colin Wilson's analysis of them is very relevant in this context, but to that we may come a little later.[8]

Meisel's assumption that in the play Shaw is inverting the antiromantic (and puritanical) Domestic Comedy convention of vindicating the husband and castigating the lover-intruder is a tempting but misleading proposition, after all, in the long run. It is dangerous by virtue of being nearly true. Meisel assumes that Shaw repeats the plot with inverse implications, that Eugene's exit is really a triumph which Shaw means to accrue to the poet, the artist. But the truth may not have been as simple, for Shaw indeed goes beyond this position, it can well be seen, and works out a further referential somersault. It is true that on the surface, Morell feels humbled; true also that he does not retain Candida to himself by means of a dashing show of strength (as would be the case in a 'domestic comedy'), but rather is himself found retained mercifully by Candida. It is also no less true that Eugene does not leave the floor till he has floored his opponent. Yet, here is more than meets the eye. The action on the surface level moves in one direction and means one thing while a contrapuntal action runs on underneath, that is, at the level of the deeper structure of the story which only a jealous and minute attention to the Shavian use of semiotics would bring to one's notice.

Contrary to Meisell's thesis, Shaw's departure from the traditional paradigm of 'Tristan and Isolde' and 'Lancelot and Guinevere' is in a different way than that of the Domestic Comedy of his day. Whereas Domestic Comedy ultimately exposes the lover as the villain of the piece and so very 'morally' lets the husband thrive in the end, Shaw does something else quite. On the surface his plot is a look-alike of that of the Domestic Comedy—the unsuspecting and possessive husband suddenly in for bad weather because of the over-arching romantic pressure generated on his conjugal life by a paramour; a contest ensues in which the wife ultimately swings back to her husband and the lover has to bow out of the scene flustered. The Domestic Drama inverted the theme of romantic adultery in the way of domesticity and sought thereby to fight philistinism. Shaw's intentions are never so simple. For, in his play, Morell tastes defeat apparently, and the poet looks a better *homme* and a genuinely romantic man whose glamour is neither belied nor curbed till the end. Shaw is not bothered at all by questions of domestic virtue in the moral and pious strain; his assertion hinges entirely on wit and intellect. Apparently, the husband is saved through defeat, even if doubt remains as to what kind of conjugal felicity he might hope to glean in future consequent of this stunning dispossession of his dignity as a man and a husband.

This would be the ultimate meaning of the comedy of Candida if we had not taken care of Shaw's own beliefs and sayings in other contexts, and more importantly, if we had not known Shaw's talents for self-contradictions. That simplification looks suspect which assumes that whereas Domestic Comedy made the anti-romantic thesis in one particular manner Shaw is just caricaturing that model and drawing out another anti-romantic thesis by gleefully making the Domestic Comedy paradigm walk on its stomach. When we are stressing Morell's discomfiture in the Auction' Scene as an anti-romantic affair, we are in some danger of closing our eyes on another fact, that Candida's rejection of Marchbanks's overture and her cosseting of Morell as a protege actually upholds the incipient romance between husband and wife in their domestic life. Indeed, I think it does not require much imagination or detective instinct to follow Shaw's reverse flick as a comedist: he is actually upholding romance in the play by giving the lie to the philanderer's romance, the poetic wooing that is, and validating the substance of conjugality by providing it the due correction it needed from the (complacent) husband's side. The play is a play basically, between Morell and Candida, and not, as Shaw with ironic mischief misled the 'romantic' reader to assume hastily, a play on love between eighteen and thirty-two. Eugene is the heroical non-hero, in almost a comic duplication of the arch-adversary in *Paradise Lost*. Morell is the non-heroical hero—a witty Shavian variation on the concept of 'Hero'. Shaw's deeper ironic counter-intentions are seen when we judge the character-conjurations in Shaw from multiple perspectives.

First, in *Arms and the Man*, the conflict has been pretty straightforward.[9] Bluntschli is intelligent and in the correct, Sergius is neither. But in *Candida* our sympathies are divided because both Morell, and Marchbanks are intelligent, each in his own way. And Morell does love his wife and does not stoop to any indecency even in the face of great crisis. Secondly, Shaw's growing faith in the gospel of efficiency, more, and more, disagreed, even while admiring, with the poetic vision of Morris the pre-Raphaelite and Yeats the upholder of the 'tragic generation'. Yeats, conceived of the poet as sitting on a knoll apart. This idea takes a severe beating, in Shaw's hands. Thirdly, the tempting misprising about Candida as a gillflirt is headless since the tenor of the play makes it plain that sex never comes to the fore of the play. Candida is the very antithesis, in motive and not so much in action, of the silly 'romantic wife' of convention. If she is tempted by anything, it is not the masculinity or the sex charm in Eugene but by the need of poetry in life. Morell is sedated by habit as husband; this habit had poetry rolled out of focus in their conjugal life. The woman in Candida does not sleep on it and the poet-lover's passion and poetry ensures much-needed ventilation in her claustrophobic life. Let Morell see his own insensateness and mend himself in time, otherwise the so-called moral-religious constructs of 'marriage' and 'chastity' cannot, potentially, deter Candida from quitting him. A heartless marriage bond carries no meaning for Candida. She makes it plain to Morell while chiding him for his stunted, convention-bound sensibility:

> "Ah, James, how little you understand me, to talk of your confidence in my goodness and purity: I would give them both to poor Eugene as willingly as I would give my shawl to a beggar dying of cold, if there were nothing else to restrain me. Put your trust in my love

> for you, James; for if that went, I should care very little for your sermons: mere phrases that you cheat yourself and others with everyday." (*Candida* 57)

All this is not an index of Candida's laxness of morality, but rather of her obeisance to a morality of a different sort—the truth of love—which gives her a dual freedom: freedom from any vulgar appetite for sex as also for any romantic illusion and at the same time from a superstitious subjection to the convention of piety and impiety. In this dual freedom from romance and conjugal servitude she is really "the Virgin Mother and nobody else." [10] Here is the new conception of a virgin mind, untampered either by custom or by illusion. In a letter to Huneker, Shaw speaks on this conception in his inimitable style:

> "Don't ask me conundrums about the very immoral female Candida. Observe the entry of W. Burgess Candida's father: 'You're the lady as hused to typewrite for him.' 'No.' 'Naaow: she was younger.' And therefore Candida sacked her. Prossy is a highly selected person indeed, devoted to Morell to the extent of helping in the kitchen but to him the merest pet rabbit, unable to get the slightest hold on him. Candida is as unscrupulous as Wagner's Siegfried: Morell himself sees that 'no law will bind her.' She seduces Eugene just exactly as far as it is worth her while to seduce him. She is a woman without 'character' in the conventional sense. Without brains and strength of mind she would be a wretched slattern and voluptuary. She is straight for natural reasons, not for conventional ethical ones. Nothing can be more coldbloodedly coldbloodedly reasonable than her farewell to Eugene: 'All very well, my lad; but I don't quite see myself at fifty with a husband of thirty-five.' It is just this freedom from emotional slop that makes her so completely mistress of her situation."[11]

In the light of this clarification coming from Shaw himself, we may now understand Candida's a-moral, intellectual base all the better. Candida's self is neither 'moral' nor 'immoral'; she is neither the 'paragon' of the Victorian 'virtue' (like the 'magdalen' heroines) nor the pure-hearted but vulnerable wife of the Domestic Comedy, nor also the sex-and-romance-crazy woman of the Sex-Farces or Bedroom Farces. All these constructs have been apparently aspected slantedly by the witty mischief of the dramatist while crowning none of them and ultimately getting beyond them with slightful strides of intellectual ideality. Shaw's gyres of intentions keep dispelling the facile conventional constructs of woman as either a domestic 'angel' (in the Christian and bourgeois sense) or a 'slattern' by mimicking and then negating the different genres through which such images used to come down on the, viewers; and in the Candida image he ultimately takes us to a 'new woman' who lays stress on the chastity of heart's affiliations rather than on physical chastity in formal conformity to conventional imposition.

As Shaw intends it, Candida's morality is dictated and towed by her primal instinct which is *in essentia* maternal. This instinct is guided by the pragmatics of need and protection to where it is due. As such this morality predates society and all its variedly evolved notions of morality with changing dates and climes. Shaw's betakenness with the 'mother' goes far indeed to influence his discourse on Woman, or New Woman, both in this play and in others. Colin Wilson in *Bernard Shaw: A Reassessment* points out the relevance of Shaw's devotedness to his mother, Bessy Shaw:

> "This is a deduction from two known facts: that his mother had no very deep feelings about him, and that he adored his mother. 'I never knew love when I was a child', he told Ellen Terry. 'My mother was so disappointed in my father that she centred all her care on my younger sister, and she left me to fend for myself.' Percy Smith has argued convincingly that he, not only idolised his mother but that all the women in his plays from *Candida* on are mother figures. Shaw made no great tragedy about the lack of maternal affection (Henderson's statement that he

> was 'permanently embittered' by it has no foundation), but it certainly needs to be taken into account in trying to grasp his personality....
>
> I would suggest it is arguable that, just as an excess of mother love may produce homosexual tendencies in talented sons, so a certain deficiency—provided it is not too marked—may produce the opposite effect: intellectuality, enthusiasm for ideas. Well's relations with his mother were curiously similar to those of Shaw with Bessy Shaw. Other names that come to mind in this connection are Russell, Whitehead, Einstein, Beethoven, Shelley and Joyce."[12]

Taking cue from Wilson, we may then affirm that in Candida Shaw clothes an idea, intellectually. That Woman is not just a sex-object, nor is she to be lost under the heaps of household chores and then reduced into a pet under the protection of her husband. Shaw divides the male identity into two faculties and then places them respectively in Morell and Marchbanks—romantic passion and yearning for woman as well as instinctive dependence on woman—simply to uphold two glaring facts staring us in the face all the while: men depend for their very existence and sustenance on the very women whom they mistakenly subsume as protegees and properties of men; and the 'mystery' of Woman (Shaw calls *Candida* a 'mystery play') is that she understands man in his puerile weakness and vanity while man remains basically ignorant of the inside core of Woman. It is to her credit completely (and she is naturally gifted with this disposition) that for all his tardiness and unpreparedness, she takes man along the road with her, keeps him and endures his nonsenses with a motherly salubrity. The Victorian androcentrism with its bourgeois moral package remains inert and insensible to this universal truth, true for all time and space. Shaw unearths this truth which had lain under heaps of rust contributed by the conventions and shines it up with his brilliant wit and dramatic insight. He brings the perennial identity of Woman out, with the force of an apocalypse in the end of the play Shaw has no large quarrels with the newly risen socio-political construct of the New Woman; while in public life and at the outdoor space woman may justifiably get their rights and spaces ensured on an equal footing, the idea of Woman's centrality at home also needs to be driven home emotionally, intellectually and aesthetically. It is not enough that, politically, we see women as co-equals of men, for we have not seen the ultimate truth about woman until we have recognized that she is our superior, aesthetically. Home does not thrive merely by politics; it has to depend on true emotion which is aesthetic, and that way intensely moral, though this morality does not come down from the stale archive of convention. The achievement of Shaw is thus no short of iconoclasm—changing our ways of apprehension and rewriting our sensibility. Only great literature has access to this august prerogative. Shaw's success at that has been patent and broad enough. The word of praise comes from A.C. Ward, over half a century after the first publication of *Candida*:

> "After more than half a century its 'mystery' and its 'secret' still hold the attention of the audiences. It is 'still entertaining and amusing; and although the New Woman long ago ceased to be new, Candida has enough of the nature of every woman of her class and country to have survived many changes of fashion in ideas and attitudes. She has a heart as well as a mind, and in any competition for the naming of the favourite heroine in Shaw's plays Candida would come second only to Saint Joan."[13]

It seems we have had an inkling of Shaw's real intention with the 'love-triangle'; there is a paradigm shift in it in keeping with the Shavian idea of Woman. An attestation of this comes from Shaw's own letter which he wrote to Golding Bright:

> "'Candida' is the poetry of the 'Wife and mother—the Virgin Mother in the true sense....'"[14]

Thus, not only Bessy Shaw but Virgin Mary as the Mother went into the concept of Candida. In another letter, this time to Ellen Terry, Shaw emphasised that Candida is "the Virgin mother and nobody else". Maurice Valency is of the opinion that Shaw did conceptualise Candida not so much in realistic terms as in symbolic terms; therefore it is "A Mystery" and written in the Pre-Raphaelite spirit and attitude. Valency observes:

> It was doubtless a tribute to the obtuseness of his audience that Shaw retitled *Candida* 'A Mystery'. This epithet has been generally explained as a reference to the poet's 'secret'. But it is more likely that Shaw had in mind the medieval mystery plays as a prototype of Pre-Raphaelite attitudes in the theater. Possibly he saw in the Candida situation an analogy to a play about Mary, Joseph and their unruly son. In that case he might have done better, to have called it a Morality, for its symbols, if symbols they are, come closer to the personification of the medieval moral plays than to the Bible stories enacted in the mystery cycles.[15]

The significance of the Auction Scene now should stand in the clear. Bernard Shaw makes ideas and actions rally up to this climactic scene where the apocalypse of "the Wife and Mother—the Virgin Mother in the true sense" takes place; Morell as Joseph belongs to her, while Marchbanks profiles as the 'unruly son,' for does not Candida affectionately call him a lad, a boy? She even at one time scolds him: "You bad boy": Maternity gleams on the ring of this affection, and Marchbanks is petted and scolded and guided affectionately by the lady only to bring him to the point of maturity and self-reliance. The play thus is both a Mystery and a Morality: And Shaw is the new Baptist of this Faith in the wake of the modern era.

Note

All citations from the text have been taken from Shaw's *Candida,* with Introduction and notes by A.C. Ward, Mumbai: Orient Longman (The Orient Edition), 2001. (London: Constable, 1955).

References

1. George Meredith, *An Essay on Comedy and the Uses of the Comic Spirit,* London: Constable, 1913.

2. *Essay on Comedy*, 62.
3. Meredith, *The Egoist*, with Introduction by Lord Dunsany, London: OUP (The World's Classic), 1948.
4. Elain Showalter, "Towards a Feminist Poetics" in M. Jacobus ed. *Women Writing about Women*, Boston: Croom Helm Ltd., 1979.
5. Henrik Ibsen, *A Doll's House*, in *Four Major Plays*, tran. in English by James Macfarlene and Jens Arup, London: OUP, 1981.
6. Quoted in Martin Meisel, *Shaw and the Nineteenth Century Theatre*, New York: 1984.
7. Meisel, *Shaw and the Nineteenth Century Theatre*; 159.
8. Colin Wilson, *Bernard Shaw: A Reassessment*, London: Macmillan, 1969.
9. Shaw, *Arms and the Man,* with Intro. and Notes by A.C. Ward, New Delhi: Orient Longman (The Orient Edition), 2003. (London: Constable, 1954).
10. Letter to Ellen Terry, in *Bernard Shaw: Collected Letters*, 1874-1897, edited by Dan H. Laurence, New York: 1965; 632.
11. Quoted in Colin Wilson, *B.S.: A Reassessment*; 132.
12. Colin Wilson, *B.S.: A Reassessment*; 28.
13. A.C. Ward in his Introduction to *Candida*.
14. Letter to Golding Bright, in *B.S.: Collected Letters*, 1874-1897; 623.
15. Maurice Valency: *The Cart and the Trumpet,* New York, 1973; 132.

5

The Country-City Opposition in Blake: A Study of *Songs of Innocence and Experience*

Kenneth Usongo

Late 18th century British society was largely stratified with the wealthy, on the one hand, enjoying many privileges to the detriment of the poor who were generally victims of exploitation. Beyond the rosy images depicted in some of the literature and paintings of this era lay several injustices, namely, discrimination, poverty, and misery. Consequently, moral crusaders like William Blake appealed for a more tolerant and humane society, one that can curb class barriers and their attendant ills. Like others before him such as the Society for the Reformation of Manners, the Society for the Propagation of Christian Knowledge or the Abolitionist movement that castigated some of the evils of this time, Blake also denounces some of these reprehensible practices, be they in the city or country, in "Songs of Innocence and Experience." In this regard, his graphic verse is very revealing about the political, social and economic climate of his age; he expresses his opposition to some of the ills of his society through art.

Blake's perception of the city, like that of Romantic poets such as William Wordsworth and Samuel Coleridge seems to mean smoke and slums, its factories, its businessmen, and its false religion that empties men, women and children of their individual lives and fills them with its annihilating smoke and ugliness (Michael 16). According to Raymond Williams in *The Country and the City*, the country has gathered the idea of a natural way of life: of peace, innocence, and simple virtue; the city has contrarily gathered the idea of an achieved centre: of learning, communication and light. There is generally an ideological separation between the processes of rural exploitation which have been, in effect, dissolved into a landscape, and the register of that exploitation, in the law courts, the money markets, the political power and the conspicuous expenditure of the city (46). However, Blake, in his poetry, shifts the traditional polarity between the city and the country that is often synonymous with vice and virtue in depicting both milieus as rosy and evil simultaneously. More importantly, Blake rewrites the country-city binary by exploring it as a manifestation of the conflicting states of mind. My submission is that a critical look at the country/city binary reveals Blake's somewhat ambivalent attitude towards both settings. Interestingly, Blake first wrote "Songs of Innocence" before appending those of Experience and this possibly underlines the transition from innocence to experience that the mind is exposed to, and the poet's inclination towards the country than the city. Nevertheless, it would have been too quixotic, in my mind, for the poet-painter to have represented the one as all glamorous and the other as totally negative.

Jennifer Davis Michael, like Sir Geoffrey Keynes, Northrop Frye, Harold Bloom and others, insists that Blake rejected the mystifying fetishization of nature because it too denied the existence of anything beyond the material world (18). She echoes other critics in saying that if nature and civilization are both human constructs, then, the dialectic of country and city is questionable because both indicate the unstable synthesis of human artefact and organic environment. Indeed, Blake was very ambivalent in his beliefs and actually embraced intellectual and emotional ambivalence (Mason XV). Truly, his mythology was very complex, bordering at times on contradictions which, in line with the poet's thinking, were a display of a moral imperative. As an infant, he saw visions of angels, an experience that was in sharp contrast to the terrifying dishonesty in this epoch. In discussing the country-city divide in Blake's poetry and art, I shall rigorously employ Marxist criticism.

Marxism reads a text in the light of an all-informing philosophy in which the idea of a class struggle is central. There is interdependence between literature and the economic structure of society. Even though a uniform critical response is not expected, Marxist criticism is varied and lively. I argue that Blake reveres art which he uses to point out the faults of his society. Indeed, Marxism is simply one way of relating the text to a view of the social reality of the time in which it was written (Peck and Coyle 192). Through this method, the Marxist critic looks critically at problems and contradictions within a bourgeois culture, bringing to the fore disruptive or inadequate ideological values.

Blake's poetry is seen as revealing of class struggles in the late 18th and 19th centuries British society, and this perception is partly informed by the understanding that it is difficult to find an artistic form that is void of a political or social tinge. As a matter of fact, Stewart Crehan in *Blake in Context,* aligns Blake with English Jacobinism that embodied politically conscious artisans and small tradesmen who were opposed to the monarchy, aristocracy, and various distinctions of rank (18). Employed as an engraver by the bookseller Joseph Johnson into a milieu that included dissenting radicals like Thomas Paine, Mary Wollstonecraft and William Godwin, Blake shared the belief in reason and universal principles of justice (Williams 215).

Blake does not envisage a Manichean view of life. If one were to historicize his literature, the poet-artist would have probably opted for the countryside than for the city. This likelihood is buttressed by the compelling images of joy, solace, and beauty evoked in the country poems and paintings as opposed to the haunting imagery of suffering, blood, and disappointment enshrined in the city poems and drawings. He would have likely shared Wordsworth's statement that the primary laws of nature, namely, virtue, kindness, and sympathy were more prevalent in the country than in the city.

This opinion is grounded in the understanding that, with the exception of a few poems such as "Upon Westminster Bridge" that examines the city from a somewhat positive perspective, most of Wordsworth's poetry, particularly *The Prelude*, gives an unpalatable view of the city. Blake's poetry appears to fault more the city than the country, an apparent indication that while both settings need reformation, the case of the city seems more expedient than that of the country. It is this message that he graphically illustrates in his verse that, on the one hand, celebrates the splendour of nature and, on the other hand, vilifies the cruelty and evils of his generation. After all, allegorical readings of Blake tell us that while he wrote poetry, what he really meant to say was something about the historical events of his time, or about religion, or about psychology (Halmi XXXIV-XL). In other words, Blake can be judged as a committed writer in that he uses his poetry to castigate certain evils of 19th century England, be they exploitation, child labour or tyranny. It is decidedly this critical position that gives a revolutionary twist to his art.

Innocence and experience, externally and generically, apply to the condition of man before the Fall; internally and psychologically to the child who has not experienced the inner divisions of human life. It should be recalled that Blake's Innocence has its roots in the thought of the Swedish visionary, Emmanuel Swedenborg. In this regard, the conception of Innocence is seen as an inner state of mind, taking images such as the child and the lamb. At the other extreme, Experience is externalized in a world of images like chain, thorns, spears, and blood, all of which correspond to the harsh realities of life (Paley 3-4). At this level, the treasured concept of benevolence is now replaced by deceit and exploitation.

"Songs of Innocence" are products of a mind in a state of innocence and an imagination unspoiled by stains of worldliness. Contrarily, "Songs of Experience" protests against and satirizes a state of affairs which need not exist. The voice in the poems, especially in "Songs of Experience," is that of a reformer whose indignation is roused by the confrontation of unnecessary barriers to a state of life in which man can be joyful and free; the bitterness is not against life, but entirely against kings, priests, and the church (Hirsh 93). Blake's art that is grounded in suffering can be seen as radical; he seems to be infusing rebellious drives in the downtrodden class as a solution to the various injustices to which they are subjected. As intimated by Andrew Lincoln, Blake shares the philosophical historian's interest in exploring relationships between economic, social and religious developments, and sympathizes with the 'conjectural' historian's interest in reconstructing the major stages of social evolution (Clark and Worrall 73). In other words, by depicting the suffering of poor and unprivileged people, as is the case of 'London,' he appears to be stimulating people towards rebellion as a solution to injustices, in the same way that Soyinka conscientizes Igwezu or Ngugi wa Thiong'o and Ngugi wa Mirii activate Kiguunda and Wangeci in *I will Marry when I want*. Like these authors, Blake can be seen as an engaged writer who condemns the exploitation of children by oppressive forces like the church and the king. The poet is deeply aware of the social and historical climate of his age and, in his 'city poems,' appeals for a halt to some of the evils perpetuated by powerful, economic classes.

Blake intertwined painting and poetry to the extent that it is difficult to make a separation between both; in fact, he sacrificed time and money in this endeavour that he considered ornamental, grand and unique. In making colourful representations of his poems, Blake is perhaps envisaging an English society that can ape his attractive designs in the forms of humaneness and love. He uses one element of form to complement the other resulting in a melody that runs from voice to voice, and can be developed in a scene (Hagstrum 10-12). His colours can be deeply suggestive and can serve to heighten meaning. For example, a red streak represents sunrise and blue, like the case of "Songs of Experience," suggests night; the borders provoke a flight of the imagination as the beholder muses from one realm of joy to another. In the case of "Songs of Innocence and Experience," the former have fresh and attractive vegetation while the latter is saturated with dead or dying foliage. To Jean Hagstrum, the tree of Innocence is large and healthy; its branches entwined in a natural embrace while the same tree in Experience is dry and dying; its withering branches form round arches over the page (83). The need to study his paintings as an index to his poetry cannot be overemphasized; indeed, to Uvedale Price (4),

> ...the use, therefore, of studying pictures is not merely to make us acquainted with the combinations and effects that are contained in them, but to guide us by means of those general heads (as they may be called) of composition, in our search of the numberless and untouched varieties and beauties of nature.

As a matter of fact, like the great artists such as L. da Vinci, M. Angelo, Raphael and others who saw pictures as shedding light on the history, poetry and arts of a society, Blake verse can be seen as representative of 19th century England.

In fact, the prose language of "Songs" is a reenactment of radical songs that were popular among the working class in the 1790s. In this regard, David Worrall states that these poems should be appreciated against the background of political contrariety in which the songs competed for ideological supremacy in a society undergoing political polarization (194-211). As proof of his attachment to the working class, Blake seemed to have conceived visual designs in his illuminated books in the hope of reaching an audience beyond those sufficiently cultured to read his complex poetry. Put differently, he thought of the poor working class as target audience susceptible to revolt against oppression. Hence, his graphic paintings were perhaps conceived as a means to conscientize the suffering masses; pictures of exploited children, weary old people in the streets of London were intended to haunt a potential audience of revolutionaries. Taken as a whole, these paintings were also part of Blake's scheme to circumvent arrest for propagating revolutionary ideas. After all, a majority of "Songs of Experience" were written in the spring and summer of 1792, at the start of Pitt's Terror and shortly before the institution of the Association for the Preservation of Liberty and Property against Republicans and Levellers (Lincoln 224).

"The Echoing Green," arguably cast in the country and suggestive of Blake's concern for the country and the helpless, reinforces a communion of joy between children and nature; both seem to be inextricably linked as not only man, but birds all respond enthusiastically to the beautiful rays of the sun:

> The Sun does arise,
> And make happy the skies;
> The merry bells ring
> To welcome the Spring;
> The skylark and thrush,
> The birds of the bush,
> Sing louder around (ll. 1-7)

This poem traces the cycle of human life in two realms: natural life represented by natural day and old age by the evening. Childhood is seen as prophetic because in it is stored intimations of immortality. Wordsworth expresses this idea in his famous paradox of the child being father of the man, an issue that Old John seems to acknowledge as he 'laughs away' while the children play. It is the same spirit of joy that animates the poem "The Lamb" as it highlights the comfort of an Immanent God who is distinguishable in terms of tenderness and meekness. The country setting of this poem articulates the charming voice of the lamb in the same way that the echoing green reverberates with the happiness of the playful children. The cumulative force of the poem attests the supreme joy radiating between the lamb and the child who questions it. And this is reinforced in the painting that shows a child stretching his hand towards the lamb in a gesture of comradeship. The picture of a cottage near them hammers at the pastoral background that resonates with glee, a vivid depiction of the joys associated with the countryside.

"Laughing Song" is another pastoral poem that presents a charming, peaceful world of Innocence, a world seemingly void of capitalist exploitation as the Speaker enjoins the reader to partake of this unique experience of uncontested happiness, especially:

When the green woods laugh with the voice of joy,
And the dimpling stream runs laughing by;
When the air does laugh with our merry wit,
And the green hill laughs with the noise of it; (ll. 1-4)

There is a contrary feeling evoked in "Nurse's Song" which somehow bridges the world of the child (Innocence) and that of the adult (Experience). As the child whiles away his time in nature, the adult cautions him on the dangers of protracted play in the evening: "Then come home, my children, the sun is gone down,/ And the dews of the night arise;"(ll. 5-6). The absence of dialogue between the Nurse and the children, the metaphors registered in the words "day" and "night" insinuate tyranny and jealousy on the part of this Nurse as she discourages these children from playing. This is unlike the case of Nurse's Song (Innocence) that celebrates total communion between the children and the Nurse as marked by dialogue between both parties; the length of this poem is also suggestive of the spirit of camaraderie between the Nurse and children as against the severe tone of Experience that the poet obliquely identifies with oppression. Alternatively, innocence and experience are perceived as states of the mind and, in this case, reflected in the child and adult respectively. E.D. Hirsch aptly comments that the basic understanding here is that man is vulnerable and dependent, and that the innocence of the child is the highest wisdom man can attain (33). In this connection, in order for a man to curb his exploitative and selfish desires, often associated with Experience, a return to the virtues of Innocence represented in childhood is imperative.

In the accompanying poetic painting, we notice an adult nurse torn between reading and watching children play. It is as if the children, like those in Wordsworth's "The Tables Turned," are instructing the nurse to discard his books (barren leaves) and derive inspiration from nature. These children seemingly do not need any instruction from him; instead, the latter appears to draw peace and joy from the former who are cast against a rural and natural backdrop as opposed to the urban setting of the proceeding poem.

"Holy Thursday" describes a historical event that occurred in London where actual attendance at a charitable school peaked five thousand. This poem is symbolic of unpleasant memories of destitution that plagued the Speenhamland Relief System that was intended to alleviate poverty. Prior to this attendance, the children were scrubbed and dressed in their best outfits for purposes of decency: "'Twas on a Holy Thursday, their innocent faces clean" (1). Their multicoloured attires: red, blue, green are indications of their deplorable state; their innocence and brightness seem to infuse hope in the forsaken London city: "O what a multitude they seem'd, these flowers of London town!" (5).

It is paradoxical that while late 18th century London teems in abundance of wealth, children are subjected to hardship as evident in "Holy Thursday" experience. This overtly partisan and simple poem chastises the mistreatment of children. There is a marked division between the affluent and the destitute, and this can be redressed through a redistribution of the wealth of the nation and not by creating charity schools. Blake challenges this practice as a panacea to the plight of children because it is unnatural in the first place. The design on this poem harbouring a horrified woman pointing at naked children registers a strong note of protest. The poem is an indictment on industrial England for abandoning children to themselves while, ironically, the parents have gone to church to pray. Writing at the time of the passage of the "Chimney Sweepers' Act" of 1788 when newspapers and reformers like Jonas Hanway were publicizing the treatment of the sweeps, Blake expresses his deep outrage, obliquely and ironically, through the understated discourse of boys who, in the symbolic context of "Songs of Innocence and Experience," have, to Martin Nurmi, somehow preserved their humanity in the face of the dehumanizing treatment inflicted on them (Frye 15). In fact, the child in "The Chimney-Sweeper" Innocence is apparently naïve about his exploitation, but is aware of it in "The Chimney-Sweeper" Experience: "And because I am happy and dance and sing,/ They think they have done me no injury" (ll. 9-10); an indication of the complexity between the states of innocence and experience that seem to infringe on each other. The church along with the Priest and King constitute an unholy trinity that exacerbates the discomfort of children; this telling irony underscores the poet's indignation at this abysmal state of affairs and, of course, a reversal in the form of a revolt against this state of things seems to be Blake's message.

Essentially, Blake's "Songs," particularly the Chimney Sweeper poems, are a subtle denunciation of man's alienation from labour, which in this case seems to be the bedrock of capitalism. In protesting against this view of work, Blake manifests his preference for purposeful art that can draw attention to societal ills and not exploitative labour that sustains capitalism. Once more, the poet's disapproval of the exploitation of children and the working class by the rich and the powerful is unmistakable.

Children are morally superior to the adult nurse in "Nurse's Song" in that while they derive solace in playing on the green, she objects to this practice. She fails to understand that landscape signifies a seductive mixture of peace and solitude with security and visual pleasure (Pugh 1). This scenario makes the countryside enviable hence Blake's portrayal of it in a positive sense. Perhaps the Nurse's conspiratorial whisperings retrace her uneventful youthful past that makes her jealous of the rollicking children.

"London" is unarguably Blake's most poignant attack on the city. The powerful message of the poem is that of social and political revolution. A Marxist reading of the poem reveals the polarization of the city between 'the haves' and 'the haves-not' thereby enough reason for a revolution by the oppressed against the oppressor. In stressing economic and social differences, this poem somehow challenges the financially disadvantaged class of society into opposing their unfair treatment. Human reason has created the evil triumvirate of church, monarchy and marriage. Again, to Hirsch, without a church which sustains social injustice by promises of Heaven, there would be no chimney sweeps; without kings who wage war for their private interest, empire would be no more; without marriage, there would be no "unacted desires" and therefore no harlotry (94). Therefore, the situation can be redressed when the suffering masses fight for an improvement in their welfare. The chartered street and Thames, the Infant's cry of fear, the mind-forged manacles seem to depict the heart of darkness, a justification for a social revolution that will ultimately benefit the exploited class(es) of society. The disquieting array of human suffering, depicted in the poem, was partly occasioned by industrial explosion:

> But most thro' midnight streets I hear
> How the youthful harlot's curse
> Blasts the new-born infant's tear
> And blights with plagues the marriage hearse.
>
> (ll. 13-16)

The design of a hoary old man being led by a boy through a desolate London street reiterates woe that has overwhelmed these city dwellers. And the image of blood in the poem, to David Erdman, is an apocalyptic omen of mutiny and civil war involving regicide (495). Decidedly, a revolution will result in a representative redistribution of wealth in a manner that embraces all segments of society, in a manner advocated in Blake's poetry.

Despondent as may seem prospects of city life, Blake does not look at both the country and the city from a mutually exclusive perspective. Instead, one appears to be nurtured and sustained by the other as noted in the duality in "The Sick Rose" whereby its sickness is the result of her ignorance. Stated differently, the rose's evil is both within and without; its naïvety is exploited by the worm. Put allegorically, neither the city nor the country are totally free of vice or virtue; what makes each setting different is the degree of goodness or evil that each inhabits.

Innocence and Experience represent the contrary states of the human mind; Innocence refers to the state of the human soul before greed and nonchalance claimed their victims in Experience. Perhaps as an illustration of his commitment to Innocence, Blake made a total of twenty-seven paintings which, to Sir Geoffrey Keynes, are products of a mind in a state of innocence and of an imagination unspoiled by stains of worldliness. Thereafter, public events and private concerns conspired to convert Innocence into Experience, producing Blake's preoccupation with the problem of Good and Evil (XIV). Indeed, "Songs of Innocence" are to be taken at their face value as the outpourings of a naïve and childlike spontaneity, and the "Songs of Experience" as the bitter disillusionment resulting from maturity (Halmi 12). Stated differently, Blake's poetry reflects traces of virtue and vice in both the country and the city; the poet does not view the one as charming and the other as completely evil. Instead, both environments have their strengths and weaknesses; the difference only comes in terms of degree. Nonetheless, the case of the country and city poems, as earlier discussed, attest a preponderance of virtue in the country than in the city.

To Harold Pagliaro, unself-consciousness, typified by Innocence, is a failure on the part of the child to perceive inimical elements in the world while Experience implies both a complexity of cautionary restraint in the mind's contours and the mind's occasional forgetfulness of such complexity (9-13). Put differently, the states of Innocence and Experience are conflicting; the one does not negate the other. Both states interact with one another resulting in greater exposition from this interplay. Innocence is the married land Blake called Beulah while Experience is the harsh, but vital world of generation. Harold Bloom synthesizes this duality in that Experience exposes the precarious unreality of Innocence whereas Innocence censures the duplicity of Experience's realities; the world of Innocence shows God as loving and Nature as a benevolent mother as opposed to the contraries of these qualities registered in Experience (17-30).

In line with Raymond Williams' assertion in *Marxism and Literature* on art reflecting not 'mere appearances,' but the 'reality' behind these (95), so too can it be said that Blake's "Songs" give us social and historical insights into late 18th century England, a depiction that shows the virtues and the vices of the country and the city in the wake of various transformations such as the industrial and agrarian revolutions. The plight of the chimney sweepers, the cries of infants, the happiness of children as they play in the green, as evinced in "Songs of Innocence and Experience," attest the shifting boundaries of virtue/vice and country/city that Blake is most concerned.

In fact, the relationship between the city and the country is an old classical concern, one where both settings were initially viewed from two diametrical perspectives whereby the country was perceived as virtuous and the city vicious. Progressively, as evident in "Songs of Innocence and Experience," both settings appear to be interwoven, sharing somehow similar qualities of goodness and evil. It is this latter vision of the country-city paradigm that Blake explores in his poetry. He studies man in four principal relationships: man and his world, man and his body, man and his fellow men, and man and his past and future. Blake believes that man either designs his world or allows himself to be brutalized by nature; a man's time is either imaginatively reformed or becomes oppressive and restrictive. Clearly, the plight of the suffering masses can be redressed when they take the initiative in resisting various injustices and oppression. It is partly a result of such a philosophy that makes a Marxist reading of his poetry justifiable. Indeed, just before his death on August 12, 1827, Blake burst out singing of the things that he saw in paradise. Symbolically, the poet-artist envisioned new ethics for England in the spirit of brotherhood and moderation in the absence of which a social revolution was inevitable.

Works Cited

Bloom, Harold. *The Visionary Company*. Garden City, New York: Doubleday & Company, 1961.

Crehan, Stewart. *Blake in Context*. Atlantic Highlands, NJ: Humanities Press, 1984.

Erdman, David V. *Blake Prophet Against Empire*. Princeton, New Jersey: Princeton UP, 1969.

Frye, Northrop, ed. *Blake: A Collection of Critical Essays*. Englewood Cliffs, N.J.: Prentice-Hall, Inc., 1966.

Hagstrum, Jean H. *William Blake: Poet and Painter*. Chicago: The U of Chicago P, 1964.

Halmi, Nicholas, ed. *Northrop Frye's Fearful Symmetry: A Study of William Blake*. Vol. 14. Princeton: Princeton UP, 1947.

Hirsch, E.D. *Innocence and Experience: An Introduction to Blake*. New Haven: Yale UP, 1964.

Keynes, Sir Geoffrey, ed. *Songs of Innocence and Experience*. Paris: The Trianon Press, 1967.

Lincoln, Andrew. "Blake and the History of Radicalism" in Nicholas M. Williams ed. *Palgrave Advances in William Blake Studies*. New York: Palgrave Macmillan, 2006.

——. "Blake and the 'Reasoning Historian'" in Steve Clark and David Worrall eds. *Historicizing Blake*. New York: Macmillan, 1994.

Mason, Michael, ed. *William Blake*. Oxford: Oxford UP, 1988.

Michael, Jennifer Davis. *Blake and the City*. Lewisburg: Bucknell UP, 2006.

Nurmi, Martin K. "Fact and Symbol in 'The Chimney-Sweeper' of Blake's 'Songs of Innocence'" in Northrop Frye ed. *Blake: A Collection of Critical Essays*. Englewood Cliffs, NJ: Prentice-Hall, Inc., 1966.

Pagliaro, Harold. *Self-hood and Redemption in Blake's Songs*. University Park: The Pennsylvania State UP, 1987.

Paley, Morton D., ed. *Twentieth Century Interpretations of Songs of Innocence and of Experience*. Englewood Cliffs, N.J.: Prentice-Hall, Inc., 1969.

Peck, John and Martin Coyle. *Literary Terms and Criticism*. New York: Palgrave, 2002.

Price, Uvedale. *An Essay on the Picturesque, as Compared with the Sublime and the beautiful; and, on the Use of Studying pictures, for the purpose of improving real landscape*. London: J. Robson, M.DCC.XCVI.

Pugh, Simon, ed. *Reading Landscape*. Manchester: Manchester UP, 1990.

Williams, Raymond. *The Country and the City*. Oxford: Oxford UP, 1973.

——. *Marxism and Literature* .Oxford: Oxford UP, 1977.

Worrall, David. "Blake and the 1790s Plebeian Radical Culture" in Steve Clark and David Worrall eds. *Blake in the Nineties*. Houndmills: Macmillan, 1999.

Yeats, William Butler ed. *Poems of William Blake*. New York: Boni and Liveright, n.d.

6

Baldassare Castiglione's *Book of the Courtier in Renaissance England*

Carole Rozzonelli

It had become a common habit in England in the XVIth century to send young men of position on the *Grand Tour* to complete their education. The English young gentleman had no textbook to teach him the accomplishments that were thought requisite to all those of noble birth. The first noblemen to have created this ideal were the Italian Dukes of the Renaissance. A new type of courtier had appeared in Italy. The courts of Urbino, Mantua, and Ferrara were the most famous. There, a new conception of the "companion of the Prince", as they called the courtier, was created. This ideal was then taken up by the Princes of Europe (François 1er, Henry VIII); then, by their courtiers and all the upper classes. The Renaissance ideal of the gentleman and lady undoubtedly affected the inclination of all persons who were, or who wished to be considered gentlemen and ladies. Of course, this ideal, product of a changing civilization, received many definitions in the XVIth and XVIIth centuries, of which a few including those of Thomas Elyot, Baldassare Castiglione, Roger Ascham, and Peacham may be taken as representative. However, the most famous book to express this ideal was *The Book of the Courtier* by Baldassare Castiglione.

The Book of the Courtier is the most famous Renaissance treatise on courtly manners. Castiglione's Courtier was drafted in 1508, written in Rome and Mantua between 1513 and

1518; it was finally printed and published in 1528. The book circulated for some time before that in manuscript. From the literary point of view the book is one of the outstanding books of the century. It expressed what was thought in Renaissance Italy. It found immediate favour outside Italy and was translated into many languages. Long before the book was translated into English by Thomas Hoby in 1561 it was exercising its influence in works like Sir Thomas Elyot's *Governour* (namely *The Boke named the Governour* which dates back to 1531).

Since the first pages Baldassare Castiglione reminds us the reason for the composition of *The Book of the Courtier*. It seems that he wanted his society to be always present in everybody's mind. It was a means to immortalize a society in which he lived and which had to be part of eternity in his eyes. The second reason why he wrote this book was the coming of Pope Julius II who was back from one of his victorious expedition in Bologna:

> Now after Julius II had by his presence and with the help of the French brought Bologna under the rule of the Apostolic See, in the year 1506, he passed through Urbino on his way back to Rome.[1]

In his introduction, Baldassare Castiglione also presents his work telling us his purpose; these are his words:

> "[...] I should describe what, in my view, is the form of courtiership most appropriate for a gentleman living at the Courts of princes, by which he will have the knowledge and the ability to serve them in every reasonable thing, winning their favour and praise of others. In short, you want to know what kind of man must be one who deserves the name of a perfect courtier and has no shortcomings whatsoever". (39)

Later, he proposes to create:

> "a courtier so perfect that the prince who is worthy of his service, even though his dominion is small, can count himself a truly great ruler". (40)

So as he says, he:

> "recounts some discussions which once took place among men who were singularly qualified in these matters". (40)

The book is written in dialogue form. We read long discourses which are held during four days at the court of Urbino at the beginning of the XVIth century, between the hostess the Duchess Elisabetta Gonzaga and her ghests to clear up boredom. There is an atmosphere of a feast throughout the whole book. In the XVIth century, conversation was considered as a fine art; it was a real entertainment, what they called "conversational entertainment". In the opening pages, we read about the usual procceding. The main woman is elected to be the person who will direct the conversation.

The assembly decides for a topic of discussion the latter being here, we quote:

> "I would like our game this evening to be this: that one of us should be chosen and given the task of depicting in words a perfect courtier, explaining the character and the particular qualities needed by anyone who deserves such a title. And, just as in philosophical disputations, if anything is said which does not seem appropriate, each of us may be allowed to contradict." (p.51)

Thus, each member will be assigned to speak in turn and in this manner all the ideas and opinions of the age will be expressed.

Apart from this dialogue form, *The Book of the Courtier* is divided into four parts, namely four books. It deals successively with the perfect courtier, the relationships between the courtier and the Prince, and the noble lady. It is necessary to stress that Baldassare Castiglione examines the physical and moral qualities which suit best the perfect courtier but also the perfect gentlewoman because the latter position changed too.

The dialogue form with the numerous participants makes difficult the understanding of the points developed. The most part of the theses held by each characters are opposed. They expose in minute details the acts and attitudes of the courtier. And it is hardly possible to assert that it is Baldassare Castiglione's thinking that we read.

First of all, the book must be regarded as an autobiography. At this point Baldassare Castiglione's life has got some kind of importance. Let us survey rapidly the most important facts.

Baldassare Castiglione was born at Casatico, near Mantua, on Dec. 6, 1478 and died in Toledo on Feb. 2, 1529. He was educated in Milan at the humanist school of Giorgio Merula and Demetrius Chalcondyles. He became a diplomat and was often referred to as Count Castiglione. He had been successively at the courts of noblemen during his lifetime. His masters were first Ludovico Sforza, nicknamed "Il Moro"; in 1499, he entered the service of Francesco and Isabella Gonzaga (Francesco was marquis of Mantua); in 1507 that of Guidobaldo da Montefeltro, Duke of Urbino. He remained at Urbino until 1513, and after Guidobaldo's death (in 1508), he continued to serve his successor, Francesco Maria della Rovere. He was sent to England in 1506 to receive the Order of the Garter on behalf of Guidobaldo. In 1509, he followed Della Rovere, commander of the papal army, in the war against Venice; in 1511 he took part with Julius II in the siege of Mirandola. For his services, he was made count of Novilara, near Pesaro. As Ambassador of the Duke of Urbino, he went in 1513 to the court of Leo X in Rome; in 1516, he was back in Mantua where he married Ippolita Torelli (d. 1520). He served Federico Gonzaga in Mantua; later, Pope Clement VII who appointed him in 1524 apostolic prothonotary. In 1525 he was sent to Spain as papal nuncio to Charles V. After the sack of Rome by the Imperialists in 1527, he was accused by Pope Clement VII of not having foreseen it, but he succeeded in proving his innocence of treacherous intention.

Thus, we retain from this summary that the book can be considered as an autobiographical work. Indeed, we cannot forget to point out that Baldassare Castiglione is the perfect gentleman like the one he describes in his book. Castiglione has dwelt among courtiers at the court of several noblemen and princes. He has been at the same time a warrior, a diplomat; he knew the greatest men of his time: Pope Julius II, Leo X, François 1er, Emperor Charles V, Princes such as Ludovico II Moro, Isabella of Este and so on.... So, he spent the most part of his lifetime with politicians, warriors and courtiers.

In the opening pages of his book, he stresses the fact that he was absent from the conversation which took place in Urbino:

> "Even though I did not take part in them in person (being in England when they were held), they were faithfully reported to me soon after my return by someone who was present, and I shall endeavour to reproduce them as accurately as my memory allows so that you may discover what was held and thought on the subject by eminent men whose judgement can always be trusted completely." (40)

This is obviously a literary artifice Baldassare Castiglione uses for the sake of the fiction of the book. It is said that he was handsome and above all a nobleman. He learned the art of chivalry at the court of Ludovico Sforza. Not only did he know the art of arms but he also fought. Moreover, he was learned in art and was a good friend of Raphael. He was learned in music, drawing, singing and dance. He also liked the letters and often attended the literary Academies in Rome. And, of course, he had as a friend the greatest literary man of his time Pietro Bembo who is a character of his book.

As it has been already mentioned, Baldassare Castiglione served numerous masters. And it is in the court of Urbino that he met Pietro Bembo, Bernardo Bibiena, Giuliano de'Medici, l'Unico Aretino (Bernardo Accolti), Ludovico da Canossa, Ottaviano and Federico Fregoso, who eventually became the interlocutors of his *Book of the Courtier*.

So, we can really come to the conclusion that he put a lot about himself although he negates this idea pretending he was absent from the meetings. Besides, although he does not personally appear in the meetings his presence can be guessed at from time to time in one character's mouth.

It seems that the book is a document relating history. Indeed, we get a precise idea of the setting, the characters present, and the historical events. Everything is given with great precision. Baldassare Castiglione proves precise when he describes in great details the town of Urbino and its palace:

> "On the slopes of the Appennines, almost in the centre of Italy towards the Adriatic, is everyone knows, the little city of Urbino. Although it is surrounded by hills which are perhaps not as agreeable as those found in many other places, none the less it has been favoured by Nature with a very rich and fertile countryside, so that as well as a salubrious atmosphere it enjoys an abundance of all the necessities of life." (40)

However, his description is very conventional. Baldassare Castiglione does not suggest much. He only says that it was surrounded with a beautiful and fertile countryside. Further, we get a picture of the palace:

> "[...] Duke Federico built on the rugged site of Urbino, a palace which many believe to be the most beautiful in all Italy; and he furnished it so well and appropriately that it seemed more like a city than a mere palace. For he adorned it not only with the usual objects, such as silver vases, wall-hangings of the richest cloth of gold, silk and other similar material, but also with countless antique statues of marble and bronze, with rare pictures, and with every kind of musical instrument; nor would he tolerate anything that was not most rare and outstanding. Then, at great cost, he collected a large number of the finest and rarest books, in Greek, Latin and Hebrew, all of which he adorned with gold and silver, believing that they were the crowning glory of his great palace." (41)

Concerning the characters, we can say that Federico Guidobaldo's court has been immortalized by Baldassare Castiglione who in honour of a sophisticated society chose the characters who used to be part of the salon of Duchess

Elisabetta Gonzaga, a learned and witty gentlewoman ("so great and talented woman" p.43). In describing the characters of his book he makes real portraits. When we consider their physical and especially moral features these characters seem false. Obviously, Baldassare Castiglione flatters them. And, indeed, it has been proved that their moral qualities were deficient. The Duchess "a very great lady", to quote Castiglione again, was said not to be virtuous at all and Signora Emilia Pia with whom she was always was said to be merciless. Further, Castiglione does not mention that the prefect had committed crimes, or that the Duke died of a sickness, or that Unico Aretino was always acting like a clown, and that Pietro Bembo who defended platonic love had children.

However, the book can pass for a testimony of the time because it seems to be a detailed observation of the Italian civilization of the Renaissance. Baldassare Castiglione as if he wanted to draw an historical document gives us pieces of information on his own culture and on some literary and artistic problems of his time. For instance, his society was preoccupied with question such as that of the national language. So, one part concerns the national language. We know that in Italy there existed numerous dialects and most important there was no unity so, the difficulty was to create a language or rather decide which one was the best. It is said that modern languages such as French and Spanish were more important than the national language that is Italian and Latin. It seems that there was a controversy between Tuscans and Italians. Then, we find an argument about the letters and the arms and a secondary one on the hierarchy of the arts; here the controversy was on the superiority of letters on arms and of paintings over sculpture.

Concerning history, Baldassare Castiglione describes also the great historical events which happened such as the Italian wars. There are also a great deal of precise allusions to great men that is historical figures such as François Ier and Charles V.

Somewhere, we find allusions to the psychological features of the Spaniards and the French. Baldassare Castiglione deals even with the corruption of the Church and makes a real satire of religion. His characters seem to desire no submission to a god. We understand they despise and feel anger towards religion or at least the Church of the time.

Finally, at one point we find an analysis of the different forms of governments existing in Italy. We do not have to forget the historical context in which Castiglione wrote his book. He published his book at a moment when Italy was divided in several independent states.

Here is the new theory of the courtier as it presented itself to the Italians of the Renaissance according to Baldassare Castiglione. We have to bear in mind that during the Renaissance, the supreme power of the state concentrated in the person of one sovereign prince. Around this prince gathered the courtiers who were the descendants of feudal Lords. Thus, court life in the Renaissance became important and as Lewis Einstein declares:

> "More and more the activities of the nation centred around and emanated from it. While during the Middle Ages every castle was a miniature court, complete in itself, the life of the nation was now focused so to speak, around one sovereign, about whom there gathered the best in the land. The court became almost the only means of entering the service of the state, which at that time depended so largely on royal favor. It led as a stepping-storm to the great career of arms, diplomacy and administrative employment. Whoever found favor in his prince's eye might well hope to be entrusted with the command of an army, the charge of an embassy, or the government of a province."[2]

Here we find the substance of Castiglione's purpose which is to form a perfect courtier, one who would know how to serve his prince in every reasonable way and gain his favour. Thus, he gives his courtier every desirable human quality: discretion, power to please his fellows, wisdom in counsel, good birth, beauty, wit, grace, and so on.

Thus, we find the idea that nobility must be by birth alone. The courtiers should be a gentleman born and of good family:

> "So, for myself, I would have our courtier of noble birth and good family, since it matters far less to a common man if he fails to perform virtuously and well than to a nobleman. For, if a gentleman strays from the path of his forbears, he dishonours his family name and not only fails to achieve anything but loses what has already been achieved. Noble birth is like a bright lamp that makes clear and visible both good deeds and bad, and inspires and incites to high performance as much as fear of dishonour or hope of praise; and since their deeds do not possess such noble brilliance, ordinary people lack both this stimulus and the fear of dishonour; nor do they believe that they are bound to surpass what was achieved by their forbears. Whereas to people of noble birth it seems reprehensible not to attain at least the standard set them by their ancestors. Thus as a general rule, both in arms and in other worthy activities, those who are most distinguished are of noble birth, because Nature has implanted in everything a hidden seed which has a certain way of influencing and passing on its own essential characteristics to all that grows from it, making it similar to itself." (54)

Castiglione scorns those courtiers with delicate features who seek a womanish beauty by curling their hair, picking their eyebrows. He asks of his courtier only that he be of a good shape, well proportioned in his limps, showing strength, lightness, and quickness for the exercises of war. And, tennis is for him good for such qualities.

Castiglione teaches how a courtier must use wit. It consists in telling funny stories or being pleasant without hurting people and being coarse. Also, he does not have to use the artifice of imitation too much.

Grace should accompany all actions. But this grace is unteachable but happily and naturally possessed ("a natural,

God-given gift", 65). Of course, grace can be achieved by diligence and thus the courtier must devote to bodily exercise.

Aptness for arms and all physical exercises suited to a gentleman such as wrestling, swimming, vaulting, running, riding, casting the stone, and tennis, come next.

His courtier will be well versed in liberal studies, history, oratory and poetry, sufficiently skilled himself in the arts of speaking, writing prose and verse in Latin, Greek, and the vernacular, drawing and painting, music and dancing, in order to say well what he would to be a good judge of the works of the masters, to fill his leisure hours when alone with pleasurable occupation. He should practice all this also to furnish his share of delightful pastimes in company. Most important he will show all his knowledge and skill with a grace and ease that will cover up pains and show the spontaneous aspect of his performance because the way of a gentleman must never be the way of a professional. Here, Castiglione lays down the famous rule of Aristotle that he who would be most impressive in the exercise of his art must appear to use no art at all:

> "[...] that true art is what does not seem to be art;" (67)

Or:

> "[...] to practice in all things a certain nonchalance which conceals all artistry and makes whatever one says or does seem uncontrived and effortless." (67)

So, the idea is that you have to acquire great skills in doing things but do not show great care in doing them. Let us take a concrete example that of music. Baldassare Castiglione is enthusiastic with music, trusting on the whole the good judgement of the properly educated courtier to keep him from abusing an essential accomplishment. In other words, Castiglione cautions against display by the courtier of real mastery in music. Further, he warns him not to learn to play and sing well (see 95-96).

One last point we have to make is that all the intellectual and moral virtues are necessary to the perfect courtier:

first of all virtue was part of a nobleman of famous lineage but particularly courage which Castiglione names among the virtues of the mind (see 123).

The last question raised is to know what the end to which all this perfection works is. For Castiglione the desired end was to win the good will and favor of the prince:

> "I want the courtier not only to make it clear on all occasions and to all persons that he is of the quality we have already described but also to devote all his thought and strength to loving and almost adoring the prince he serves above all else, devoting all his ambitions, actions and behaviour to pleasing him." (125)

In fact, there is the idea that the courtier must be and is perfect to serve as a model for the prince who has to be virtuous. The prince is not virtuous, so the task of the courtier is to educate the prince and to guide him towards virtue. Also, the courtier must speak the truth to the prince on every matter without fear or danger of displeasing him. And even when he sees that the prince is bent on some action unfitting for him he may have courage to stand up to him and dissuade him from ill and tell him to do good. Thus, he must be persuasive.

Next, according to Castiglione the will of the prince is really important. At this point a major problem arises. It is to know to what extent a courtier must obey a prince. We notice that Castiglione does not foresee the potential tyrant: he seems convinced that good courtiers only serve good princes. So even if there is evil the courtier has to obey and act.

Besides, thanks to his goodness, pleasantness, wisdom, wit, knowledge of letters and many other things we have already developed the courtier will understand how to conduct himself in all circumstances in order to show his prince what honour and profit will come to him. Let us examine Castiglione's conclusion:

> "In my opinion, therefore, the end of the perfect courtier (which we have so far left untouched) is, by means of the accomplishments attributed to him by

> these gentlemen, so to win for himself the mind and favour of the princes he serves that he can and always will tell him the truth about all he needs to know, without fear or risk of displeasing him. And, if he knows that his prince is of a mind to do something unworthy, he should be in a position to dare to oppose him, and make courteous use of the favour his good qualities have won to remove every evil intention and persuade him to return to the path of virtue. Thus, if the courtier is endowed with the goodness these gentlemen have attributed to him, as well as being quick-witted and charming, prudent and scholarly and so forth, he will always have the skill to make his prince realize the honour and advantage that accrue to him and his family from justice, liberality, magnanimity, gentleness and all the other virtues befiting a ruler, and on the other hand, the infamy and loss that result from practising the vices opposed to these virtues. Therefore, I consider that just as music, festivities, games and other agreeable accomplishments are, so to speak, the flower of courtiership, so its real fruit is to encourage and help his prince to be virtuous and to deter him from evil. Then we must consider that the merit of good deeds consists in two principal things: to choose a truly virtuous end for our intentions, and to know how to find convenient and suitable means for its attainment. And so, it necessarily follows that a man who strives to ensure that his prince is not deceived by anyone, does not listen to flatterers or slanderers or liars, and distinguishes between good and evil, loving the one and detesting the other, aims at the best end of all." (284-85)

What we must retain from this dealing with the prince is the following ideal: one must succeed but to succeed one has to be liked or loved. So one has to adopt lies and serve blindly.

The art of conversation is also part of the courtier's accomplishments. During the Renaissance was invented conversational sports and pastimes such as the discussions that form the body of Castiglione's book. Storytelling and even talks on the sayings of philosophers and wise men were common activities held at courts.

These conversations helped to give a new status to the ladies at court. The consideration of the lady at court comes last in Book III. The ladies played a minor part at court except in indoor amusements for leisure hours. The lady of the palace, as Castiglione calls her is the counterpart of the courtier. In Castiglione's view of her she represents the perfection of womanhood (as the courtier represents the perfection of manhood). When Castiglione comes to propose the shaping of a companion for his courtier he raises the question of the position of women of the court. Let us quote Cesare Gonzaga's answer:

> "[...] there is no court, however great, that can possess adornment or splendour or gaiety without the presence of women, and no courtier, no matter how graceful, pleasing or bold, who can ever perform gallant deeds of chivalry unless inspired by the loving and delightful company of women, so any discussion of the courtier must be imperfect unless ladies take part in it and contribute their share of the grace by which courtiership is adorned and perfected." (210)

In fact, Castiglione does not make his gentlewoman of court resemble the courtier in all aspects. He reserves for her a special place but he makes her equal to him. He endows her with perfection also and does not deny her the fundamental human qualities which are essential to perfection in the courtier. He, also tries to find the special quality that belongs to a woman who lives at court. Let us quote one passage of great importance:

> "Leaving aside, therefore, those virtues of the mind which she must have in common with the courtier, such as prudence, magnanimity, continence and many others besides, and also the qualities that are common to all kinds of women, such as goodness and discretion, the ability to take good care, if she is

> married, of her husband's belongings and house and children, and the virtues belonging to a good mother, I say that the lady who is at the Court should properly have, before all else, a certain pleasing affability whereby she will know how to entertain graciously every kind of man with charming and honest conversation, suited to the time and the place and the rank of the person with whom she is talking. And her serene and modest behaviour, and the candour that ought to inform all her actions, should be accompanied by a quick and vivacious spirit by which she shows her freedom from boorishness; but with such a virtuous manner that she makes herself thought no less chaste, prudent and benign than she is pleasing, witty and discreet. Thus she must observe a certain difficult mean, composed as it were of contrasting qualities, and take care not to stray beyond certain fixed limits." (212)

Castiglione presents the ladies of the court of Urbino, both the Duchess and the other ladies such as Emilia Pia in a particular function. In fact, we understand that a lady would not exist if the circle of courtier did not exist. A proper lady is to be found in the company of bright men. These intelligent and witty women might be supposed to be able to discourse on most if not all the subjects with the same ability and grace as the courtier.

Special qualities are assigned to her. First of all, she will not show her dislike of company and conversation for it may easily be thought that she pretends to fear other may discover something about her she wants to hide:

> "Nor in her desire to be thought chaste and virtuous, should she appear withdrawn or run off if she dislikes the company she finds herself in or thinks the conversation improper. For it might easily be thought that she was pretending to be straitlaced simply to hide something she feared others could find out about her." (212)

Castiglione goes on on the same page, saying that she should not show herself free and pleasant, or speak unchaste words or adopt a certain loose familiarity of manner to make men believe of her what is perhaps not true. Castiglione suggests that if she finds herself in the midst of talks she finds improper, she should listen with little blush and shame (see quotation above). Likewise she will not participate in evil reports of other women.

We can very well understand that the lady's main function was that of the conversation. Among the numerous subjects ladies and gentlemen discussed was that of love (the favorite subject). In the book, we get the debate over the ends that lovers seek. The question is to know if sexual intercourse was necessary for perfect human love. In Castiglione, we find a beautiful picture of a union of minds only:

> "So he should ignore the blind judgement of these senses and enjoy with his eyes the radiance, the grace, the loving ardour, the smiles, the mannerisms and all the other agreeable adornments of the woman he loves. Similarly, let him use his hearing to enjoy the sweetness of her voice, the modulation of her words and, if she is a musician, the music she plays. In this way, through the channels of these two faculties, which have little to do with corporeal things and are servants of reason, he will nourish his soul on the most delightful food and will not allow desire for the body to arouse in him any appetite that is at all impure. Next, with the greatest reverence the lover should honour, please and obey his lady, cherish her even more than himself, put her convenience and pleasure before his own, and love the beauty of her soul no less than that of her body. He should, therefore, be at pains to keep her from going astray and by his wise precepts and admonishments always seek to make her modest, temperate and truly chaste; and he must ensure that her thoughts are always pure and unsullied by any trace of evil. And thus, by sowing virtue in the garden of her lovely

> soul, he will gather the fruits of fautless behaviour and experience exquisite pleasure from their taste. And this will be the true engendering and expression of beauty in beauty, which some say is the purpose of love." (334-35)

Pietro Bembo encourages the courtier to love in a platonic manner instead of feeling an ordinary love. He celebrates the highest form of love. Love is no more sensual. Love is a desire to unite with the beautiful. We get in fact two kinds of love developed: one is divine or sacred (the one defined by Plato) that is a union with the beautiful; and the other love was flirting, that is lovers were advised to converse. Here, Castiglione teaches lovers how to play the love game. He analyses the ideal quality of the lover and his lady. Let us describe the game: the courtier tries to get the lady yield by showing his passion but the lady has to be secret and take her distance (see 335-36). Of course, the task of estimating the truth of the lover is difficult; especially for the lady because of her life. She is almost secluded and does not have to show her feelings, she has to hide her nature. Thus, it is difficult to know her. As we can see it is a real vicious circle. However, external signs are here to help for a solution.

In Book IV, there is an obvious glorification of love: Pietro Bembo spiritualizes love and gives the idea of uplifted love (union is based chiefly on the kiss); it means union of souls rather than bodies:

> "Consequently, the rational lover delights when he joins his mouth to that of the lady he loves in a kiss, not in order to arouse in himself any unseemly desire but because he feels that this bond opens the way for their souls which, attracted by their mutual desire, each pour themselves into the other's body in turn and so mingle that each of them possesses two souls, and it is as if a single spirit composed of the two governs their bodies. So the kiss may be called a spiritual rather than physical union because it exerts such power over the soul that it draws it to itself and separates it from the body. For this reason, all chaste

> lovers desire a kiss as a union of souls; and thus when inspired to love Plato said that in kissing the soul cornes to the lips in order to leave the body." (336)

This was the theory of courtiership for the gentleman and the lady that for a century circulated in the courts of Europe. Castiglione's book is typical of the Italian influence in the Renaissance. And the question now may be to know what the effect of this book on England was, in other words what was its impact. Did it bring into England new ideals of manners?

Castiglione's book after its diffusion had a certain impact on England. The question of what constituted a gentleman was a living problem of the age. It was even at the end of the XVth century that Italian influences began to appear at the English court. It is said that the Dukes of Ferrara and especially that of Urbino were friends with Henry VII. England, as other Northern European nations became familiar to the new type of courtier which had been created in Italy. The English court tried to act as France and Spain did welcoming the Italian courtiers. Thus, Henry VII had numerous Italians in his service. They observed Italians at home or abroad and also acquired knowledge of the courtier's education through the translation of Italian books. As we have already mentioned, many handbooks of courtesy and even guides of conversation were published during the XVIth century. The influence of those manuals was really European and as Lewis Einstein asserts:

> "Il Cortegiano may almost be said to have given voice to the undefined mass of Italian influences at the Tudor court, and assisted in forming in England the new type of courtier."[3]

And, indeed,

> "The court of England is in these days one of the most renowned and magnificent courts that are to be found in Europe."[4]

The English courtiers were usually of noble birth, skilled in military arts, dancing, and sports. Sports they practiced included tennis, bowls, archery, billiards, wrestling, fencing, hunting and riding. Courtiers were skilled both in the use of weapons and in the art of refined social intercourse. They had experience in the arts of poetry (the sonnets of Shakespeare, Thomas Wyatt and Philip Sidney appeared during this period) and music (they played the lute, the viol, the virginals and other instruments). They had familiarity with painting and the sciences. The courtiers appeared very studied. They were well-educated in classical and modern languages such as French, Italian or Spanish. They were gracious in conversation. Versatility was common among courtiers: they developed physical and spiritual capacities. Moreover, the main purpose of courtiers was to serve a prince and tell him the truth:

> "What is a courtier?
> 'An attendant upon majesty, a companion of nobility, a friend to virtue and a hope of honour'."[5]

Court life involved fierce competition for the favor of the sovereign. Courtiers were competitive in order to win admiration from a prince or the King himself. They made lots of efforts to gain his favor. However, English courtiers also enjoyed gossip, flirting and political maneuvering; as a consequence, the English court was an aggressive world.

As a conclusion, we can go as far as to say that the central theme of the book is in our opinion the problem of history and the idealization of the Italian society. Indeed, Baldassare Castiglione seems to remind us only of the best aspects of his society. We can truly say that this book is a capital testimony on the small Italian courts of the XVIth century. Castiglione gives a complete and precise representation of his society and its customs. He gives a real picture but it seems to be an idealized image. It is obvious that in reality court life was different. Probably, we can go as far as to say that Castiglione wrote this book to protest against the harsh reality of court life. Thus, he proposed a type of man which could be different from what could be witnessed.

The book says much but it also seems to omit some elements. The book of the courtier can be considered as a testimony but it must also be regarded as a literary masterpiece which contains lies, omissions, or even literary embellishments.

Castiglione does not tell us everything and tells only positive aspects. Thus, he is close to reality but at the same time he escapes from reality. Castiglione must have ignored or even transformed the historical reality of the time, because he was a man of letters who only considered what was pleasant in his society. Probably, Castiglione does not question the society in which he lives because he was born at court, taught at court and for him there might be only courts on earth as a form of society.

First of all the national problem is just evoked and not at all developed. This is a paradox when we think that the national conscience of the country was a problem at the heart of the time. For instance, one character begins to evoke the rather ill-state of the Italian nation and another character intervenes to change the topic of the conversation.

When somebody examines the inferiority of the Italian military force, somebody diverts again the conversation. When one examines the religious question that is the corrupted side of religion somebody tries to speak in praise or in defense of churchmen. Halfway through the book, one speaks of the bad princes to condemn their vices and crimes but of course somebody avoids the subject. This is paradoxical when we think that at this time princes were unfaithful, criminal, and this was also the case of courtiers. A good example is Francesco Maria della Rovere who served at the same time two masters or even Castiglione himself who committed dishonest actions and parted from his masters because of other interests he had found at others'. He served as we have already seen successively as a courtier the Gonzagas, the Montefeltros, and again the Gonzagas and finally Pope Clement VII. In fact, courtiers used immoral means to reach their aims.

Castiglione only evokes the wars but does not go into them in deep details. Indeed, he gives us a charming image of a time which was full of problems. Moreover, the description he makes of court is partly wrong. We have to bear in mind that court was the favorite place for treason, corruption, and crime. One of the best examples we can give is the following contradiction: the characters say that the courtier is not a flatterer but we constantly read praises of the princes.

Also, Castiglione creates an intellectual and moral man, a kind of aesthete. He asks for such and such quality. Thus, to our eyes his courtier is too much accomplished. It must be impossible to find all these qualities in the same man. The description proves to be untrue. However, Castiglione is careful when he despises this perfection through some of his characters' invention. In fact, Castiglione's ideal is a formal and individual perfection. It will never be a general one.

The overall impression we get after reading this book is that, it is not entirely a testimony but rather a treatise on the Italian Renaissance. The fact that we read long descriptions showing Castiglione's desire to be precise proves the idealization. It is true that the characters debate on concrete problems to which they give solutions, but the solutions they give are in our opinion, most of the time really extravagant and inapplicable. We can go as far as to say that the book reflects part of the Italian Renaissance, but it seems that Castiglione believed so strongly in an ideal he wanted to institute that this courtier sometimes is unreal. So the perfect courtier is for us a myth, a myth representing perfection because it is obvious that this portrait of the courtier has been embellished for the sake of literary artifice. Of course, Baldassare Castiglione might have been conscious that this ideal of perfection was not a reality. At the basis of Castiglione's Book there is an ideal and it is because of this ideal that the book had a great amount of success in England whose civilization was changing. The book, to a certain extent, helped conditioning the behaviour of the English courtiers.

References

1. Baldassare. Castiglione, *The Book of the Courtier*, translated by George Bull, England, Penguin Books, 1967, 44. Other quotations in our article.
2. L. Einstein, *The Italian Renaissance in England*, New York, The Columbia University Press, 1902, 58-59.
3. L. Einstein, *op. cit.*, 61.

4. A. Nicoll, *The Elizabethans*, Cambridge, Cambridge University Press, 1957, 41.
5. *Ibid.*, 41.

Bibliography

Text

Castiglione Baldassare. *The Book of the Courtier*, translated by George Bull, England, Penguin Books, 1967.

General Background

Burckhardt Jacob. *La civilisation de la Renaissance en Italie*, 3 tomes, Le Livre de Poche, Traduction de H. Schmitt, revue et corrigée par R. Klein, Paris, Librairie Plon et Club du meilleur Livre, 1958.

Burckhardt Jacob. *The Civilization of the Renaissance in Italy*, (1860), England, Penguin Classics, 1990.

Chamberlin Eric Russell. *Everyday Life in Renaissance Times*, London: Batsford; New York, Putnam's, 1965.

Delumeau Jean. *La civilisation de la Renaissance*, Paris, Arthaud, 1967.

Hay Denys. *The Italian Renaissance in its Historical Background*, Cambridge, University Press, 1961.

Hyder E. Rollins & Herschel Baker, eds. *The Renaissance in England*, D.C. Heath & Co., Lexington Mass., 1954.

Plomb John Harold. *The Penguin Book of the Renaissance*, New York, Horizon, 1965.

Specific Aspect

Briggs, Asa. *A Social History of England,* Viking Press, New York, 1983.

Dutton Ralph. *English Court Life, From Henry VII to George II*, B.T. Batsford Ltd., London, 1963.

Einstein Lewis. *The Italian Renaissance in England*, New York, The Columbia University Press, 1902.

Emerson, Kathy. *Wives and Daughters: Women of 16th Century England,* Whitson Publishing Co., New York, 1984.

Emmison, F.G. *Tudor Secretary, Sir William Petre at Court and Home*, Longmans, London, 1987.

Erickson, Carolly. *The First Elizabeth*, Summit Books, New York, 1983.

Fox-Davies, Arthur Charles. *A Complete Guide to Heraldry*, Bonanza Books, New York, 1978.

Hibbert, Christopher. *The English: A Social History, 1066-1945*, Grafton Books, W.W. Norton & Co., New York, 1987.

Loades, David. *The Tudor Court,* Barnes & Noble, New Jersey, 1987.

Morris, Christopher. *The Tudors*, B.T. Batsford Ltd., London, 1955.

Nicoll Allardyce. *The Elizabethans*, Cambridge, Cambridge University Press, 1957.

Rowse, A.L. *The England of Elizabeth: the Structure of Society*, Madison, Wisconsin, The University of Wisconsin Press, 1978.

——. *The Elizabethan Renaissance: the Life of the Society*, New York, Charles Scribner's Sons, 1971.

Scott, A.F. *The Tudor Age*, Thomas Y. Crowell Company, New York, 1975. (selections from primary sources.)

Smith, Lacey Baldwin. *The Elizabethan World,* Houghton Mifflin, 1972.

Williams, Penry. *The Later Tudors, England 1547-1603,* Oxford University Press, 1995.

——. *The Tudor Regime,* Clarendon Press, Oxford, 1979.

Youings, Joyce. *Sixteenth-Century England, The Pelican Social History of Britain*, England, Penguin Books, 1984.

7

Imagery in Shakespeare's Histories

Sanjay Kumar Sinha

The study of imagery in Shakespeare's History plays makes a very interesting study. It is worth considering in the Histories significant threads and patterns of imagery—the recurrent themes through whose study and correlation the full meaning of the work as a whole emerges. It not only fixes and defines but tends always to enlarge its subjects, causes it to expand beneath the reader's eye and invests it with a wider range of meaning. Some images belong primarily to literary convention, others impress us as deeply personal in their effect; some, again belong exclusively to the dramatic personage in whose mouth they are placed and to the situation in which he finds himself, others seem to answer more directly to the expression of the author's own experience. The poetic image, more particularly as used by Shakespeare in the Histories, is living and not a dead thing. They cannot be abstracted from their context: they live, develop and change by their very nature.

The function of imagery in Shakespeare's plays has been studied by a number of modern critics. Caroline Spurgeon's *Shakespeare's Imagery and What it Tells Us* was the first of the several projected volumes. She analyses the results of her systematic tabulation of all Shakespeare's images from which she deduced the characteristics of the poet's mind and personality, and also, from the repetition of images drawn from one field, the theme of each play. F.C. Kolbe in *Shakespeare's Way* seeks to arrive at the meaning of the plays by counting the frequency of key words—a mechanical method which is not often fruitful. Edward A. Armstrong in *Shakespeare's Imagination* has revealed a number of image clusters, repeated from play to play and all connected with birds, which throw light on the working of Shakespeare's mind. Wolfgang Clemen in *Shakespeare's Bilder* has written a valuable account of the dramatic function of Shakespeare's imagery, less scientific but more critical than Miss Spurgeon's. Wilson Knight, however, is primarily concerned with the analysis of poetic-symbolism and the subordination of character to the poetic meaning of the play. He is more concerned with the pattern of each play than with the chronological sequence of events. He tends to describe Shakespeare's meanings in terms of 'themes' rather than in terms of motive, character development, and so on and considers the themes spatially rather than temporally. Wilson Knight speaks of cutting below 'the surface crust of plot and character' and considers the logic of imaginative correspondence as more significant and more exact than the logic of plot. He also, of course, tells us that we should not look for perfect verisimilitude to life, but rather see each play as an *expanded metaphor*, by means of which the original vision has been projected into forms roughly correspondent with actuality.

Shakespeare has used Bird-life very significantly in his history plays. These images and impressions exist mainly in direct relation to all essences, which may be, metaphorically, considered ethereal and volatile. Bird-life suggests flight and freedom and swiftness; very often it also suggests pride. Birds are usually gentle and sweet, and in many instances accompany love; but they may also be evil, as in *Macbeth*, where, however, they yet harmonize with the ethereal and spiritual theme, the swiftness, and the dizzying flight. Bird passages may be related to the human spirit particularly ethereal and aspiring. In this relation we find, particularly the falcon and the eagle. Then we have the lark, bird of dawn, observing its close association with light and music. They may also be related to more general thoughts of the human spirit and to mythological figures such as Phaethon, Icarus, Mercury and angels generally.

The falcon is continually used to suggest 'pride.' However, pride may well be either pleasing or a repellent quality: it may tend towards fine aspiration or insulting insolence. We hear of Coriolanus's 'soaring insolence'[1] and Hamlet's 'towering passing'.[2] We may as well have just a proud confidence: It is this that makes Bolingbroke boast in arrogance in *Richard II*.

"As confident as is the falcon's flight
Against a bird, do I with Mowbray fight,"[3]

A not so different suggestion is probably behind such a passage from *1 Henry VI* where Pucelle laments the loss of confidence before Angiers.

"Now the time is come
That France must vail her lofty—'plumed crest.'"[4]

Richard II is rich in these images: "How high a pitch his resolution soars!"[5] says King Richard, fearing Bolingbroke's ambition. He repeats the idea when banishing the two rivals, Bolingbroke and Mowbray:

"And for we think the eagle-winged pride
Of sky aspiring and ambitious thoughts,
With rival-hating envy, set on you,
To wake our peace...."[6]

Here the bird is an eagle. The eagle specially harmonizes with the words 'sky-aspiring,' and often suggests the grand indomitable aspiration of noble mankind towards excellence. Sometimes such aspiration is blameworthy, sometimes it is not; but pure aspiration is at the heart of most of these images, though each be coloured differently by its context. Caesar's ambition likewise receives falcon imagery:

"These growing feathers plucked from Caesar's wing
Will make him fly an ordinary pitch.
Who else would above the view of men...."[7]

We have another significant pride-falcon association in *3 Henry VI*:

"Neither the king, nor he that loves him best;
The proudest he that holds up Lancaster,
Dares stir a wing, if Warwick shake his bells."[8]

Wolsey's pride is 'high-blown,'[9] in *Henry VIII*. Such towering birds then suggest pride of place and ambition. Naturally, they are often associated with kinship. Here, the eagle tends to replace the falcon: In Richard II we see York confessing about Richards.

> "Yet looks he like a king; behold, his eye
> As bright as is the eagle's, lightens forth
> Controlling majesty."[10]

In *King John* we find a fine bird passage showing the king-eagle association powerfully:

> "No: know the gallant monarch is in arms
> And like the eagle o'er his aery tow'rs
> To souse annoyance that comes near his nest."[11]

The king of birds is, clearly, an apt associate for the kings of men: partly because of his sky-aspiring flight, his towering place, as well as his majestic appearance and leonine strength and reputation.

The whole of Shakespeare's work, indeed, continually emphasizes this quality in man: aspiration. In some form or another it recurs powerfully in nearly every play and this quality is to be related to the eagle and the falcon. The eagle may, indeed, be related to divine inspiration:

> "Was Mahaomet inspired with a dove?
> Thou with an eagle art inspired then;"[12]

Birds are, on the whole, favourites of the Shakespearean imagination. They suggest fine or sweet qualities usually. Especially the union of docility and natural strength in the falcon appears to give it high honours so that it is ranked, beside other such creatures, hounds and horses; for, though dogs as a whole come off badly, yet hounds receive very different treatment. Here are all three together, significantly juxtaposed with girls in *1 Henry VI*.

> "Somerset: Judge you, my lord of Warwick, then between us
> Warwick: Between two hawks, which flies the higher pitch.

Between two dogs, which hath the deeper mouth
Between two blades, which bears the better temper
Between two horses, which doth bear him best;
Between two girls, which hath the merriest eye."[13]

In *2 Henry IV*, Northumberland speaks to Bardolph:

"The times are wild; contention, like a horse,
Full of high feeding, madly hath broke loose
And bears down all before him."[14]

So we find falcons, horses and hounds somewhat idealized in Shakespeare. Horses especially are vividly admired, on account of physical beauty, on faithfulness, as in the description of 'roan Barbary' in *Richard II*:

"Come, let me taste my horse,
Who is to bear me like a thunderbolt
Against the bosom of the Prince of Wales;
Harry to Harry shall, not horse to horse
Meet and ne'er part till one drop down a corse."[15]

Shakespeare's use of mythological figures in the history plays, such as Phaeton and Icarus is equally significant. Phaeton may be used in relation directly to kingship. Richard II compares himself to Phaeton:

"Down, down I come; like glistering Phaeton,
Wanting the manage of unruly jades."[16]

Similarly the story of Icarus is used by Talbot in *1 Henry VI*. He addresses his son:

"Then follow thou thy desperate sire of Crete
Thou Icarus."[17]

In the next scene in the same act we have—

"And in that sea of blood my boy did drench
His over-mounting spirit, and there died,
My Icarus, my blossom, in his pride."[18]

The image of 'Mercury' also is important for our purpose. He is a winged god; and is powerfully imagined by Shakespeare. Mercury blends directly with the idea of 'angels.' This superlative passage from *1 Henry IV*, starting with fine birds and 'young' animals and leading up to Mercury and angels is worth taking into account:

> "All furnished, all in arms;
> All plumed like estridges that with the wind Baited like eagles having lately bathed;
> Glitering in golden coats, like images;
> As full of spirit as the month of May
> And gorgeous as the sun at midsummer;
> Wanton as youthful goats, wild as young bulls. I saw young Harry with his beaver on,
> His cuisses on his thighs, gallantly armed,
> Rise from the ground like feathered Mercury,
> And vaulted with such ease into his seat,
> As if an angel dropp'd down from the clouds, To turn and wind a fiery Pegasus
> And witch the world with noble horsemanship."[19]

The young athletic prince in grace of early manhood is compared with 'feathered Mercury'—a symbol of active masculine strength.

So, in Shakespeare's imagery of those excelling qualities in men, his aspiring pride, his soldiership, his athletic grace, beauty of form, all that is 'air and fire' rather than sluggish 'earth and water', we pass from birds, through metaphysical ideas of swift and winged intuitions, to more vivid and concrete embodiments in terms of Mercury and angles.

Importance is given by the *Histories* to the virtues of 'prudence' and 'economy.' These are the essential qualities together with strength of character kingliness—for a ruler's governance both of himself and his realm. Their opposites—carelessness, excess, waste, and disease—are to be found in the sequence running from *Richard II* to *Henry V*. It is with the themes of good husbandry, extravagance, through the metaphoric language of this tetralogy and particularly of *Richard II*, that these images are chiefly concerned to bring out a unified design. From Richard's "I wasted time, and now doth time waste me,[20] to *Henry V*'s weighing time, the concept of good husbandry presides like a central concern. The assumption behind this emphasis seems to be that *life and power are precious gifts and to squander them is a crime against God and State* (emphasis mine). A negligent and heedless prince like Richard II creates a vaccum of power, which invites disaster.

Throughout the *history plays*—'waste' and 'destruction' and its antithetical theme—'fatness' or 'excessive growth' go hand in hand. Both are the extremes of which economy is the mean. Even a word or metaphor deepens into character and extends into plot. In *Henry IV* the pervasive imagery of extremes is embodied both in a lean king of state, literally worn away with anxiety, and a fat king of revels—Falstaff. Shape is partly an index to character. Everywhere the ideal king, the figure of God's majesty, is contrasted with

"the ugly form
of base and bloody insurrection...."[21]

Frequently, fast follows feast, early death follows premature growth, in emphatic contrast. The prince and Falstaff engage in the matching of "unsavory similes"[22] of fatness and leanness. The Chief Justice talks to Falstaff, "Your means are very slender, and your waste is great"[23] to which Falstaff promptly replies "I would my means were greater and my waist slenderer."[24] The care-worn John puns on his own name before Richard II:

"For sleeping England long time have I watched;
Watching breeds leanness, leanness is all gaunt."[25]

Usually in the history plays the responsible man and the state are thin, the heedless usually fat. Honour seeking Hotspur is presented in a beautiful image "amongst a grove the very straightest plant."[26] Falstaff on the other hand is presented—"Out of all order, out of all compass"[27]—who reduces 'honour' to a 'word'. Indeed, imagery of over-eating is applied both to the rightful ruler and the usurper. Henry IV is made "portly" by the help of the Percies:

"...did oppress our nest;
grew by our feeding to so great a bulk
That even our love durst not come near your sight
For fear of swallowing...."[28]

The eaters are eaten and the would-be physicians become centres of contagion. The lean may wax and the fat wane, but all go to extremes. Implicit everywhere is the idea of Aristotelian norm and ideal of moderation or of equilibrium among opposing forces. Henry IV, like Richard before him, becomes increasingly a helpless observer of a malady he cannot cure:

"Then you perceive the body of our kingdom,
How foul it is; what rank diseases grow,
And with what danger, near the heart of it."[29]

He further says:

"The commonwealth is sick of their own choice;
Their over-greedy love hath surfeited."[30]

Themes of negligence, excess and waste are developed in *Richard II* primarily through several strands of imagery—those of time, the garden and sickness, and the farm and death. Richard finally sees with unusual clarity that he himself has abused time.

"How sour sweet music is
When time is broke and so proportion kept!
And here have I the daintiness of ear
To check time broke in a disordered string; But,
for the concord of my state and time
Had not an ear to hear my true time broke.
I wasted time, and now doth time waste me";[31]

In still other closely related group of images, Richard's garden becomes a farm and his land his deathbed. In Gaunt's most famous speech and in several passages on divine right, the play gives us two of the most exalted pictures of England and the divinity of kingship in Shakespeare. Gaunt proceeds from his praise of "This other Eden, demi-paradise"[32] to a terrible indictment, "This blessed plot", [33] is "now leas'd out.... Like to a tenement or pelting farm".[34] It is bound in not with "triumphant sea"[35] which keeps it from 'infection'[36] but with "inky-blots and rotten parchment bonds."[37] Thus the conqueror of others made a shameful conquest of itself. Gaunt is eloquent about the crime of turning a royal realm into real state:

> "Why, cousin wert thou regent of the world
> It were a shame to let this land by lease."[38]

As the demi paradise becomes a farm, the king becomes a mere overlord:

> "Landlord of England art thou now not king."[39]

The Gardener speaks of the

> "wholesome herbs
> Swarming with caterpillars",[40]

and in one of the speeches in the play that unite several of its major strands of imagery, Gaunt identifies the sickness of the king with that of his land. In metaphors like these, perhaps for the first time, Shakespeare has brought the chronicle of a king and his kingdom into perfect unity.

> "Thy deathbed is no lesser than thy land,
> Wherein thou liest in reputation sick."[41]

The doctor who should be bleeding the sick body of the realm is himself laid out sick upon it, at the mercy of the physicians who "first wounded"[42] him.

> "A thousand flatters sit within thy crown,
> Whose compass is no bigger than thy head; And
> yet, incaged in so small a verge,
> The waste is no whit lesser than thy land."[43]

The waste (Waist) of the king's 'controlling majesty'[44] is the waste of the state. The caterpillars, by eating away Richard's power to govern, are devouring the green garden of England. Richard's failure as watchful gardener and physician bequeaths to his successor a realm fat and very sick.

Bolingbroke's watchful shrewdness collaborates with Richard's ineffectuality to turn Fortune's wheel. The two men, like other protagonists in Shakespeare, are functions of each other and of their total situation. They are locked in a grim dance in which Richard's weakness opens the way to power for Bolingbroke, and Bolingbroke's silent strength matches Richard's expectation of annihilation. Metaphors of water and moving bucket suggest a Bolingbroke on high poised and ready to flood a royal reservoir that empties itself. But judgements in the later histories and binder to the wasteful Richard than to the politician Bolingbroke, whose usurpation and killing of a king are thought more heinous than all of Richard's folly. Though a trimmer Bolingbroke cannot weed his own garden for "his foes are so enrooted with his friends,"[45] troubled Henry sees Richard's blind rioting recapitulated in his son Hal, perhaps as a punishment for his own 'mistereadings'.[46] This comparison between Richard and Hal affords us a convenient vantagepoint for pursuing thematic imagery of waste and excess through succeeding plays of this group.

After the excesses of Richard's reign, the Lancastrians reject fatness and imprudence in both man and commonwealth. The Prince's first soliloquy-

> "I 'll so offend, to make offence a skill
> Redeeming time when men think least I will,"[47]

clearly paves the way for the later banishment of Falstaff. The sympathy of the world has always been with the fat knight. The Prince's turning point from plump Jack—'banish plump Jack and banish all the world,"[48] is a rejection of fuller life in favour of power. Falstaff claims that the royal blood or soil in Hal was originally "lean, sterile and bare"[49] and had to be "manured, husbanded, and till'd"[50] with "fertile sherries"[51] to make Hal "valiant."[52] The sustained imagery we have been following and Shakespeare's characterization of Falstaff emphasize a darker side of this hill of flesh and illuminate his profoundly functional role in this entire cycle of plays. Shakespeare rapidly found the imagery drawn from nature and animal life which is so marked a feature of the style of *Henry VI* and far more subtly, of *Richard II*, inadequate for his increasingly complicated meaning. He chanced upon another and far more expressive vehicle for the overgrown garden. The final evolution of the metaphor of the fat garden and of the sick body politic is probably the fat man. Falstaff is both the sickness of the state, the prince of the caterpillars praying on the commonwealth and the remedy for some of the ills. His role dramatizes the gulf between the essential virtues of the private man. Timeless Falstaff is in a curiously reciprocal relationship with time-serving Henry IV: for they are the principal competitors for the Prince's allegiance. The usurper who disdained to follow the example of rioting Richard finds his eldest son rioting with Falstaff—a kind of embodiment of Henry's inability to weed his own garden. Both the politician and the reveler must disappear from the world of young Henry V before he can find his own voice somewhere between them. He had to befriend Falstaff to know this man's gifts and language and, in the perfectness of time, he had to act to arrest the threat of such gross terms to the kingdom. The rejection of Falstaff marks the new king's turning from the negligence and excess that had nearly destroyed England since the reign of Richard II. As the young king dismisses one tutor and cultivates another in the Chief Justice he cultivates his garden in "law and form and due proportion."[53]

Derek Traversi, another explorer of meaning in Shakespeare's play is agreeable to concede pioneering position to Wilson Knight in analysis of the plays of Shakespeare. Although Traversi has his own methods of assessing Shakespeare as a dramatist, he recognizes the special position that Wilson Knight has achieved through his analysis of recurrent images in Shakespeare's play.

Wilson Knight, to an eminent degree, and Professor Spurgeon, in her own possibly more pedestrian way, has greatly extended our understanding of Shakespeare. It is worth looking a little closely at the 'methods,' so to call them, upon which these real discoveries are said to be based. Traversi says: "In case of Professor Spurgeon, the 'method' consists of card-indexing and counting images to establish their relative frequencies and drawing the corresponding conclusions. The image 'X' appears so many times and the image 'Y' so many: from the preponderance of either, we can draw all kinds of conclusions, which seem to be 'scientifically' based, perhaps about the dramatist's own tastes and certainly, it is suggested, about the intentions which underline a given play. However, we find that the poetic image, even if we accept it as a kind of ultimate constituent of poetry, is not readily susceptible to this kind of treatment. Some images belong primarily to literary convention, others impress us as deeply personal in their effect; some belong exclusively to the dramatic personage in whose mouth they are placed and to the situation in which he finds himself, others seem to answer more directly to the expression of the author's own experience. Above all, the poetic-image is, more particularly as used by Shakespeare, a living and not a dead thing; and it lives, not dissected and placed in a card-index, but in a context, in relation to the intensity with which it is conceived, to the rhythm of the verse that conveys it, and to the total conception of the play in which it is found. Images, in fact, cannot be abstracted from their context, or counted up by a mechanical process as if they were all identical or similar in value. They live, develop, and change by their very nature, and it is in fact the life, the development, and the change which escape classification and call for the critic, or more simply the theatregoer, to make his similarly living response. If the result is, as it must surely be, something less than a scientific certainty, that may be considered by some a pity; but the rest of us may derive some encouragement from the reflection that there are certain areas of life which are, of their very nature, irreducible to the card-index and its overgrown and monstrous successor, the computer."[54]

Wilson Knight and Caroline Spurgeon have one thing in common. Both start from a consideration of the poetic image and its function in the complete dramatic effect. We may have certain reservations against Knight's conclusions, but there is nothing of the card-index or the computer about Professor Wilson Knight's work. "It is necessary to say," opines Derek Traversi, "that there has been probably no writer on Shakespeare, who has opened out more new fields of vision to an understanding of the dramatist in his full life and complexity. Practically everyone who has since written on Shakespeare has had occasion to express his disagreement with many of Wilson Knight's conclusions, in which highly personal application of ideas derived, in varying degree, from Nietzsche and from Christian tradition, play a large part; but practically all those who have done so have also repeated or developed findings that he was the first to express."[55]

An appreciation of the complexity within the unified structure of Shakespeare's histories has been greatly aided by studies of their imagery. It is frequently pointed out that such studies run the danger of treating plays as poems, but though the warning is salutary, it should not suggest that the method is invalid. Since there is no true dichotomy between plays and poems, the fact that Shakespeare's plays are eminently actable, even eminently theatrical, does not prevent them from being poems in the sense of intricately organized verbal artifacts. The best studies of imagery in the history plays have shown how intimately verbal patterns are bound in with theatrical effect.

Notes and References

1. Shakespeare, William. *Coriolanus, II.* i. 236.
2. Shakespeare, William. *Hamlet, V.* ii. 80.
3. Shakespeare, William. *Richard II,* I, iii. 61-62.
4. Shakespeare, William. *1 Henry VI*, V: iii. 24-25.
4. Shakespeare, William. *Richard II*, I. i. 109.
6. *Ibid.*, I. iii 129-32.
7. Shakespeare, William. *Julius Caesar*, I. i. 72-74.
8. Shakespeare, William. *3 Henry VI*, I. 145-47.
9. Shakespeare, William. *Henry VIII*, III. ii. 361.
10. Shakespeare, William. *Richard II*, III. iii. 68-70.
11. Shakespeare, William. *King John*, V. ii. 148-50.
12. Shakespeare, William. *1 Henry VI*, I. ii. 140-41.
13. *Ibid.*, II. iv. 10-15.
14. Shakespeare, William. *2 Henry IV*, IV, i. 39-40.
15. Shakespeare, William. *1 Henry IV*, IV. i. 119-23.
16. Shakespeare, William. *Richard II,* III. iii. 178-79.
17. Shakespeare, William. *1 Henry VI*, IV. vi. 54-55.
18. Ibid., IV, viii. 14-16.
19. Shakespeare, William. *1 Henry IV*, IV. 197-210.
20. Shakespeare, William. *Richard II*, V, v. 49.
21. Shakespeare, William. *2 Henry IV*, IV, i. 39-40.
22. Shakespeare, William. *1 Henry IV*, I. ii. 69.

23. Shakespeare, William, *2 Henry IV*, I. ii. 126.
24. *Ibid*., I. ii. 128-29.
25. Shakespeare, William, *Richard II,* II. i. 77-78.
26. Shakespeare, William, *1 Henry IV*, I. i. 82.
27. Ibid., III. iii. 16.
28. *Ibid*., V. i. 61-64.
29. Shakespeare, William, *2 Henry IV*, III. i. 38-40.
30. *Ibid*., I. iii. 87-88.
31. Shakespeare, William, *Richard II*, V. v. 42-49.
32. *Ibid*., II. i. 42.
33. *Ibid*., II. i. 50.
34. *Ibid*., II. i. 59-60.
35. *Ibid*., II. i. 61.
36. *Ibid*., II. i. 44.
37. *Ibid*., II. i. 64.
38. *Ibid*., II. i. 109-10.
39. *Ibid*., II. i. 113.
40. *Ibid*., III. iv. 46-47.
41. *Ibid*., II. i. 95-96.
42. *Ibid*., II. i. 99.
43. *Ibid*., II. i. 100-03.
44. *Ibid*., III. iii. 70.
45. Shakespeare, William, *2 Henry IV*, IV. i. 207.
46. Shakespeare, William, *1 Henry IV*, III ii. 11.
47. *Ibid*., I. iii. 192-93.
48. Shakespeare, William, *2 Henry IV*, IV. iii. 106.
49. *Ibid*., IV. iii. 107.
50. *Ibid*., IV. iii. 108.
51. Ibid., IV. iii. 109.
52. Shakespeare, William, *Richard II*, III, iv. 41.
53. Traversi, Derek, *An Approach to Shakespeare*. London: Macmillan, 1967, 12.
54. *Ibid.*, 13-14, *op. cit.*
55. *Ibid.*

8

Lord Byron: The Romantic Augustan

N. Sharada Iyer

Byron set the English Muse on a pilgrimage all over the continent and proved a fruitful source of inspiration to the political revolutionaries as well as the literary aspirants of Italy, Russia and England as well. His death was viewed as a world calamity. Carlyle wrote "the news of his death came upon my heart like a mass of lead". Jane Welsh told Carlyle "If they had said the sun or the moon was gone out of the heaven, it would not have struck me with the idea of a more awful and dreary blank in the creation than the words 'Byron is dead'. Tennyson wrote upon a stone amid mosses and ferns, Byron is dead—the whole world seemed to be darkened for me."

Much of his popularity was due to the time spirit which Byron absorbed and reproduced. In an age when the forlorn hope for freedom was apparently in its last gasp, his stentorian voice rang through Europe and sent a new life coursing through the feeble hearts. The Post Revolutionary era for many was a period of scepticism and cynicism, when old values appeared to have gone bankrupt and even faith in God assumed the shape of a broken reed, life itself had become empty of meaning, and melancholy meditation was apt to dwell on the deadness of things and the ruins of what was once glorious and grand. No poet has expressed these sentiments more powerfully than Byron. His *Childe Harold* is a prolonged meditation on the transitoriness of the earthly glories and of proud ambition of the mighty monarchs, while Don Juan is a flippant and penetrating exploration of the utter hollowness of all social pretentions and glittering refinement. The force and energy of his verse full of passion and excitement of life so eminently fitted to thrill, arouse the feeling, and kindle the imagination of a generation half sunk into listlessness and emotional torpor.

More than anything, the popularity was due to the personality of the man—young, handsome and of noble birth with number of mystery and guilt round his neck and his extraordinary struggle to break himself from the fetters of moral prudery and religious hypocrisy and ultimately throwing himself heart and soul into the momentous fight for freedom in Greece. Tennyson was to remark with considerable justice "Byron however mistaken gave to the world another heart and new pulse so we are kept going. Blessed be these that grease the wheels of the old world."

Byron was a man of fascinating and enigmatic personality which aroused interest and curiosity so wide and universal that the poet for a long time was practically eclipsed by the man Byron. An estimate of his poetry is swayed by the magic and scandal clinging to him. He is a more complex figure than any of the romantics and unites the pungency of wit and irony with the noble dream and aspiration so dear to the poets of his generation. Byron was a divided personality a bundle of contradictions which accounts for the variety of his poetical work.

This peculiarity was partly due to the perversity of fortune and partly to circumstances. His father was an unbalanced spendthrift who deserted his wife and child died when Byron was only four years old. His mother a moody, quick tempered woman who "fretted him with a shower of sentimental kisses and the next moment hurt him with a cruel taunt at his lameness." Byron was handsome but lame. He was bred in Presbyterian faith and the sense of sin and fear of hell was drilled into his infant mind by his 'too pious nurse'. He inherited the noble title at an early age but lacked money and means to keep up his dignity. He found fame—he woke up one morning to find the whole fashionable society at his feet. Then came his marriage to the daughter of a wealthy noble Sir Ralph Milbanke, which proved a failure, Byron was separated from his wife and daughter.

The Lady Caroline affair, and still worse, his openly advertised relationship with his half sister, Augusta, a big scandal as it was, the English public vent its wrath upon Byron. Macaulay comments "Society capricious in its fondness flew into rage with its favoured and petted darling. He had been worshipped with an irrational idolatry. He was persecuted with an irrational fury we know no spectacle so ridiculous as the British public in one of its periodical fits of morality. In general, elopements, divorce and family quarrels, pass with little notice. We read the scandals, talk about it for a day, and forget it. But once in, six or seven years our virtue becomes outrageous. We cannot suffer the laws of religion and decency to be violated. We must make a stand against vice. We must teach libertines that the English people appreciate the importance of domestic ties. Accordingly some unfortunate man, in no respect more depraved, than hundreds whose offence have been treated with lenity, is singled out as an expiatory sacrifice. If he has children, they are to be taken from him. If he has a profession he is to be driven from it. Be is cut by the higher order, and hissed by the lower. He is, in truth, a sort of whipping boy, by whose vicarious agonies all other transgressors, of the same class are it is supposed, sufficiently chastised. We reflect very complacently on our own severity, and compare with great pride the high standard of moral established in England with the Parisian laxity. At length our anger is satiated. Our victim is ruined and heart-broken. And our virtue goes quietly to sleep for seven years more."

Byron was hounded out of England. The English society "petted and spoiled Byron, and then cast him out" in one of its periodical fits of morality. He was called a devil's disciple and incestuous ogre by the very people who had extolled and idolized him, forced him into exile on the continent which became the theatre of his action, triumph and dramatic death at the age of thirty-six". With an aching heart Byron tore himself away from England at which he must have cast a longing lingering look. The question of rejection of Byron by the English society is rather complicated. H.J.C. Grierson commenting upon it writes..."society had for Byron an attraction and authority it never possessed for Shelley, and conversely that society, even in holding up its hands in horror and indignation, was fascinated by Byron's poetry while Shelley's musical cry passed over their heads unheeded". Aristocratic society on the one hand, and pietistic Evangelical Christianity, on the other bred a conflict in Byron, which remained unresolved all through his life.

The conflict with his own sense of delinquency and the narrow creed by which he had been taught to interpret and judge of that experience was only one of many themes of his later poetry. The other principal one was his fight with the English aristocracy which in hypocritical alliance, as he deemed, with evangelical and middle class sentiment, had joined in denouncing and driving him into exile.

> The cruelty and envy of the people
> Permitted by our dastard nobles, who
> Have all forsook me, had devoured the rest;
> And suffered me by the voice of slaves to be whooped
> out of Rome.

The sport of destiny and circumstances created a deep sense of isolation and loneliness aggravated by his pride, intense egoism and made himself absorbed. But he was afraid of facing his own self, all his activities and debauchness were only escape avenues from that self which haunted him like a demon. The sense of doom that hedged round his life came from his being brought up in Calvinist faith, the sense of doom was born of his haunting sense of sin.

He was a man of immense strength and implacable will power and his passions were stormy and volcanic and he rightly defined poetry, his own poetry "as a lava of passion whose eruption prevents an earthquake". Arnold imaged him as a Titan with a war dance in his blood, waging ceaseless strife against the whole world and the laws of Man and God which reached its climax in his noble martyrdom at the altar of Greek liberty.

Byron made his debut on the poetic stage with his youthful and valueless volume of verse entitled 'Hours of Idleness'. It was a juvenile effort a mere elegant trifling of a Lord who made experiment with poetry. This work of frail character was severely criticised in the 'Edinburgh Review' Byron was infuriated and came out with his satirical poem 'English Bards and Scotch Reviewers' in which he poured his scorn on the new poetry of the Lake School describing it as something childish and absurd in comparison with the verse of Pope and the allied poets of the neo-classical school. Then came his travel to the Mediterranean which produced a rich harvest of poetry in the form of the first Cantos of *Childe Harold*. The volume was published in 1812. The description of the exotic East so real yet so strange gratified the deep curiosity which was already aroused by the works of scholars and antiquarians. *Childe Harold* made Byron famous overnight. His rise to fame had a meteoric splendour and it dazzled and bemused the men and women of his own circle. The women threw themselves in his way and Byron with his passionate and impetuous temperament, easily succumbed to their tricks and viles, who, though later they left him more often disillusioned. The young man who, but a few months ago, had dined alone off vegetables, at a dull club had the choice of many parties as he liked to attend wherever he elected to appear he was centre of interest and was generally the pursued. Lady Caroline, may not have been conscious of laying her snares, Byron welcomed her interest, of who Byron's "She is a very superior woman, and very little spoiled, which is strange in an heiress—a girl of twenty—a peeress, that is to be, in her own right—an only child, and a savante, who had always had her own way. She is a poetess—a mathematician—metaphysician, and yet withal, very generous and gentle, with very little pretentions. Any other head would be turned with half her aquisitions, and a tenth of her advantage." Byron married her in January 2, 1815, but it resulted in a disaster. Milbanke was a very sensible and considerate women tried to adjust, even to the extent of tolerating his dubious relation with his half-sister Augusta, finally she left him because she could not change him. This resulted in the English society which worshipped him with an irrational idolatry, persecuted with an irrational fury, and forced him to leave the shores of England.

Byron no doubt exploited the fame that came to him after the publication of the two Cantos of *Childe Harold*, by composing a series of brilliant verse tales—*The Giaour, The Bride of Abydos* (1813), *The Corsair, Lara* (1814). *The Siege of Corinth and Parisnia* (1815). These tales brought him into direct rivalry with Scott's romances it proved more popular by their novelty of setting and intensity of emotions.

His exile was crowned with the publication of the last two Cantos of *Childe Harold* containing scenes and description of nature and pictures of the glorious past and their melancholy relics in the present, surviving in the cities of historical renown and interwoven with personal revelations. The style has great variety and a clear stamp of maturity. In the last phase he found his best and most characteristic vein. He adopted the Italian manner of the satirical mock epic poetry and wrote *Beppo* and his masterpiece *Don Juan* the most successful social satire of the time.

Childe Harold was published initially in two cantos. The entire work seeks to describe the travels and reflection of a pilgrim who had undertaken the European tour in order to acquaint himself with the ways and manners of people living in different parts of Europe. The hero, a romantic youth reflects and gives his observation on life, people and the political happenings in different parts of Europe. The first two cantos takes the readers to Portugal, Spain, the Ionian Isles, and Albania—wild and colourful, then a quite unknown country to Englishmen, Byron was entranced by "The wild Albanian kirtted to his knee/ with shawl-girt head and ornamented gun". The canto ends with a lament on the slavery of Greece. Byron's Hellenism is political, Keats more melodramatic and less centrally cultural than Matthew Arnolds but it is a mood that worked on the English imagination in a great variety of ways throughout the nineteenth century. The second Canto of

Childe Harold struck Scott to whom it was sent to review in the 'Quarterly', described it as being like nothing Byron had hither to published. "It is wilder and less sweet, I think than the first, but contains even darker and more powerful pouring forth of the spirit which boils within him.... We gaze on the powerful and ruined mind which he presents as a shattered castle within whose walls, once intended for noble guests, sorcerers and wild demons are supposed to hold Sabbath. There is something dreadful in reflecting that one gifted so much above his fellow creatures should thus labour under such strange mental malady that destroys the peace of mind and happiness although it cannot quench the fire of his genius." In the third the pilgrim visits Belgium, the Rhine, Alps, the Jura. In the fourth impression of Italian life are presented with reminiscences of the poetry of Petrarch and Tasso.

In the Preface to canto IV Byron wrote that it was the longest and most thoughtful and comprehensive of his compositions. Its style is rich, highly coloured, full of metaphors, the result of teaming fancy. Few poems of the same length are so sustained in interest as Childe Harold. This is due partly from the mode of treatment and partly from the subject itself. It contains elements drawn from all the different branches of poetry. Its continuity is like epic at least in the style of episodic epic poetry like Odyssey. Its description of scenery and sketches of life and manner are idyllic. A lyric element is contributed by the outburst of personal life. Its rhetorical passages and soliloquies and the introduction of a supposed auditor and apostrophising the personages mentioned are dramatic. *Childe Harold* is a suggestive poem numerous subjects and meaning—topographical, historical, biographical, artistic and literary which is done in the most attractive light. Every point that is touched on is invested with romance.

W.B. Auden writes Byron spent his early years in comparative poverty with a mother who alternately hit him and covered him with kisses, a Calvinistic nurse who spoke to him of Hell fire and predestined damnation. Unhappiness sharpens a child's wit and he soon realized that his parents were violent and odd people, his ancestors were violent and odd too, and that his deformity made him different from the other children. Further as usually happens when the parents are separated, the absent one is idealized—the father. His father made him passionate; nanny made him doomed, ancestors and his lame foot bitter. All these made him a bitter enemy of society. Out of these emerged, the general Byronic hero. "He was himself the beginning, the middle and end of all his poetry, of every tale, the chief object in every landscape." Harold, Lara, Manfred and a crowd of other characters were universally considered merely as loose incognitos of Byron and Byron intended them to be considered so. Almost all, his heroes have minds which seem at variance with their fortune, and exhibit high and poignant feelings of pain and pleasure a keen sense of what is noble and honourable, and an equally keen susceptibility of injustice and injury under the garb of stoicism or contempt of mankind. His heroes are men who have arrived by different roads to the same goal of despair. They are sick of life, are at war with society, are supported in their anguish only by their unconquerable pride resembling Prometheus on the rock, or Satan in, the burning marl who can master their agonies by the force of their will and who to the last defy the whole power of earth and heaven. It appears that the heart of his heroes has withered and the capacity for happiness has gone to melancholy. They are the authors of scorn, misanthropy and despair. They are projection of Byron himself beginning with *Childe Harold* and ending with *Don Juan*, they are all lovers of freedom and critics of oppression. Childe Harold is simply the first of the many portraits of himself.

A life of self-conscious dissipation in England in 1809 was followed by a journey to Spain, Malta, Albania and Greece which lasted almost two years and provided Byron not only with abundant new material for his poetry but also with an opportunity to build up the character of the sensitive and high-minded wanderer, exiled from a society, (which he despised)—a character which he was later to develop as the characteristic Byronic hero (and also, a self-portrait). The collapse of his marriage and attendant scandal drove him into permanent exile abroad, in 1816. The travels of 1809-11 bore fruit in the first two cantos of Childe Harold's Pilgrimage 1812. The heroes travels follow Byron's and Childe Harold's himself, for all Byron's disclaimers, he is a projection of the poet—A sensitive, disillusioned, generous minded character prone to rhapsodize over history, and to exhort degenerate nations to rise and recover their lost glory. He is also the disenchanted libertine.

For he through sin's long Labyrinth had run
Nor made atonement when he did amiss
Had sighted so many though he loved but one
And that loved one, alas could ne'er be his—

racked by "disappointed passion" who has been alone and unloved in the midst of the wildest revelry.

The third canto of *Childe Harold* appeared in 1816 and the fourth in 1818. Here, Byron drops the mask—quite openly in the fourth canto—and the character of Childe Harold gives way wholly to that of Byron. There is a curious coming together of art and life here with life imitating art. Byron has been acting out his own melodramatic imagination, becoming more and more the Byronic hero he had created: he is by this time, a genuine outcast from society, at least from upper-class English society, and he has genuine reasons for remorse and self questioning. The energy of these cantos is a fiercely egotistical energy, and though these are objective set pieces of rhetorical or descriptive virtuosity the real life of the poem comes from Byron's exploitation and manipulation of his own moods. Byron and all his troubles and inner conflicts face to face with Nature and—with human history and great men are themes of the third canto. The description of men and scenery are interrupted again and again to give voice to his own wrongs and the conflict in his soul, the consciousness of his own wrong doing and the passionate conviction of being more sinned against than sinning. As the exile wanders by the field of Waterloo, the Ardennes, the Rhine, the Alps, the Swiss lakes and in the cities and landscape of Italy musing on man and on nature, recalling local heroes and moments of history, the tone becomes more assured, the point of view with which he contemplates the human and natural world becomes steadier. Towards the end of Canto III he sums up his position,

I have not loved the world, nor the world me—
But let us part fair foes; I do believe.
Though I have found them not that there may be
Words which are things, hopes which will not
deceive,
And virtues which are merciful, nor weaves
Snares for the failing; I would also deem
Ov'r others' grief that some sincerely grieve;
That two, or one, are almost what they seem
That goodness is no name, and happiness no dream

In Canto IV, the past and present of Italy moves him to new heights of eloquence and the Byronic pose merges into genuine emotions conveyed by a verse at once passionate and elegiac.

In Venice, Tasso's achoes are no more
And soundless rows the songless gondoliers
Her palaces are crumbling to the shore,
And music meets not always now the ear;
Those days are gone—but Beauty still is here.
States fall, afts fade—but Nature doth not die
Nor yet forget how Venice once was dear
The pleasant place of all festivity
The revel of the earth, the masque of Italy.

The contemplation of Venice rouses him to special eloquence, he devotes over twenty stanzas to an evocation, at once nostalgic and comforting, of the city's past and a contemplation of its present. It is in such passages that Byron's kinship with the other romantics can be easily traced. The latter cantos of *Childe Harold* take the romantic Byron as far as he can, but he still has to find a medium in which the whole man can speak...he does that only in Don Juan the theme brought the man and masque together. The wonder of the outer world, the Tagus with the mightly fleets of England riding on its bosom, the flower of cintra over hanging the shaggy forest of Cork trees and willows were all the background to one dark and melancholy figure, the figure of Byron.

C.M. Bowra in *The Romantic Imagination* notes that from the European point of view, Byron is the chief exponent and most renowned figure of the whole movement. The man who summed up in himself its essential qualities, and by his inspiring example, imposed them on the civilized world. But from the usual English point of view, he is hardly a Romantic at all, but survival of the 18th century and an enemy of what most romantics thought holy. Byron was different from the other romantics. Though he was touched by Romanticism, he never was a poet of romantic movement in the sense Wordsworth, Coleridge, Shelley, Keats were. What fascinated the Romantic poetry was imagination and a love for fairy romances and dreamy lands of medievalism. But in Byron there is little of that imagination and reflectiveness which we find in Shelley and Keats. Byron is essentially a poet of instinct rather than of imagination. Byron could not be a romantic poet. Byron gave up the romantic view of imagination and adopted a new realistic art, that is why "on the central article of the Romantic creed, the importance of imagination, Byron is regarded as a heretic by such good judges as Keats and Burke and he would not have denied that accusation" notes Bowra.

The Romantics except the idealists like Shelley were not interested in realism and the description of the actual. Wordsworth wandered like a cloud over hills and dales, Coleridge wrought his weird dreams and was wrecked in a mist of opium, Scott with his pen lifted the veil that kept shrouded the enchanting past of the country. Shelley wove out his myth and remained wrapped up in his vision and wished to be 'the trumpet of prophecy' and Keats sought his beauty in Gothic arches and Grecian Urn. It was Byron who was of the earth and wedded to the actual realities of the mundane world.

With Keats it was the past, with Shelley the future, with Byron it is the present that really interests and grips him. His ardent fancy allied with the past on occasions but he is most at home with the England of the day, the Europe of his day, its social hypocrisies, its literary convention and affectations.

Byron scorned to leave his time for as Symons writes, "He loved the world for its own sake." Grierson writes, "Byron never quit the earth from the first to the last he is concerned with realities, and nothing but realities—mundane realities, real persons scenes and happenings." It is this realism so passionately touched and expressed in *Don Juan* that distinguishes him from the other romantics. Of all the great poets of the time, Byron presents the peculiar and poignant combination of an ardent romantic imagination and an intellectual outlook essentially worldly and matter of fact. He expresses more than a sceptic's impatience with metaphysical and theological speculation. In all this he aligns himself with his Augustan predecessors than with his Romantic contemporaries.

He was undoubtedly one of the most powerful and vigorous of English romantic poets. Born in the age of romantics and composing poems in the style of his contemporaries he had his sympathy for the Augustans, and adored Dryden and Pope more than Wordsworth and Coleridge. He had a peculiar fascination for the poetry of Pope and considered him a prince among English poets. Like Pope, his too was not in imagination reflection or aerial flights in a dream, utopia of poetic creation, but sought to present the social, economic political life of the countries he travelled. In *Don Juan* he wrote:

> I mean to show things as they really are.
> Not as they aught to be, for I avow
> That till we see what is fact, we're far
> From much improvement.

His poetry is fierce and vigorous. He is an actor not a dreamy philosopher. He thundered and volleyed and shook Europe by his utterances. He often cursed and abused, spared none. In *Childe Harold* he calls upon God to punish those who are responsible for these ills. He speaks to humanity in its own voice heightened to a pitch which carries across Europe. No poet had ever seemed to speak to men so directly. And it was this directness of his vision of the world that made him a poet, and he made a new thing of poetry. It is Byron's fundamental sincerity that accounts for his greatness. Byron was one of the chief forces who made a breach for romanticism in the fortress wall of custom and prejudice.

Byron's genius was neither lyrical nor dramatic, it was satiric. In satire, Byron found the suitable medium for his rebellions and passionate nature, it is to satire that he turned most joyfully from his early days. He had a great liking for Pope and Gifford, his worthy successor. He closely imitated them and all his satires were written under the influence of Pope, Gifford and Swift. Byron began and ended his poetic career as a satirist, beginning with *English Bards and Scotch Reviewers* and ending with *Don Juan*. "He was a poet in his manner and measure a prophet, who spoke the truth as it presented itself to him, even if he was moved to do so by imperfect motives. There is an element of truth in Byron's arrangement of the Evangelical Protestant doctrine of retribution, there is power in Byron's satire of aristocratic society and aristocratic government in England and Europe," wrote Mazzani in his book *Byron and Goethe*.

Byron expressed himself as a strong avenger of wrongs.

> And though I hope not hence unscatched to go
> Who conquer me shall find a stubborn foe.

He directed his satire particularly against the Lake School—Southey and Wordsworth. Wordsworth's constant use of 'Pedlars', 'Boats', Waggoners in Excursion irritated Byron:

> A drowy frowsy poem called the Excursion
> rit in a manner which is my aversion.

He bemoans the fall of English poetry from the heights of Pope and Dryden to the banality of Wordsworth which is:

> "Pedlars" and "Boats" and "Waggoners" oh ye shades
> Of Pope and Dryden are we come to this.

Byron found greater delight in following this mood and method rather than toeing the essential romantic dreaminess and visionary idealism. *The English Bards and Scotch Reviewers* is a complete triumph of Byronic classicism, and this high spirited, satire is indeed the Dunciad of romanticism. "When the romantic principle of the new school seemed triumphant everywhere, Byron came forward as a dauntless champion of Pope and when he essayed drama he turned his back upon Shakespeare and sat at the feet of Alfieri. He never wholly broke away from the Augustan poetic diction (Moorman Article on Byron in *The Cambridge History of English Lit.* Vol. XII).

The octova rima, used with the colloquial flexibility, in *Beppo* and *Don Juan* was the making of Byron the poet. His reputation on the European continent had long been of the very highest, but in England the contradiction between the poseur and the satirist, as well as that between the facile exploiter of emotion and the mock heroic poet, has often led to critical doubt and confusion. There was something Augustan in the cast of Byron's poetic personality and he might have best suited in the reign of Queen Anne. He needed a tradition and emotional discipline more than most poets, and he lived in a time when neither was easily available in the end he did discover his own and found a way of counterpointing egotism and self-mockery in the Augustans which no other Romantic poet discovered. It was a remarkable enough achievement. He was the one important Romantic poet who defended the eighteenth century poetic tradition against his own age.

Byron, the melodramatic exploiter of his own emotions, the rhapsodist of Nature, the liberal idealistic deploring political oppression the satanist deliberately reversing accepted moral attitudes, the patrician observer contemplating history, one can find parallels to this Byron sometimes in Blake, sometime, even in Wordsworth and in Scott, Byron the ironist, the critic who wrote in *Don Juan*:

> Thou shall believe in Milton, Dryden, Pope
> Thou shall not set up Wordsworth, Coleridge, Southey…

the master of colloquial tone in verse, the inventor of a species of discursive narrative poetry loose enough to contain an intermittent ironic commentary on contemporary life and manners as well as on himself, his fate and taste and prejudices, the wry hedonist who refuses to take himself or anybody seriously—this Byron seems an altogether different character, and one more difficult to associate with the Romantic movement as popularly understood.

Despite his differences with the Romantic poets Byron was a child of his age "Though Byron abandoned Romantic view of imagination and practised a new realistic art and he did not altogether abandon such themes and ideas which meant most to the Romantics notes Bowra. Like the Romantics he had a deep and intense love for nature, freedom, passion, melancholy and romance. He was more revolutionary than Shelley. The note of romanticism is pointedly sounded in such verses as "I would I were a careless child", "I roved a young Highlander" and the lyrics and the elegiac poems, and the melancholic note in them are saturated in the romantic tradition.

Lacking the intensity of Wordsworth, the subtlety of Coleridge, the receptivity of Keats, the aerial fire of Shelley Byron possessed a breath and vigour of imagination beyond that of any of his contemporaries. His attitudes to nature has no meditative musing, little sense of mystery, but very live sense of wonder and delight in the energising glories of Nature. Nature to him is a splendid background against which human activities depict themselves, Byron's greatest and most important contribution to English romantics was the addition of passion. Wordsworth brought poetry back to Nature. Coleridge introduces us to supernaturalism as a psychic phenomenon. Byron imparted to it, 'tone of passionate feeling' indeed the note of passion is Byron's most essential contribution to the reawakening of English poetry.

W.H. Hudson writes "with all his carelessness and his many faults, he has amazing vitality and power, and in his most impassioned moods his verse rushes on like a torrent. He is at his best in description, especially when he blends description with meditation. As a poet of nature he is most at home with nature's wilder aspects, he loves mountains and storm and he glories in the sea." If the Byron lyrics have not the lyric lightness of the best of Scott, or the lyric cry of Shelley, they have a weight and impetus of their own. He wrote as if to release his heart from the grip of imperious passion and found repose in ordering his mental delirium into rhyme. His lyrics are marked by force and vigour of elemental passion. It was in poems like 'Giaour', 'The Bride of Abydos', 'The Siege of Corinth', which were inspired by Scott that a new gale of passion blew through English poetry—startling and arresting. And the passions of love and hate gave to Byron's verse a weight and speed which distinguishes it from Scott's flowing and at time facile verse. Byron's language was natural, the flow most rapid—the note of passion and romantic setting gave to Byron's poetry a rare charm.

The poetry of Byron broke upon the public of England and of Europe with a startling effect which was difficult to comprehend either in character or in range. Of the Romantic poets, none except Byron attracted much attention abroad. The French showed none of the interest to Wordsworth, and Coleridge and later to Shelley or Keats that they had shown to Pope and Swift, Thomson and Young, to say nothing of writers who interest were not mainly literary—Locke, Newton, Shaftesbury, Hume, Adam Smith. The quickening influence of Byron's poetry was felt from one end of the continent to the other, about whom Goethe said 'Byron alone I let stand by myself, Walter Scott is nothing beside him.'

The reactions were more conflicting something like it had been evoked in, though in a narrower range by Marlowe, in *Tamburlaine, Faustus and The Jew of Malta* which had presented something of the same challenge to accepted conventions—religious, ethical and social. Whatever be the literary merit of the tales which Byron poured forth in the year following his return from the Mediterranean, they brought into poetry a new note of passion, passion its own justification, such as had not been heard since some of the Elizabethan dramatics Marlowe, Webster, Ford. There was something at once stimulating and releasing in the absorbing self-forgetting passion of such a song as that of Medora in 'The Corsair'.

> Deep in my soul that tender secret dwells
> Lonely and lost to light evermore
> Save when to thine my heart responses swells
> Then trembles into silence as before
> There in the centre, a sepulchral lamp

Burns the slow flame eternal—but unseen
Which not the darkness of despair can damp
Though vain its rays as it had never been.

What compared with such intensity of feeling, were the mild bleating of Bowless sonnets or the poems inspired by them in the volumes of joint work of Coleridge, Lamb and Llyod. Byron's poetry tempts and compels surrender to that which is beyond the common self. He lacks the penetrative vision of Wordsworth, the subtle and aerial light and shade and the concentrated verbal density of Keats, the ethereal music and imagery of Shelley, but the music of Byron's poetry is sonorous and torrential, it stuns us into submission and impels us forward like a tidal wave to create a lasting reverberation. It is in *Don Juan* that Byron found himself and hit upon a form which in matter and manner, in tone, flexibility of verbal texture, is destined to remain a lasting monument to his genius and art.

Byron wandered through the world, sad gloomy, and unquiet, wounded and bearing the arrow in the wound. Solitary and unfortunate in his infancy, unfortunate in his first love, and still more in his ill advised marriage, attacked calumniation both in his act and intention, without inquiry or defence, harassed by poverty; forced to quit his country, home and child, friendless, pursued even on the continent by a thousand absurd and infamous falsehood, and by the cold malignity of the world that twisted even his sorrows into crime, he yet, in the midst of inevitable reactions preserved his love for his sister and his Ada, compassion for the misfortune; his fidelity to the affection of his childhood and youth, from Lord Clare, to his old servant Murray, and his nurse Mary Gray. He was generous with his money to all whom he could help and serve, from his literary friends down to the wretched libeller Ash. Though impelled by the temper of his genius, by the period in which he lived, and his efforts for poetic individualism which had to face all obstacles he still tried to set up a standard. That he presaged the future with the provision of his genius is proved by the definition of his poetry in his journal "Poetry is the feeling of a former world and of a future". Poet as he was, he preferred activity for good to all that his art could do. His poetry is the poetry of the future; of humanity; potent in new harmony, unity and life.

A witness of the progress of the Restoration and the triumph of the principles of the Holy Alliance, he never backed out from his courageous opposition, he preserved and publicly proclaimed his faith in the rights of the people and in the final triumph of liberty. He stigmatised baseness, hypocrisy and injustice, wherever they sprang. He seemed at time a transformation of that immortal Prometheus, of whom he has written so nobly, whose cry of agony, yet of futurity sounded above the cradle of the European world, and whose grand and mysterious form transfigured by time, reappear from age to age, to wail forth the lament of genius tortured by the presentation of things it will not see realized in its time.

Thus lived Byron, ceaselessly tempest tossed between the ills of the present and yearning after the future; often unequal, sometimes sceptical, but always suffering often most so when he seemed to laugh and always loving even when he seemed to curse. He is the poet, who threw his fortune, his genius and this life at the feet of nationality and liberty he loved. Byron fulfilled on the continent the European role given by him to English Literature. Before he came all that was known of English literature was the French translation of Shakespeare and the anathema hurled by Voltaire against the 'intoxicated barbarians'. It is since Byron that one has learned to study Shakespeare and other writers on the continent. From Byron dates the sympathy of the entire true hearted for England—the land of liberty. He led the genius of Britain on a pilgrimage throughout Europe.

References

Evans, Ifor. *Portrait of English Literature* (London: Sidlewick and Jackson, 1979).

Grierson, Herbert and Smith, J.C. *A Critical Study of English Poetry* (London: Penguin, 1962).

Bradley, A.C. *Oxford Lectures on English Poetry* (London: Oxford University Press, 1909).

Hazlitt, William. *Lectures on the English Poets* (Edinburg, Everyman, 1887).

Hough, Graham. *The Romantic Poets* (London: Arrow Books Ltd., 1961).

Mair, G.H. *English Literature 1450-1900* (London: OUP, 1969).

Symons, Arthur. *The Romantic Movement in English Poetry* (New York: Phaeton, 1963).

Rickett, Arthur Compton. *History of English Literature* (London: Thomas Nelson and Sons Ltd., 1963).

Dowden, Edward. *Studies in Literature 1789-1877* (London: Kegan Paul, Trench, Trubner Co. Ltd.).

Prasad, Brijesh. *A Short History of English Poetry*, (Delhi: Macmillan, 1971).

Rai, V. and Dwivedi. *Landmarks in the History of English Literature* Vol. II (Benaras: Motilal Benarasi Das, 1962).

Hough, Graham. *The Romantic Poets* (London: Arrow Book Ltd., 1961).

Mair, G.H. *English Literature I450-1900* (London: OUP, 1969).

Symon, Arthur. *The Romantic Movement in English Poetry* (New York: Phaeton, 1963).

Compton Rickett, Arthur. *History of English Literature* (London: Thomas Nelson & Sons Ltd., 1963).

Arnold, Mathew. *Essay's in Criticism Second Series* (London: Macmillan & Co. Ltd., 1915).

Legouis and Cazamin. *A History of English Literature.*

De Selincourt, Aubrey. *Six Great Poets* (Oxford: Oxford University Press, 1940).

9

Response to the Seventies: The Characterization of Rose and Frances, Heroines of Margaret Drabble's Novels *The Needle's Eye* and *The Realms of Gold*

Arpa Ghosh

In seventies, England had lesser influence on the political and artistic scenario of Europe than the England of the pre-war years. The swinging sixties had witnessed a surge of youth emancipation and the emancipation of women with the growing use of the contraceptive pill and growing acceptance of the single parent family. The euphoria of the sixties subsided in the seventies, but some basic social changes stayed. Teenage cultures, originating in the working class, spread to all ages and all classes. Their distinctive blend of gaiety and suppressed violence found an echo in the music, clothes, and speech of social groups of all classes, but chiefly, young professionals and executives. The British for the first time threw off the mantle of Victorian morality that had restricted them up to the Second World War and beyond. Young people in particular sought and found a new cultural and moral independence. Family, sex and marriage would never be the same again. The sights and sounds of British life changed drastically. One-parent families, though still suffering considerable hardship, were accepted publicly and even supported to a reasonable degree by public services. Pre-marital sex became common among all classes, aided by family planning clinics. Homosexual couples openly set up house. In all the print and electronic media, on stage and on screen, the range of topics handled and the manner of their treatment was more extensive and freer than ever before. The Education Act allowed bright children of the working class to enroll into the high-browed universities. Society seemed to be moving to a new classless phase. The middle class held out the promise of expanding to include large chunks of the working classes. Meritocracy seemed to be the order of the day. Radio changed its character to cater to niche audiences. No longer was there a blanket programme offered by the BBC. In fact from the seventies the BBC lost out to the new Circe, the television. Supermarket strategies ruled both TV and radio as amusement and public demand scored over the nation's responsibility to offer healthy and ethical entertainment to the British masses. Mass culture to a great extent replaced the elitist cultural ethos of pre-war Britain. The chief advocates of elitist culture had been T.S. Eliot and F.R. Leavis. In the seventies and eighties however we find the Leavisite dicta of the Great Tradition with its system of canonization being flouted at several levels.

The seventies are characterized by slump and recession, a general depression after the excitement of the sixties. One crisis after another hit Britain. The defeated withdrawal of Western forces from the Vietnam, the political scandal of Watergate, the international oil crisis leading to a worldwide economic recession sapped the vitality of the sixties. Britain lost its preeminence to the Unites States gradually becoming dependent on the bullying solicitude of Big Brother.

The seventies saw the emergence of remarkable women writers—Doris Lessing, Iris Murdoch, Muriel Spark, Margaret Drabble, Fay Weldon, Penelope Fitzgerald, Barbara Pym, Beryl Bainbridge, Maureen Duffy, Nell Dunn—but during the seventies and into the eighties the serious reader of British fiction also saw a period of self-conscious invention of a newly feminist fiction which meant, amongst other things, a reappraisal of what was on offer, and what had been repressed, in the female tradition. From the sixties onward, the novel breaks up in two channels; one the intellectual tradition that keeps a niche, elite audience in mind, the other the sociological novel that targets the middle-brow audience. To the former group belong Iris Murdoch, Muriel Spark and A.S. Byatt. Drabble categorically identifies herself with the latter group. In the sixties, Drabble limits herself to the 'condition of women' novel using exclusive female experience like single motherhood and post parturition depression as material for her novels. Drabble is a pioneer in the use of this kind of material, but unfortunately her early novels are limited in scope, claustrophobic and quite tedious in their unrelieved portrayal of the unenviable social predicament of the university educated, socially maladjusted woman. From the seventies onwards Drabble widens her scope. In this decade she writes her famous "condition of England" novels *The Needle's Eye* (1969), the quasi-fantasy novel *The Realms of Gold* (1975) and *The Ice Age* (1977). In the eighties, Drabble writes the sociological mosaic-like novels, *The Middle Ground* (1980) and her trilogy *The Radiant Way*, *A Natural Curiosity* and *The Gates of Ivory*.

For several reasons, Margaret Drabble is a convenient peg on which, to latch a discussion of the sociological novel of the seventies. Even though she secured a double first in English literature from Cambridge, Drabble posits herself against Leavisite elitism that was so fashionable in her years in the University. She claims to feeling constricted by Leavis' hegemonic delineation of the Great Tradition, a forceful and compelling canon formation that Drabble finds quite stifling. Second, Drabble while discussing her own work admits to her predilection for Arnold Bennett's novels, Bennett who is snobbishly dismissed by Virginia Woolf in her 1919 essay on modern fiction.

> Our quarrel, then is not with the classics, and if we speak of quarrelling with Mr Wells, Mr Bennett, and Mr Galsworthy, it is partly that by the mere fact of their existence in the flesh their work has a living, breathing, everyday imperfection which bids us take

> what liberties with it we choose.... Mr Bennett is perhaps the worst culprit of the three, inasmuch as he is by far the best workman. He can make a book so well-constructed and solid in its craftsmanship that it is difficult for the most exacting of critics to see through what chink or crevice decay can creep in. There is not as much as a draught between the frames of the windows, or a crack in the boards. And yet—if life should refuse to live there?[1]

Drabble on the contrary draws attention to Bennett's humble origins, eye for stark detail and faith in documentation when it comes to the unspoken, unsung lives of the quotidian commoner.

> "He [Bennett] has a great respect for ordinary life and ordinary people who don't necessarily achieve much or lead glamorous lives, although they may aspire to. He came from a very poor background himself, as did my family, and he never forgot it. And because of this grounding in knowledge of ordinary people, which Virginia Woolf for example did not have, Arnold Bennett tells you things that Virginia Woolf simply did not know. Although I suppose Virginia Woolf is a greater writer."[2]

Drabble's engagement with contemporary reality develops interesting social ramifications in the seventies even while she retains her interest in strongly etched female characters. If we look for a common motif running through her fiction, in her own words it is, "weathering into identity." In the complex, variegated life of the economically embarrassed England of the 1970s in which migration to the States is a growing menace, welfare politics buttressed by Keynesian economics increasingly unfeasible, unemployment a growing problem, the hiatus between dream and reality, the territory of the mind and the territory of the body widens.

Interestingly, in the two traditions we referred to a little while ago, the same problem of disillusion is dealt with in different ways. Niche writers withdraw from the world of quotidian reality often creating their own fictive worlds. Iris

Murdoch's and Muriel Spark's negotiation with their own times is often indirect and philosophical, to some extent escapist.

Margaret Drabble, Anthony Burgess, Angus Wilson and David Lodge on the other hand grapple with the day-to-day problems of urban life with the energy of a Dickens and the breath of vision of a George Eliot. Drabble's strength is her insider's knowledge of multiple layers of English society. A chief motif in Drabble is a woman's survival and quest for meaning in the arid desert of urban existence. We find the author selecting as her setting a section of urban society that neither belongs to the upwardly mobile capitalist class, nor to the downtrodden working class. Her heroines are often gutsy, energetic women who by virtue of their intellectual prowess, resourcefulness and superior life force claw their way out of their working class origins to inhabit the cultural fringe of London life, unable to return to their roots yet too critical and open-eyed to identify with the pretentious upper classes. Fringe existence is a recurrent motif in Drabble. Located in a cultural hinterland, Drabble's heroines are in an ideal position to observe and comment on the social and economic undercurrents of seventies' and eighties' society. Throughout the seventies Drabble quibbles with this motif of the cultural and social hinterland. Her heroines are surrounded by an aureole of magical grace (a word I use for want of a better word) even while inhabiting the drab, dreary world of seventies London. Part of this aura comes from their social flexibility, their outsider's point of view, and their intellect enriched by experiential knowledge. But part of it is also Drabble's negotiation with avant-garde forms of stream-of-consciousness, magic realism, fantasy, and feminist narrative techniques that she combines with a strong base of classic realism to give a grainy, rough-hewed texture, and a positive, hopeful thrust to her narratives. Drabble's technique is not a verbatim or blind imitation of the classic realist technique of the Victorian times. What Martin Amis refers to as "postmodern trickiness" is to be found with checks and balances in Drabble's seventies' novels.

The trajectories of Rose Vassilou, heroine of *The Needle's Eye* and Frances Wingate, the heroine of *The Realms of Gold* run opposite to each other. Francis lives in an exalted status of social superiority, academic excellence, success in career by securing the distinction of discovering the prehistoric city of Tizouk and what is even more fascinating, state of perfect mental and emotional bliss in which she has it all: an absent husband whose nuisance value she has ciphered by paying him off, completely devoted children, a distinguished and besotted lover who satiates her sexually and emotionally, yet who is safely married to a perfectly inadequate, totally messed up woman who can never be Frances' rival but who, wonder of wonders, evinces a confidence in Frances even while hating her husband who has made a mockery of her marriage. In a nutshell Frances represents a fecund and supple life-force that combats sterile, negative and stunting forces.

The world inhabited by Frances is a post-war, post-industrial, disintegrated world, but Frances possesses the strength to imbue her world with meaning. She is bothered with social niceties but only to a certain extent. Human bonding and emotional dependence on loved ones is of prime importance to her.

Frances occupies a special place among the Drabble heroines. She is a character who almost attains mythic proportions, as admittedly in her case, Drabble moves beyond the realm of the purely factual to portray an affirmative philosophy of life.

In creating Frances, Drabble veers away from her usual materials. Though Frances is a brilliant student and a Northerner like Drabble's other heroines, she does not hail from an impoverished lower-middle class background as does Kate Armstrong and Liz Ablewhite heroines of Drabble's later novels *The Middle Ground* and *A Radiant Way*[3]. Rather Frances is the daughter of well-to-do academicians. Both her parents have achieved success in their respective fields. Moreover, Frances though endowed with energy, resourcefulness and vitality, is cursed by a family disease—a proneness to periodical mental depression. Therefore, whereas, later Drabble heroines struggle against poverty and hegemony of the pedigreed Londoner, Frances struggles against emotional and pathological problems. Also Frances's reputation in her field has reached almost legendary proportions—something which the average Drabble heroine never quite manages to achieve. Frances, in more ways than one, has been presented larger than life. No wonder, Carey Kaplan[4] sees in her the archetypal matriarch—the all-powerful mother-figure. Drabble, in this novel at least, ignores the demands of realism to an extent in order to project a powerful picture of a strong female who has mastered the secret of achieving familial and social harmony.

The methods Frances uses to combat negative and stunting influences are disarming in their simplicity. Survival for her entails balance and symmetry of vision. It entails viewing life in the long and short perspective. Frances is capable of flexible perspectival vision.

She is an integrated person who even after achieving legendary success and recognition in her chosen field relishes the comparatively modest pleasures and responsibilities of family life. She is the rare successful conglomerate of the keen professional—the archaeological discoverer of Tizouk,—mother, sweetheart and tender, grieving niece who gently probes the past of a mad, provincial relative who has died of starvation.

To Frances, her profession is an organic part of her personality. Her work takes her far and wide across the deserts of Africa. Inhabiting hotel-rooms and living out of suitcases, Frances sometimes finds the going pretty tough. But, she enjoys travel, enjoys inhabiting new spaces and extending the boundaries of the known. Frances thinks of archaeological excavation as the exploration of the earth's secrets and the creation of new spaces, and most importantly, a connecting of the present with the past. Tizouk is the city of her imagination. She has researched meticulously for years, but it was in a flash of feminine intuition that she knew exactly where to look.

In her words:

> "I imagine a city, and it exists. If I hadn't imagined it, it wouldn't have existed." All her life, things had been like that. She had imagined herself doing well at school, and done well. Marrying and had married. Bearing children, and had borne them. Being rich, and had become rich. Being free, and had become free. Finding true love, and had found it. Losing it, and had lost it. (31)[5]

The parenthesis infuses Frances' professional and private lives till they become inseparable. A spark of intuition inspires Frances to spot the location of Tizouk. However, when she explores the ruins thoroughly she realizes that the lives of the Phoenicians did not differ so much in kind as in degrees from that of modern man. Continuity rather than hiatus, similitude rather than dissimilitude, characterizes human existence. The myth of Phoenician cruelty, especially their propensity to slaughter their own children is something that Frances seeks to explode. She brings the same imaginative flair to bear upon both her personal life. The same motive to unearth the basic connecting links between alienated beings and the main-spring of life, fuels her to probe into the mystery of her aunt Connie's death. Her aunt's death is very much in the realm of her own personal life. As she herself experiences fostering links with nature, so she seeks to find such links, such vindication of life around her.

> At Connie Ollerenshaw's cottage, Frances goes through the debris of an obscure existence that characterizes her professional life. Connie's history, as it unfolds, fills Frances with deep satisfaction as it proves that the will to live among the Ollerenshaws is not a freakish occurrence. Connie had chosen to live and die alone, a courageous personal choice, and Frances respects her for that. In vital ways Connie is Frances' mirror-image, her true ancestor. Going through Connie's memorabilia Frances discovers traces of a fully lived, self-sufficient existence.

> It did not seem to her too bad, the way her great aunt had lived and died. And the cottage felt all right. It even had a feeling of home. It was contained, it was a secret.... Nature had enfolded it, had embraced it and taken it and thicketed it in, with many thorns and briars; nature had wanted it, and had not rejected it. (295)

Connie, Frances feels, is a woman, who, like her, has lived life in her own terms. Though Frances feels an immediate affinity to her dead relative, the resemblance, in all fairness, should not be stretched too far, as Connie excludes community from her life, whereas community is a vital ingredient in Frances' existence.

Realms of Gold is a celebration of life in fiction at a time when the real world has turned drab and depressive. Frances Wingate has been portrayed as larger than life, almost as the earth mother:

> She was brown and yellow. Her skin was golden, and it was an interesting mixture of coarseness and sensitivity: it had been weathered...by sun and sand like an ancient monument. (93)

Described in such a manner, there is something awesome and deathless about Frances. The 'brown' and 'gold,' as well as the concept of weathering, align Frances to the slow, timeless, geological rhythms of the earth's surface. That Frances is a large woman who has a voracious appetite for food and drink, and all the other pleasures life has to offer, is emphasized repeatedly: "She is a large woman and could drink more than was good for her.... It was true that she had a happy constitution, a metabolism able to deal with a large quantity of foreign substances..." (11). Frances is very clear in her conception of life. Life is not complex at all; it is truly of an "unfair, terrifying, rigid, irreducible, wicked, amoral simplicity." (184)

Frances is strongly backed by authorial approval. A strong, humanistic viewpoint is projected and pitched against the bleak, disoriented and disintegrated aspects of twentieth century life. The inner, intuitive will to live is Drabble's concern as is the need to seek one's individual destiny while remaining an integral part of one's drab social community. To this end she creates a powerful and vibrant female figure and endows her with extraordinary energy and an extraordinary capacity to love.

Rose, the heroine of *The Needle's Eye*, on the other hand is a woman who undertakes the reverse journey from wealth to obscurity, not out of a sense of mission but because she is driven by a compulsive need for personal grace and salvation that makes her a fugitive of the upmarket chic London society of which she is a member by virtue of being born as the daughter of a millionaire. Resolutely turning her back to her inheritance Rose seeks in the shoddy, violence-ridden life of the seventies London down-market locality her personal destiny as mother and as renunciant.

A confused, pathologically nervous and indecisive person, a victim of parental bullying and domestic violence, Rose is a woman who persists in inhabiting the fringes of urban life, refusing to let wealth infringe on her life. Rose rejects money and the privileges it brings often wrongly and wrongfully. What is meaningful to Rose is the bond of motherhood. She clings to it with pathetic anxiety and stubbornness. Her estranged husband Christopher draws a telling picture of Rose's unique personality:

> She undermined me...from the beginning, she had no trust in me, she panicked as seen as she married me, she only did it to give herself a real fright and then she couldn't face it when I turned out alright, when I was loyal to her...she could have taken anything in me except my efforts at good behaviour.... (232)[6]

According to Christopher, Rose had feared that life with an established husband would turn her attentions from the pursuit of grace. By marrying him, a penniless, crude, immigrant Greek, she had deliberately chosen the hard stony path of life, rejecting her father's wealth and security. But when later Christopher tried to provide her with the same wealth and security, Rose fought shy and rejected him too. Christopher's bitter words: "You've no idea...how absolutely wicked and selfish people are when they get hold of this idea of being good," (232) highlights the other side of the picture. Self-fragmentation is a distinct feature of Rose's character. On one hand the voice of common sense seeks to dissuade the mother from following her vision. On the other hand the fanatical streak in Rose seeks grace at all cost:

> O God said Rose, munching her salad angrily, I don't care. You can die for all I care. I'm going to go back now and soon I can collect Maria and Marcus from school...and the woman rose to her feet, white and wailing. In Rose's mind she wailed, like a soul in hell. On the bottom right-hand corner of the day of judgement she wept and writhed her hands across continents. (264-65)

With a keen and clear eye for detail, Drabble impartially delineates Rose's character, showing that while there is something grossly impractical and selfish in Rose's perception of individual destiny, yearning for grace can be strong enough for a weak and emotionally confused woman to resist the money-culture of seventies patriarchy. Aversion of wealth in Rose goes hand in hand with a strong desire to eke out a respectable existence for herself and her children without money acting as a buffer. "I was glad to cut myself off from all that stuff. I'd always believed that one could not get rid of money that it would stick like a leech or parasite, and breed and breed even if one tried to cut it out" (93). In fact, Rose is an instance of a woman eking out for her self a separate existence by painstakingly tutoring herself in the art of survival outside the economics of money culture. Pointing at her shabby, shoddy neighbourhood she confides in a friend:

> I hated it for years, but I believed in it, and now I love it. All this you see I created for myself. Stone by stone and step by step. I carved it out, I created it by faith, I believed in it, and then slowly, it began to exist. It's like God. It requires faith. (35-36)

Rose makes an attempt to carve a niche for herself on the fringes of patriarchal materialist society. The street where she lives is emblematic, for it houses feys, waifs and immigrants who are made to feel their alienation from mainstream British society every moment of the day. Yet like the typical Drabble heroine Rose is neither at home with them nor with the hypocritical upmarket crowd who invite her to their evening parties where she is treated as a museum piece. Part of Rose seeks the down slope of a modest, status-free existence, but the rest of her lacks the strength to see her through this kind of life. One part of her seeks to renounce. But another part of her lacks the strength to do so. The only time she rises above her indecisiveness and wins a victory in terms of decisive action is, when out of her free will, she renounces her intense desire to leave for Africa and instead settles down with Christopher and the children denying her missionary self. It is not so much Rose, the martyr and the fanatic to interests Drabble, as does Rose the woman who despite her psychic excesses, recognizes and responds to her social and family responsibilities. In spite of her individualism Rose is doomed to live life in half-measures.

The interesting point about the characterization of Frances and Rose is the author's effort to provide an alternative reading of the seventies situation with its growing stress on consumerism and upward mobility. Frances is an exaggerated study of success while Rose is an exaggerated study of failure and eccentricity by any pragmatic standard. Yet, in a scenario of universal desiccation and mammon worship, growing impotence of a once powerful and glamorous nation, and erosion of human values and morality, Frances and Rose breathe new life, vitality and promise into their lacklustre surroundings. Both women resist commodification by asserting their humanity strongly and uniquely. Frances never loses touch with nature and the small joys of life:

> The very ditches were a source of delight. It was full of creatures.... Frances ..would lie there on her stomach with her face against the frontier of water and peer for hours and hours, wondering what God had bothered to make it all for, and pondering at the origin of species; coming near at times to an apprehension of a real answer: God had done it all

> for fun, for joy, for excitement in creation, for variety, for delight. Why seek to justify? There it all was". (102-03 - ROG)

While Frances takes an intense pleasure in the diversity of life, Rose is absorbed in her private, spiritual world while performing her duties as mother and social being:

> All alone I arrest the course of nature. I arrest it. I divert the current.[7] (104 - NE)

In both cases, something spills over and above textual representation and takes the characters of Rose and Frances to an allegorical level. Both characters defy categorization. Rose becomes the lonely chalice bearer in the midst of the faithless, sometimes inspired and sometimes thwarted, but never led completely astray in her quest for spiritual grace in an age that has lost touch with its spiritual self. Frances on the other hand is the earth mother, self-contained in her unique perception of the world. She has all the trappings of material success, but does not really require any of them.

Uterine imagery, for example, dormant volcanoes, archeological excavations, tooth cavities, and sewerage pipes with their disturbing, fecund smell, breathe a natural vitality into an otherwise effete, ineffectual and impotent setting. The significant image clusters are the ancient city of Tizouk and Connie Ollenrenshaw's cottage in *The Realms of Gold* (both discussed and quoted above) and a description of Rose's house in the shabby suburban district in *The Needle's Eye.*

> It took her years to realize that it was not neglect that had patched up the sash cards and filled the cracks in the wall with putty and stuck pieces of varnished paper over major structural faults, but on the contrary a yearning impoverished solicitude without money that can never rebuild or reconstruct, but can merely patch and cover and stop up each breach as it occurs. (52 – NE)

All three descriptions go against the ethos of materialism. Connie Ollerenshaw's cottage, like her life, is closer to nature than to man-made society. The ancient city of Tizouk that

Frances unearths is a fabulous and timeless escape from the niggling worries of quotidian life. And the shabby, pasty house in which Rose stubbornly go on living in spite of her father's and husband's requests that she live with them in their up market accommodations, is a manifestation of her desire to fashion an alternative way of living for herself. These images reinforce the desire of the two heroines to form meaningful communities that have the vitality and strength to fight the desiccating effects of materialistic society. Survival for both women denotes individual initiative, familial and filial warmth, a benevolent fate or simply faith in the larger forces of nature and the individual's sense of being connected to history.

An interesting feature of Drabble's novels is her closure or lack of it. Like life, her novels peter out without a significant, decisive closure and this combined with her powerful feminist imagery makes her style part of *ecriture feminine*, or feminine writing as defined and illustrated by French feminists. The seventies urban life is tackled with great narrative vigor, but realism in Drabble is not unmixed. Rather it is combined with feminist imagery and modernist narrative techniques. The realist in Drabble seeks to capture the diversity of social existence in mosaic form. But at the same time she realizes that individual ego and destiny are too well-etched at this point of history to be completely subsumed in the matrix of society. The form and content of Drabble's sociological fiction is therefore irrevocably affected and altered by the modernist movement that defies and challenges the certainties of classic realism.

References

1. (86-87) *20th Century Criticism* edited by David Lodge.
2. Margaret Drabble's interview with Diana Cooper-Clark, "Margaret Drabble: Cautious Feminist." *Atlantic Monthly*, Nov. 1980, 24.
3. *The Middle Ground*, London: Weidenfield and Nicholson; NY: Knopf, 1980.
4. *The Radiant Way*, London: Weidenfield and Nicholson; NY: Knopf, 1987.

5. Kaplan, Carey. "A Vision of Power in Margaret Drabble's *The Realms of Gold*", *Journal of Women's Studies in Literature*, 1, No. 3, Eden Press, Summer 1979.
6. All quotations from *The Realms of Gold* are borrowed from the London: Weidenfield and Nicholson; NY: Knopf, 1975, edition.
7. All quotations from *The Needle's Eye* are borrowed from the London: Weidenfield and Nicholson; NY: Knopf, 1969, edition.

10

Moral and Religious Gnosis in Plays of Samuel Beckett

Anita Myles

The first performance of Samuel Beckett's *Waiting for Godot*[1] in 1953 created a storm in the theatre world. Initially, the play appeared to be incomprehensible to the audience while critics and academicians dissected it mercilessly probing for latent meanings and implications. Consequently, inspite of controversies and disagreements, *Waiting for Godot* was branded a moral and religious allegory though the playwright himself firmly denied the nuances. While Beckett produced more plays, the critics stubbornly continued their struggle to implicate a steady and persuasive moral and religious note in each one. Possibly, the inclination for interpreting Beckett's plays from the moral and religious perspective was rooted in his upbringing in the Protestant tradition especially as the dramatist felt deeply moved by the intense pain and suffering that he witnessed in the world around him. Understandingly, such negative observations resulted in a loss of faith in religion, forcing the dramatist to question often the existence of a superpower who was unaware and unconcerned about the plight of helpless mankind. Nevertheless, in spite of his lack of faith in religion, Beckett's plays are replete with examples and references extracted from *The Holy Bible*[2], Christian theology and mythology. At the same time, his characters freely exhibit knowledge of and familiarity with religious texts and religious customs.

When Samuel Beckett began writing, existentialism was in full sway. Christian existentialists followed Kierkegaard's concept that in God, man may find freedom from tension; in Him the finite and the infinite are one. In his book *Fear and Trembling* (1843) Kierkegaard stated that Divinity and its Will are ultimately unknowable to human consciousness; hence a Christian must have unquestioned faith in order to maintain his or her belief, emphasizing rightly that the nature of individual human experience remains incommunicable to others, rendering the person absolutely alone in the world. On the other hand, the atheistic existentialists, disciples of Jean Paul Sartre and Martin Heidegger believed that man suffers alone in this godless world but he can achieve much by his will power. Both groups of existentialists exhibit deep concern for man's being feeling that reason is insufficient to understand the mysterious world with the awareness of anguish being a universal phenomenon and concluding that the idea of morality gains momentum only through positive participation. Literary texts, if analyzed from this point of view, contain characters experiencing some kind of mental or spiritual breakdown beginning to question the meaning of reality and existence. Samuel Beckett was well-versed in European thought from Rene Descartes and Arthur Schopenhauer to Nietzsche, Ludwig Wittgenstein, and Sartre. Naturally, his writings revolve around the phenomenological themes of the elusive nature of human consciousness. He plunges into the existential suffering of man prompted by the absurd situation of an infinite mind trapped in a finite body and the incommunicability of individual human experience. Beckett, with his percipient insight evolved a style that would help him to express the human dilemma and the existential themes that preoccupied him for long. The Second World War Europe witnessed the disappearance of religious and moral values without any alternative and the masses became aware of their absurd existence, realizing that anticipating hope pinned on forces outside themselves was futile. Under such compulsive circumstances, shuttling between leaderless and valueless social systems of France and England, Samuel Beckett produced the monumental play, *Waiting for Godot*.

Beckett's scepticism and sense of vicissitude bred out of God's non-challant and passive observation of life's miseries gained momentum due to his exposure to German and French Existentialist doctrines but his early exposure to Christian faith prevented the playwright from becoming a follower of Greek idea of "Immanent Will".

Beginning with the title of *Waiting for Godot* critics located an affinity between the words 'God' and 'Godot'. Estragon and Vladimir, the two tramps look forward eagerly to the arrival of Godot as in him they envision a means of alleviation from their mental and physical excruciation and suffering. Godot symbolizes salvation and redemption for the tramps. Incidentally, the play appears to be more coherent if one understands Godot as God. The 'waiting' of the two tramps signifies steadfast faith and hope initially, though later they waiver.

As the play proceeds, one encounters a lot of Christian imagery compelling it to be explicated in the Christian perspective polarizing on major moral and religious issues. The tramps enter into a postulation related to the two thieves crucified along with Jesus Christ.

> Vladimir: ...Two thieves, crucified at the same time as our Saviour. One—
>
> Estragon: Our what?
>
> Vladimir: Our Saviour. Two thieves. One is supposed to have been saved and the other...(*he searches for the contrary of saved*)...damned.
>
> Estragon: Saved from what?
>
> Vladimir: Hell. (12)

Further conversation confuses the tramps making them wonder if only one or both were damned, also referring to the four Gospels of which only one mentions the incident. Beckett admitted that in creating the dramatic situation he was influenced by St. Augustine's statement and not by the Biblical text:

> Do not despair, one of the thieves was saved.
> Do not presume, one of the thieves was damned.[3]

Obviously Beckett was fascinated by the equal possibility of salvation as well as damnation mentioned in the statement as he makes Vladimir to comment instantaneously,

> It's a reasonable percentage. (11)

When Vladimir and Estragon peruse that chances for salvation and damnation are equally possible, hope rises and both decide to continue waiting for Godot, the ensuing discussion centering on Godot and what he would do for them on his arrival whereas ignoring Godot indicated punishment. They refer to the two thieves hanged along with Christ—one who accepted the magnificence of Christ gained salvation while the other who denied him was condemned. Ironically, they decide to hang themselves on a tree in the vicinity if Godot did not arrive for rescuing them. Clearly enough the coming of Godot symbolizes salvation and new life for the tramps who are similar in thought pattern to the two thieves crucified along with Christ. One was doubtful like Estragon while the other diligently sought salvation like Vladimir hopes if Godot comes.

In his apparently meaningless and unintelligible speech, Lucky, the slave too mentions the existence of a wayward though loving God. Lucky can see man waste and pine, shrink and dwindle in the absence of religious stability and excessive involvement in materialism. To quote the dramatist:

> Given the existence...of a personal God...with white beard...who from the heights of divine apathia divine athambia divine aphasia loves us dearly with some reasons unknown...are plagued in torment plunged in fire...to waste and pine...to shrink and dwindle. (42-44)

The image of God, the all knowing loving father as projected in Christian mythology is of an old man having a white beard.

The messenger boy who meets Vladimir and Estragon in Act II, gives a similar God-like description of Godot. In Act I he admits that he works for Godot emphasizing:

I mind the goats, Sir. (51)
As for my brother,
He minds the sheep, Sir. (51)

Furnishing further information the boy says that Godot doesn't beat him but he beats his brother who minds the sheep. Instantaneously references to Cain and Abel, Esau and Jacob, the two major symbolical tales of *The Old Testament* get revived in the mind of the reader.

In *Waiting for Godot*, there are repeated references to certain Christian terminology viz. On Pozzo asking his name Estragon replies 'Adam'; Vladimir scolds Lucky for 'crucifying' such a good master as Pozzo with his personal suffering; in Act II Pozzo responds to Estragon's call 'Abel, Abel,' and later to 'Cain, Cain' to which Estragon comments 'He's all humanity.' Similarly on several occasions a prayer slips out, 'God have mercy on me' and 'Christ have mercy on us'.

Vladimir incorporates the spirit of helping and caring for those in need. Vladimir covers the sleeping Estragon. Their mutual interdependence may be construed as a symbol of Christian charity. Later both help the fallen Pozzo to get up. Vladimir is conscious of the need to do good whenever an opportunity comes. He says,

> Let us do something while we have the chance! It is not every day that we are needed. Not indeed that we personally are needed. Others would meet the case equally well, if not better. To all mankind they are addressed, those cries for help still ringing in our ears! But at this place, at this moment of time all mankind is us, whether we like it or not. Let us make the most of it, before it is too late! Let us represent worthily for once the foul brood to which cruel fate consigned us. (79-80)

When Vladimir speaks about helping others, he seems to advocate the Christian doctrine: 'Love your neighbour as you love yourself.'

However, Robert Gary infers that the characters in *Waiting for Godot* are only marginally Christian as they shun the idea of repentance as a possible solution for their fears.[4] Truly, the expectation of the tramps on the arrival of Godot is not at all Christian. Vladimir says 'I'm curious to hear what he has to offer. Then we'll take it or leave it' (48). This is quite against the principles of Christianity for God knows all our needs and will fulfill them as long as we willingly submit to the Will of God. Their knowledge of The *Holy Bible* is also imperfect. Vladimir quotes 'Hope deferred maketh the something sick.' He has replaced the word 'heart' with 'something'. Vladimir does not blindly accept all that is written in *The Bible*. He questions the authority of the evangelists about their description of Christ's crucifixion. The tramps are not sure whether Godot will actually come or not, in spite of the optimistic utterance 'We will be saved' on the arrival of Godot.

Everything about Godot is inscribed with uncertainty, yet the hope that Didi and Gogo evince in waiting for him in itself exemplifies Christian virtue. Gogo is forgetful and inclined to make mistakes but Didi, stronger of the two repeatedly reminds Gogo that they are waiting for Godot. At the end of each Act, when the boy comes with the message that Godot will not come, Vladimir continues to preserve hope, determined to come back the next day to meet Godot. Didi is optimistic and hopeful about at least fifty per cent chances of being saved.

Nevertheless, a fact to be perceived in the play is that the tramps are quite wavering in their assumption about the arrival of Godot. Christianity describes God as benevolent imparting purpose and meaning to human existence. If hope is strong then man can easily overcome boredom, defeat and despair. The tramps are desperate and uncertain because their hope is not strong especially being unsure about Godot's identity. When Lucky and Pozzo arrive they mistake them for God though both mention that they had met Godot some time ago. Perhaps this stipulates the Christian concept that Christ appears to people in various guises. *The Bible* states that in helping others you are actually serving Christ—'When you do this to the smallest you are doing it to me.' Christian theology interprets this statement by claiming that Christ is already in this world: one need not wait for him; serving humanity brings one closer to Christ who says regretfully 'I was naked you did not clothe me, I was in prison, and you did not visit me.' A sense of boredom, desperation and ennui is conspicuous in the waiting of Didi and Gogo only because they lack unflinching hope. They unnecessarily wait for God who is already in this world in various guises. Vladimir admits that their waiting for Godot is from irrational habit.

An in depth analysis of *Waiting for Godot* substantiates the fact that the pay is concerned with the hope of salvation through God's grace. Vladimir's waiting signifies hope and faith. Vladimir's kindness to Estragon is seen as a symbol of Christian charity. Yet the religious interpretation tends to overlook certain relevant facts. Beckett repeatedly mentions the uncertainty about Godot's coming, also the unreliability and the irrationality involved in the process of waiting. When waiting is compounded with absurdity then it loses its religious essence. Further, the notion of suicide as a possible solution to human problems is absolutely unchristian in spirit. It eclipses the concept of faith and hope being projected by the dramatist.

If in *Waiting for Godot*, the two tramps are desperately waiting for the end, in *Endgame*[5] Hamm and his companions are stupefied because the end is approaching quickly and they fail to comprehend any fresh beginning after that. In *Endgame,* the characters lack faith in the life after death this decrypts their courage for re-encountering the odds of life while they incessantly pray to God as a matter of habit and not due to faith. However, their repeated prayers negate religion by strengthening the belief that God actually does not exist; hence it is futile to pray.

In his suffering, the blind Hamm may resemble the Biblical Job but otherwise the two are contrary to each other. Job gradually accepts his tragic situation and prays faithfully to God for courage and tenacity to overcome the pain. Hamm, on the other hand derides God. If Job accepts his suffering as the act of divine dispensation, Hamm believes that God is unjust.

In the play, Nagg narrates the story of a tailor which contains ironic and tantalizing comments on the Creator. An Englishman approaches a tailor to stitch him a pair of trousers. Each time he went to collect the trousers the tailor asked for more time to rectify a mistake that he had made in either cutting or stitching. Ultimately, the Englishman lost his patience and began scolding the tailor thus:

> God damn you to hell, Sir, no, it's indecent, there are limits! In six days, do you hear me, six days, God made the world. Yes Sir, no less Sir, the WORLD! And you are not bloody capable of making me a pair of trousers in three months! (21-22)

The story has the implication that God created the world in great haste rendering everything in a state of flux. Perhaps, man is expected to rectify the mistakes committed by God. Consequently there is constant struggle and a state of conflict between God and man. Ironically the struggle is between two unmatched partners God being more powerful has his way while man has to endure meekly supplicating invariably for God's mercy.

Hamm in *Endgame*, plays the role of the Absolute, dominating over Clov, Nagg and Nell. Hamm's fathering of Clov is analogous to God fathering man. The image becomes vivid when Hamm insists on being pushed to the centre of the stage so that he is the hub of all activities just as God exists as the focal point of all human activities according to the Christian concept. Hamm commands a disintegrating kingdom signifying man's strife in the universe. Hamm believes that death is the end of everything having no faith in life after death. Perhaps, the life long suffering of the four characters in the play weakens their faith in goodness if there is any. Hamm is old, blind, paralyzed confined to a wheelchair; Clov is unable to sit while Nagg and Nell, the legless parents of Hamm are placed in two ash cans. For these characters the world outside has ceased to exist. Naturally their speeches indicate the sense of loss which has subdued them thereby representing the gloom and chaos in a Godless world. Hence their attitude tends to be cynical and morbid.

Happy Days[6] is a play quite contrary to *Endgame* as the scepticism and despair suddenly gets replaced by faith in God and the power of prayer. Winnie who is buried in sand and is unable to move remains a vivacious and buoyant person right to the end. Hamm in *Endgame* is incapacitated so he is pessimistic, Winnie in *Happy Days* also suffers yet she is optimistic about her hopeless predicament. She makes sure that her life is nothing else but a record of 'happy days'. When the play opens, Winnie begins with a prayer:

> Winnie: (gazing at zenith.) Another heavenly day. (Pause. Head back level, ey *front, pause. She clasps hands to breast, closes eyes. Lips move in inaudible prayer, say ten seconds. Lips still. Hands remain clasped. Low.*) For Jesus Christ's sake Amen. (*Eyes open, hands unclasp, return to mound. Pause. She clasps hands to breast again, closes eyes, lips move again in inaudible addendum, say five seconds. Low.*) World without end Amen. (Eyes *open hands unclasp, return to mound. Pause.*) Begin, Winnie. (*Pause*) Begin your day Winnie. (1)

All through the day, Winnie keeps busy in sundry activities for ignoring her problems. If Winnie survives by faith and optimism, her husband Willie finds diversion elsewhere. Neither does Willie have faith like Winnie nor does he believe in prayer. Instead, he takes refuge in obscene postcards and newspaper reports. Firm faith in the existence of a superpower that keeps an eye on all percolates through Winnie all the time—

> ...someone is looking at me. (18)

Winnie tends to be a significant progression in Beckett's existential system due to her deep-rooted optimism. In spite of his religious diversion, Beckett rarely portrays such sanguine characters.

Other plays of Beckett embody similar moral and religious undertones, themes shuttling between hope and despair, faith and doubt, optimism and cynicism. For example, Dan and Maddy in *All That Fall*[7] seem to share the idea of metaphysical cruelty. The loss of their child has made Dan despondent about life beginning to realize that there is no God to extricate him from his state of dejection. Contrarily, Maddy attempts reviving faith in God by referring to certain passages in *The Bible*. She reminds him that even a little sparrow does not fall without the Will of God and man is more valuable than sparrows. Dan laughs when Maddy tells him of the text of a sermon preached at the village church: "The lord upholdeth all that fall and raiseth up all those that be bowed down" (Psalm 145).

Krapp, the old man in *Krapp's Last Tape*[8] resembles Dan, an agnostic. Krapp is a discontented man because his youthful desires have remained unfulfilled. He continuously contrasts the lost past with the sour present leading a life of total obscurity and utter loneliness. Perhaps, if Krapp developed hope and faith like Winnie in *All That Fall*, his life would have been better managed. But Krapp's attitude leaves the ultimate impression that people lacking faith and hope are doomed to suffer untold miseries.

Embers[9] is akin to *Krapp's Last Tape* in that its protagonist is an old man, Henry musing on the past. Henry is obsessed with the compulsive need to talk. Failing in accomplishing his expectations from his wife and daughter, he develops the urge to express his innermost desires to someone who would understand him overpowering his reason. He would often walk to the seashore, muttering to himself and identifying the turmoil in his mind to the waves in the sea.

In *Play*[10], a man, his wife and mistress are encased in urns with only their heads sticking out. They have been placed in urns to symbolize the fact that they have died and departed from this earth. They have led adulterous lives and go on talking in a bid to expatiate the guilt within. The three characters portray the frustration of mankind at large who suffer the burden of a guilty conscience because they have no faith in divine forgiveness.

The perusal of the plays of Beckett invariably projects the image of a Godless man who is a victim of despair, disillusionment and hopelessness. Indirectly, some characters accept the existence of God but believe that he is cruel and inconsiderate. The characters pray to God, take the name of God, beg for mercy and grace yet faith is lacking. Characters like Vladimir, Estragon, Hamm, Clov, Krapp, Dan and Maddy, Henry, Winnie and Willie turn towards God sometime or the other but in the absence of sufficient faith they continue to suffer. Beckett in these plays has portrayed the modern existentialist dilemma where each individual is guided by selfish motives which in turn give rise to mutual distrust and suspicion culminating in isolation marked by manifold miseries. Beckett seems to reiterate what Eliot had conjectured in *The Waste Land*[11] that man's misery will enhance multifariously without the anchorage of religious faith. The plays of Beckett harp on the significance of faith and hope which would make it easier to navigate through 'the iron gates of life'. The plays not only portray the plight of modern man but also offer a possible solution. Such a pattern of moral and religious gnosis in Beckett's plays opened new vistas in the traditional existential theories by attempting to bring together under one doctrine, the Christian and the aesthetic systems through the varied themes and multi-dimensional characters of his plays.

References

1. London: Faber and Faber, 1956, rpt. 1986.
2. *The New International Version* (New York: The Bible Society, 1983 edn.).
3. Ronald Hayman, *Theatre and Anti-Theatre: New Movements Since Beckett* (London: Secker and Warburg, 1979), 8.
4. "*Waiting for Godot*: A Christian Interpretation", *Critical Thought Series*—4, 45.
5. London: Faber and Faber, 1958, rpt. 1988.
6. London: Faber and Faber, 1961, rpt. 1966.
7. London: Faber and Faber, 1957, rpt. 1983.
8. London: Faber and Faber, 1959.
9. London: Faber and Faber, 1959.
10. *Collected Shorter Plays* (London: Faber and Faber, rpt. 1984).
11. *The Complete Plays and Poems of T.S. Eliot* (Norfolk: Faber and Faber Ltd., 1982 edn.).

11

"Ode to a Nightingale": Keats' Clairvoyant Journey

Purnendu Chatterjee

For I have ever thought that it might bless
The world with benefits unknowingly;
As does the nightingale, upperched high,
And cloister'd among cool and bunched leaves—
She sings but to her love, nor e'er conceives
How tiptoe Night holds back her dark-grey hood.

Keats, *Endymion*, Bk. I, ll. 826-31

A poet is a nightingale, who sits in darkness and sings to cheer its own solitude with sweet sounds; his auditors are as men entranced by the melody of an unseen musician, who feels that they are moved and softened, yet know not whence or why.

Shelley, *A Defence of Poetry*

I

The Odes, as the finest expression of Keats' genius, constitute the genuine credentials of the poet's fame. As a rare confluence of joy and sadness, the Odes record the poet's passionate search for the immutable principles of Joy and Beauty on the face of the ubiquitous operation of Time, whose face is changed and decayed. An enthusiastic pagan in his salad days, Keats began as an ardent and unsuspicious votary of Beauty and Joy, and made a simplistic equation that to squeeze out beauty from whatever sensuous object lying before the poet was the only sacred human prerogative; it was to be our nicest human destiny. "A thing of beauty is a joy forever"[1] [*Endymion*, i 1], he would exclaim as a constant refrain. He believed in the beginning that mankind has been uniformly galloping towards a millennial destiny, and that Nature presented a fun-fiesta of the senses; and such a spectacle waits only to be decoded and enjoyed by man.

When we come to the Odes, we find Keats completely changed self—a battered man with shattered nerves. The battery of trenchant criticism unleashed against him, the death of his younger brother Tom due to consumption, the emigration of his elder brother George to Canada and the long agony of his love-passion was wearing out his spirits, while his health was beginning to fail. Gone are his high, unquestioning presumptions about life, Joy and Beauty. Gregarious salvation of humanity, or even the more tenuous hope of the poet's sacred prerogative for personal salvation through a heightened sensitivity and creative imagination, seems to vanish like an embarrassing dream. He sees through the vanitas vanitatum of Love, Ambition and Poetry. In 'Ode on Indolence' the poet bids:

"...ye three Ghost adieu! Ye cannot raise
My head cool-bedded in the flowery grass
For I would not be dieted with praise."

The poet has passed through an ordeal of fire which life exposed him to. Life is hopelessly moored in the mire of time and change, and any hope of relief seems impertinence, not to speak of salvation. With life creeping on all fours and souls becoming leaden-eyed, the dream of Joy and Beauty appears to totter and shrink back almost in embarrassment—their very validity, even in terms of the swiftest imagination, is now under the shadow of doubt.

In his desperate attempt to fall back on at least some assurance, Keats in the Odes radically renovates his version of Beauty and, with it, the proposed means to achieve the same. Beauty is no longer viewed in pure sensuous terms. It now consists, as he himself owned, in the intensity and permanence of the feeling or experience evokes; for only that way one could leap out of the mortal dimensions of time and space. Of course, an intellectual conceit! Beauty that shall not die! Obsessed at the distressing limitations of reality Keats' romantic exuberance tries means after means in the Odes to grasp at some undying essence that shall beat Time in its own game. In a mode which is Shakespearean, he shifts through alternative possibilities—what if it is the bower of the nightingale or how if it could be the enduring world of plastic art? However, thanks to his artistic fidelity to his own experience and his *negative capability*, he does never forego his solid fund of common sense and declares the results of each flights of fancy as tentative and invalid. Reality cannot be finally fought off or ignored. He is always aware of the existential pathos of the human soul. It is because, Reality throughout keeps lurking in the backdrop, that his quest for Permanence and Beauty attain a greater veracity and elusive charm. The humanity of Keats is affirmed as his religion of Beauty is enveloped by an honest recognition of life's real terms.

The recognition of the harsh realities of existence is affirmed in 'Ode to the Nightingale'. The youth who grows "pale and spectre-thin" is his brother Tom, the beauty that cannot keep its lustrous eyes is Keats' general comprehension of the mutability of Beauty and the Love that cannot affirm itself beyond tomorrow is the poet's wasted passion for Fanny Brawne. Swallowed by these ghastly realities Keats enjoys an out-of-the-body experience in the Ode.

Before discussing on the out-of-the-body experience of the poet, I shall very briefly consider the present concept of the experience.

II

An out-of-body experience (henceforth OBE), is an experience that typically involves a sensation of floating outside of one's body and, in some cases, perceiving one's physical body from a place outside one's body. OBEs are often part of the near-death experience, and reportedly may also lead to astral projection. It is claimed that OBEs sometimes observe details during an OBE which were unknown to them beforehand.

In some cases, the phenomenon appears to occur spontaneously; in others it is associated with a physical or mental trauma, use of psychedelic drugs, or a dream-like state. It is possible to induce the experience deliberately, for example, through visualization while in a relaxed, meditative state. Recent (2007) studies have shown that experiences somewhat similar to OBEs can be induced by direct brain stimulation. Some of those who experience OBEs may have willed themselves out of their bodies, while others found themselves being pulled from their bodies (usually preceded by a feeling of paralysis). In other accounts, the feeling of being outside the body was suddenly realized after the fact, and the experiencers saw their own bodies almost by accident.[2]

OBEs are often initiated through lucid dreams, though other types of initiation are also used. In many cases, people claim to have had an OBE, reported being asleep, on the verge of sleep, or having been asleep shortly before the experience. A large percentage of these cases referred to situations where the sleep was not particularly deep (due to illness, noises in other rooms, emotional stress, and exhaustion from overworking, frequent re-awakening, etc.). In most of these cases, the subjects then felt themselves awake; about half of them noted a feeling of *sleep paralysis*. Some subjects report having had an OBE during near death conditions.

There appear to be two common forms of such lucid experiences. The first involves lucid dreaming, where the subject is immersed in unrealistic worlds, or in a modified form of the reality with impossible or inconsistent features. A second experience is of a more physical nature where the environment is consistent with reality; this is often called an etheric or ethereal experience. This type can be frightening, as extremely realistic physical sensations may occur, often including magnetic and vibrating phenomena, loss of balance, and confusion. The person believes he has awoken physically and panic can be caused by the realization that limbs appear to be penetrating objects.

The OBE may or may not be followed by other experiences which are self-reported as being "as real" as the OBE feeling; alternatively, the subject may fade into a state self-reported as dreaming, or they may wake completely. The OBE is sometimes ended due to a fearful feeling of getting "too far away" from the body. Many end with a feeling of suddenly "popping" or "snapping" and sometimes a "pulling" back into their bodies; some even report being "sucked back" into physical form. A majority describes the end of the experience by saying "then I woke up". However it's worth noting that even those who describe the experience as something fantastic that occurs during sleep, and who describe the end of the experience by saying "and then I woke up", are very specific in describing the experience as one which was clearly *not* a dream; many described their sense of feeling more awake than they felt when they were normally awake. One compared the experience to that of lucid dreaming, but said that it was "more real".

There are several possible physiological explanations for parts of the OBE. OBE-like experiences have been induced by stimulation of the brain and by using cameras to fool the mind into thinking that the body is somewhere it is not. The OBE has been reproduced through stimulation of the posterior part of the right superior temporal gyrus in a patient. Positron-emission tomography was also used in this study to identify brain regions affected by this stimulation.

The simplest explanation is that OBEs are exactly what they seem: the human consciousness separating from the human body and travelling in a discorporate form in the physical world. English psychologist Susan Blackmore suggests that an OBE begins when a person loses contact with sensory input from the body while remaining conscious. The person retains the illusion of having a body, but that perception is no longer derived from the senses. The perceived world may resemble the world he or she generally inhabits while awake, but this perception does not come from the senses either. The vivid body and world is made by our brain's ability to create fully convincing realms, even in the absence of sensory information. This process is witnessed by each of us every night in our dreams, though OBEs are claimed to be far more vivid than even a lucid dream.[3]

III

Keats' 'Ode to a Nightingale' reflects an OBE that leaves the poet confused at the end: "Do I wake or sleep." The Ode captures a beautiful summer evening while the actual history of its composition, as affirmed by Charles Brown, was in a completely different setting.

> "In the spring of 1818 a nightingale had built her nest near my house. Keats felt a tranquil and continual joy in her song; and *one morning he took his chair from the breakfast-table to the grass-plot under the plum-tree, where he sat for two or three hours*. When he came into the house, I perceived he had some scraps of paper in his hand, and these he was quietly thrusting behind the books. On inquiry, I found those scraps, four or five in number, contained his poetic feeling on the song of our nightingale. The writing was not well legible; and it was difficult to arrange the stanzas on so many scraps. With his assistance I succeeded, and this was his 'Ode to a Nightingale', a poem which has been the delight of every one."[4] (italics mine)

Keats did not record the "two or three hours", that Brown mentions, in 'Ode to a Nightingale.' In the poem, the Bird sings "in some melodious plot/ Of beechen green", not in a plum-tree. The time is "night" or "midnight", not a morning after breakfast. The season is summer, not spring. Keats' imagination transmutes what he experiences under the plum-tree. He acknowledges, for this reason, flying up to the Bird "on the viewless wings of Poesy" and only returning to himself when his "fancy" fails, its spell broken by a word, "forlorn".

The poem 'Ode to a Nightingale' does not begin with the Nightingale but with a description of the poet's own self. Keats' dramatic sense makes him to set up a stage, however briefly, with a description of his own sensations before introducing the consecrated Bird:

"My heart aches, and a drowsy numbness pains
My sense, as though of hemlock I had drunk,
Or emptied some dull opiate to the drains
One minute past, and Lethe-wards had sunk."

The equation between pain and drowsiness is characteristically Keatsean. In 'The Eve of St. Agnes' Keats wrote:

"Or I shall drowse beside thee, so my soul doth ache." (Stanza — XXXI)

The drowsiness, of course, is an indicator of the gradual loss of self-consciousness of the poet. The reference to Lethe not only points to the poet's Hellenic affiliations, but also it indicates the regress of the poet's psyche from extenuating and excruciating realities. The body is an integral part of reality and, as sanctioned by the theological canons of Christianity, it has been viewed as the root of all bane and suffering. The song of the nightingale that the poet heard produced in his heart a rare joy and gave him the necessary impetus to an OBE:

"'Tis not through envy of thy happy lot,
But being too happy in thy happiness,—
That thou, *light-winged Dryad* of the trees,
In *some melodious plot*
Of *beechen green*, and shadows numberless
Singest of summer in *full-throated ease*."(italics mine)

The happiness created in the poet's heart by the song of the Bird is a very subtle feeling that the poet does not enjoy while he abides consciously in the time-space continuum. Obviously, the poet feels that he is distanced from the mundane and painful realities that surround him. Hence, the nightingale does not remain an ordinary singing bird but becomes a "light-winged Dryad"—the expression, perhaps, signifying the poet's attraction for those good, old days of happy pieties. The locale of the poem is also shifted from the grass plot that Brown mentions to "some melodious plot/ Of beechen green". Besides, the glorious use of the transferred epithet—the quality of melody of the bird's song is attributed to the plot of land where the bird is singing—and the adjective "beechen" which is a favourite expression of the poet (Keats has "beechen wreath" [*Endymion*, i 159] and "beechen tree" [*Endymion*, iv 767]), the use of the adjective "some" is supremely artistic. It lends a vagueness or indefiniteness to the locale where the song of the bird is unrestricted by earthly inhibitions—the epithet "full-throated ease" signifies a freedom that may only be enjoyed outside the mortal dimensions of time and space. The vagueness of the locale is also quite commensurate with the transcendental experience that the poet would undergo.

The transcendental experience or OBE, however, does not come with a wish. The poet considers different means that would take him out of his physicality and unite him with the joyous world of the nightingale:

"O for a draught of vintage! that hath been
Cool'd a long age in the deep-delved earth,
Tasting of Flora and the country-green,
Dance, and Provencal song, and sunburnt mirth.
O for a beaker full of the warm South
Full of the true, the blushful Hippocrene."

The "O" in the beginning of the 1st and 5th line is a breathless utterance that shows the poet's intense desire to find some means to transport his poetic self to the bower of the nightingale. Keats' reference to wine and Flora may be traced back to the fact that the poet was toying with the idea that these two entities are infallible ingredients of joy. In a letter dated 1st May, 1819 and addressed to Fanny Keats, the poet wrote:

> "...—and please heaven, a little claret-wine cool out of a cellar a mile deep—...a strawberry bed to say your prayers to Flora...."[5]

The complex sensuous imagery, involving visual, auditory, olfactory and tactile sensations, suggests that the poet's psychic journey into the world of the nightingale is to be made by an intense gratification of the senses. The references to the Hippocrene, the fountain on Mount Helicon in Boeotia, sacred to the Muses, and to Provence, a place in Southern France where troubadours in the Middle Ages used to sing their love lyrics, acquire symbolic dimensions and take the poet a step nearer to his OBE. The poet is, as Leon Waldoff suggests,

> "...flying back through literary-historical and mythological regions of the mind (Provence and Mount Helicon) toward the midnight-dark and timeless region presided over by the Nightingale."[6]

Still, the poet is not completely ready for moving out of his physicality because of a particular deterrent that must be fought of before the poetic psyche can bask in the glory of an OBE. The deterrent comes from a particular virtue of the poet himself: his rationalism. Keats has enough common sense to give him an insight into human sufferings from which the world of the Nightingale is free:

"The weariness, the fever, and the fret
Here, where men sit and hear each other groan;
Where palsy shakes a few, sad, last grey hairs,
Where youth grows pale, and spectre-thin and dies;
Where but to think is full of sorrow
And leaden-eyed despairs;
Where Beauty cannot keep her lustrous eyes,
Or new Love pine at them beyond tomorrow."

Here is a catalogue of Keats' personal sufferings, as already noted in the first section of this paper. But, how can such a suffering consciousness create poetry of splendid aestheticism? The answer is found in one of the most quoted statements of T.S. Eliot:

> "Poetry...is not the expression of personality, but an escape from personality."[7]

The poet is not harping upon his personal grief. He is objectively looking at the suffering of humanity in general. It is due to his negative capability that Keats could, as it were, leap out of his own suffering psyche and view his sufferings with an air of detachment. F.R. Leavis points to the "prosaic matter of fact"[8] tone of the stanza. The tone, in fact, is caused by the objective manner in which Keats views the sufferings. Paul de

Man, commenting upon the poet's treatment of suffering, remarks:

> "Suffering...is...objectively perceived and so easily generalized into historical and universal pain that it rarely appears in subjective immediacy...his intense and altogether genuine concern for others serves, in a way, to shelter him from the self-knowledge he dreads".[9]

This detached and generalized view of human suffering produces a cathartic effect in the poet's consciousness and prepares him for a psychic flight into the world of the Nightingale.

Once personal sadness is generalized, the poetic psyche is ready to move out of the body and dissolve into the world of the Nightingale where Beauty, Joy and Immortality reside. This is a world that Keats had longed for and the sudden announcement, "Already with thee!", is an indication that the OBE has taken place, the poetic psyche has broken through physicality and is united with the Nightingale. The poetic psyche, unburdened of grief by the cathartic process, resonates with the ecstasy of the Bird's song. Once the resonance between the poet's psyche and the Bird's song takes place, the consciousness of the poet is catapulted to the Bird's immutable domain. The darkness of the Nightingale's bower—it is broad daylight outside!—makes the landscape uncertain and even the presence of the moon is conjectural. But there is no speculation about the joy that the poetic psyche feels. The Nightingale's bower with its:

> "White hawthorn, and the pastoral eglantine;
> Fast-fading violets cover'd up in leaves;
> And mid-May's eldest child
> The coming musk rose, full of dewy wine,
> The murmurous haunt of flies on summer eves"

is an idealized pastoral world resonating with the Bird's song.

The song of the Nightingale in that idealized ambience inspires a rich desire in the poetic psyche:

"Now more than ever seems it rich to die,
To cease upon the midnight with no pain,
While thou art pouring thy soul abroad
In such an ecstasy."

The first line of the quoted extract suggests that the desire for death has been a constant preoccupation with Keats. In a letter written to Fanny Brawne in July, 1819, Keats wrote:

> "I have two luxuries to brood over in my walks, your Loveliness and the hour of my death. O that I could have possession of them both in the same minute."[10]

Listening to the song of the Bird has intensified that desire in the poet. Helen Vendler rightly points that 'Ode to a Nightingale' is based on the profound desire to die.[11] But death, as Keats views it, is not a simple negation of life; it is a merger with a *higher reality*—a reality that is conceived by the poet's imagination as true and hence, that reality is a thing of Beauty. This equation between Beauty and Truth is set up by the famous line in 'Ode on a Grecian Urn': "Beauty is Truth, truth beauty." The *higher reality* in 'Ode to a Nightingale' is represented by the immortal and immutable world where the Nightingale resides. Keats' OBE makes it possible for his poetic psyche to become a part, however temporarily, of the Nightingale's immortal world.

Psychologically, as well as physiologically, it is impossible to exist in a state of consciousness that lies outside the body. Keats, with all his veracity, acknowledges the fact that the symbolic world of the Bird, characterized by immutability, will continue beyond his death. With this acknowledgement, the romance of death breaks down:

"Still wouldst thou sing, and I have ears in vain—
To thy high requiem become a sod."

"Ears" is a metaphor for hearing and hearing is a synecdoche for living. Physical death, naturally, negates all senses, including the auditory sense. The Bird will continue to sing even after the poet is beyond the graves—the "requiem," perhaps, will be for the poet—but the poet will not be able to enjoy the song of the bird.

Once this realization dawns on the poet, he immediately distances the Bird from his own self and implicitly contrasts his own mortality with the Bird's immortality:

"Thou wast not born for death, immortal Bird!
No hungry generations tread thee down;
Perhaps the self-same song that found a path
Through the sad heart of Ruth
The same that oft-times hath
Charm'd magic casements, opening on the foam
Of perilous seas, in faery lands forlorn."

The second person pronominal address "thou" shows that the poet no more identifies himself with the Bird that is "immortal". The voice of the Nightingale has traversed across the centuries, unalloyed and untainted, shedding healing drops of consolation on the stricken heart and

> "opening out sudden windows on the weird, untrodden [sic] regions of the soul, unbarring the magic casements which no other force in life is potent to unfold". [12]

The Nightingale is now viewed as a part of historical, biblical and literary tradition and is very different from the "forlorn" poet.

Keats finds himself in the final stanza of the poem, as he was in the beginning, sitting alone. He bids "adieu" to the Nightingale—this time the bird is not a symbol, but rather a real, mortal bird—as it leaves the orchard and comes to the rational conclusion:

"...the fancy cannot cheat so well
As she is famed to do, deceiving elf."

Though he sits all alone in the orchard under the plum trees, yet the impression of the OBE has not left his mind. He has not completely forgotten the fact that he, for a brief moment, had become a part of the Nightingale's bower. Of course, this thought is quite puzzling to the poet's consciousness as he finds himself in the ambience of reality. This bewilderment finds expression in the question that ends the poem:

"...do I wake or sleep?"

The question puts the validity of the fact, that Keats had undergone an OBE under the influence of the Nightingale's song, beyond doubt.

References

1. All Quotations from Keats' poetry are from *John Keats: The Complete Poems*. (Ed.) John Barnard. (3rd Edition), London: Penguin Classics, 1977.
2. Wikipedia, the free encyclopedia.htm
3. Susan J. Blackmore, *Beyond the Body: an Investigation of Out-of-Body Experiences*. London: Heinemann, 1982.
4. Charles Armitage Brown, *Life of John Keats*. (Eds.) Dorothy Hyde Bodurtha and Willard Bissell Pope. London: Oxford University Press, 1937.
5. 'Extracts from Keats' Letters', *Keats: Odes*. (Ed.) G.S. Fraser. Casebook Series, London: Macmillan, 1993, 30.
6. Leon Waldoff, 'Imagination and Growth in the Great Odes,' *Romanticism: A Critical Reader*. (Ed.) Duncan Wu. Oxford: Blackwell Publishers, 1995, 307.
7. T.S. Eliot, 'Tradition and the Individual Talent', *English Critical Texts*. (Ed). D.J. Enright & Ernst De Chickera, Oxford: O.U.P., 1962, 300.
8. F.R. Leavis, Keats' *English Critical Texts*. (Eds.) D.J. Enright & Ernst De Chickera, Oxford: O.U.P., 1962, 316.
9. Paul de Man, *The Selected Poetry of Keats*. (Ed.) Paul de Man, The Signet Classic Poetry Series, New York, 1966, xxix.
10. Quoted in *op. cit.* 6, 312.
11. Helen Vendler, The Odes of John Keats, Harvard: Harvard University Press, 1983.
12. Prof. Srikumar Banerjee, *Studies in the Poetry of Coleridge and Keats*, Calcutta: A.K. Mukherjee Publishers, 1965, p. 115.

12

Experience, Self-Realization and Artistic Vision: Stephen Dedalus in Joyce's *A Portrait*

Ernest L. Veyu

In his brilliant book, *Art as Experience*, John Dewey comments on the processes that make for the experience of the human being in general and the artist in particular. His opinion is that experience occurs continuously because the interaction of the living creature and the environmental conditions are involved in the very process of living. Life, he says, is no uniform uninterrupted march or flow. It is a thing of histories, each with its own inception and movement towards its close, each having its own particular rhythm of movement; each with its own unrepeated quality pervading it throughout (35-36). In line with this thought, we shall attempt to capture Stephen's experiences and their effect on his art as recorded in *A Portrait of the Artist as a Young Man*.

As aforesaid, it is the experience of the artist that leads him to self-realization and then to a formation of his artistic vision. The same holds true for Stephen Dedalus. Back at home from the beginning of awareness, Stephen realizes that home is ruled by threats. His father has an alarmingly hairy face and does not have a pleasant smell. In this beginning, as ever in the text, Stephen develops a bad opinion of his father. This marks the beginning of his undesired experience at home. He understands fatherhood as something which transcends the physical. To him, it is a "mystical estate, an apostolic succession" (Schutte 91). Seeing that Simon does not meet up with the expectations of Stephen, his question is, "Who and where is my father? With whom can I claim spiritual kinship? From whom can I claim understanding and protection?" (Smidt 81).

His mother, who in his infantile appreciation has a nicer smell than his father's, soon forces him into an apology for what he knows not to be wrong. For the child, what wrong is there in thinking, "When they were grown up, he was going to marry Eileen?" (*Portrait* 8). Catholic or protestant, his mother's grounds for demanding the apology, make no meaning to his infantile mind. Her insistent "O, Stephen will apologise" (*Portrait* 8), only breaches the two of them as is already the case with his father.

When later on, his mother is too much of a catholic for his liking, and wants to censor his changing ideas, the rift in their relationship increases. William Schutte points out that through his relation with his mother, his artistic role is undermined and he is left the dispirited husk of a creative artist (95). According to Hoffman, Hall and Schell, both parents fail in their role because they ought to contribute to the child's socialisation process by assuming the role of love providers and care givers; by serving as identification figures; by acting as active, often deliberate socialisation agents; by providing the bulk of the child's experiences; and by participating in the development of the child's self-concept (214).

Home for Stephen is not a place of love, and until he rejects it, he may not come to free expression in his art. Ralph Landau attests to this when he says that creativity is fragile, and the best of circumstances requires tender loving care (155). Stephen has a problem with his eyes, and wears lenses from early age. That already constitutes a problem for him. As if it is not enough, Dante, a relative of his, threatens him with, "the eagles will come and pull out his eyes" (*Portrait* 8). This threat is woven into some poetry so it sticks better on the sensitive mind of young Stephen. It settles it for him that the home is no resting-place. The constant, hot discussions and quarrels at home only make this notion more founded.

Stephen is ill at ease with the filth, squalor and the events in Dublin. This is seen in the passage below:

> His sensitive nature was still smarting under the lashes of an undivined and squalid way of life. His soul was still disquieted and cast down by the cold phenomenon of Dublin...every event and figure of which affected him intimately, disheartened him or allured and, whether alluring or disheartening, filled him always with unrest and bitter thoughts. (*Portrait* 78)

He falls sick when Wells shoulders him into a pit of scum. Generally, a thought of the slimy pit sends him ill. His home is not different from the general state of things. As Litz describes it, after a meal the smell of fried herrings fills the kitchen, the bare table is strewn with greasy plates onto which lie glutinous fish bones and crusts are stuck by a congealing white sauce. Clammy knives and forks are abandoned here and there. A big soot-coated kettle which has been drained of the last dregs of shell cocoa lies in the midst, *et cetera* (133-34).

Mr. Simon Dedalus is a spendthrift, flirt and given to vanity. At home these habits get the family from one state of poverty to another, and they have to move houses time and again, each time to a less comfortable one. To make ends meet, Mr. Simon takes Stephen along a trip to sell the family property. But on the evening of the day the property is sold, Stephen follows his father about the city from bar to bar. His father, a kind of the prodigal son, begins to squander the money with the sellers in the market, the barmen and barmaids, and gives some to the beggars who importune him for a gift (*Portrait* 93). To young Stephen, this is an ordeal to bear.

At Newcombe's coffee-house, Mr. Dedalus' cup rattles noisily against the saucer, and Stephen tries to cover the shameful sign of his father's drinking-bout by moving his chair and coughing. One humiliation succeeds another, for example, the false smiles of the market sellers, the curvettings and oglings of the barmaids with whom his father flirts, the compliments and encouraging words of his father's friends.

This to a level-headed and thinking boy who does not bother about such nonsense is nauseating. His shame grows when he is told, "Your father was the boldest flirt in the city of Cork in his day. Do you know that?" (*Portrait* 94). A little later on, he too is to spend his lust on whores.

Any allusion made to Stephen's father by a fellow or by a master puts his calm to rout in a moment. His own description of his father is that he is: A medical student, an oarsman, a tenor, an amateur actor, a shouting politician, a small landlord, a small investor, a drinker, a good fellow, a story-teller, somebody's secretary, something in a distillery, a bankrupt and at present a praiser of his own past (*Portrait* 241). With this state of things at home, he is affected as follows: "his childhood was dead or lost and with it his soul incapable of simple joys, and he was drifting amid life like the barren shell of the moon" (*Portrait* 94).

A Portrait of the Artist as a Young Man may actually be described as growing in Catholic Ireland. There is the protestant Church, but Catholicism, if anything, is the state religion. Stephen grows up under the influence of this religion back at home and in school. All along, he attends Jesuit schools and for some time is expected to join the order and train to become a priest.

In school, he is taught to attend church, pray and to lead a God-fearing life. Most of it is indoctrination since he does not really grasp the meaning of the issues: "He could think only of God. God was God's name just as his name was Stephen" (*Portrait* 16).

He is unsettled as to who is right about the Virgin Mary controversy—the Catholics or the Protestants? He remembers that the protestants make fun of the litany of the Blessed Virgin; "Tower of Ivory. House of Gold! How could a woman be a tower of ivory or a house of gold? Who was right then?" (*Portrait* 35).

In school he receives an unjust punishment from father Dolan, the Prefect of Studies, who calls him a lazy, idle, little loafer. He remarks that the punishment is unfair and cruel because the doctor has told him not to read without glasses and he has written home to his father to send him a new pair of glasses. In addition to all this, Father Arnall has instructed that he should not study till the new glasses came. He is totally at odds with having been called a schemer before the class and to be pandied when he is a good student by all standards and the leader of the Yorkists (*Portrait* 94).

This is a crime against him from a man of the church and this sets a number of questions in his mind: How is he to ever trust the church and its men if they can be so cruel and unjust? How comes Father Dolan does not take into consideration the fact that he is a serious student and the leader of the Yorkists? The prefect of studies says the story of breaking his glasses is all a trick. How does he know that it is a trick? (*Portrait* 52). The more he thinks along these lines, the faster he comes to conclude that the church and its men are unjust and cruel. Furthermore, they cannot be trusted for patient investigation unto the truth.

It is the same men of the church who have betrayed Parnell. There has been a meddling of the church with politics, making the house of God into a polling-booth. Mr. Casey says, "We go to the house of God, in all humility to pray to our Maker and not to hear election addresses" (*Portrait* 31). But then we find that church and state are indivisible, since the priests find it their duty in warning the people, and in directing their flock in other issues as now in politics.

His relationship with the church along time and experience is fitting with Joyce's, who at first accepted Roman Catholicism as the fish accepts the ocean, a world to which he had been born and which was his natural element. But as time passed and increasing capabilities of ratiocination toughened his mind, he began to view the church in a different light. Furthermore, the sense of sin, of guilt, of worldly defilement and the cleansing power of absolution became painfully vivid to his adolescent nature, especially when he reached the age of puberty (Gorman 47).

Stephen remembers the shouts at the Christmas party at home and Mr. Casey's words: "No God for Ireland. We have had too much God for Ireland. Away with God.... Away with

God I say" (*Portrait* 32). He finally becomes something of a heretic. In a composition which he writes in class, the teacher notices traces of heresy, which Stephen, however, explains away by a play of words.

C.H. Peake comments on the impact of the hot Christmas Party discussions on Stephen as follows:

> Stephen is a bewildered onlooker in a scene of violent political and religious passion and, apart from occasional passages expressing his bewilderment, there will be little point tracing what is going on in his head. It is the total image of the scene which fills him with terror: he asks himself, "who was right then"?, but he has no means of knowing. What shocks him is the destruction by violent passions of the adult world, the family circle, and the happy occasion to which he had looked forward. It is an entire experience, a dramatic scene which plunges directly into his imagination without passing through the understanding. (104)

Stephen is inclined to love Parnell who is not loved by the clergy. Since the clergy represents the church, this inevitably calls for a choice, however mild, from the start. He even writes a paper in relation to the treatment Parnell has received. He hates foreign rule as well. But as he grows up, the compelling artistic urge takes so much of him that he does not pursue his political opinions. The family, the church and the state all frustrate his expectations. By personality and disposition he is an artist, but he discovers that none of these institutions is encouraging to his views. He soon comes to terms with himself and with his vision.

In a quest for self-knowledge, he goes into his mother's bedroom and looks at his face for a long time in the mirror of her dressing-table (*Portrait* 71). Earlier on in school Stephen makes his first attempts at situating himself within the cosmos. His first problem is coming to terms with his name, and accepting it. It is evident to him that it is not a common name; sounds strange, and his friends say so. The name alone becomes an epiphany as it leads him to an artistic end, a creative one, like Dedalus the old artificer. Accepting the name is tantamount to accepting a call and a career. When at last he accepts it, he has accepted himself and his role as artist.

There is another side to accepting the name Stephen; it is accepting the possibility of dying for his convictions. The historical Stephen dies as a martyr. He too may suffer and give his life for his faith in art. The historic Stephen sees heaven open and the Son of man standing at the right hand of God the Father. It is possible that he receives his vision of art supernaturally too.

Perhaps not pleasurable to him, but Dedalus is also his father's name. Bearing it is identification with Simon. It is an acknowledgement of Simon's blood that runs in his veins, and the possibility of becoming like him. This he does not want, denies son-ship to Simon, and goes in search of a father.

In his determined aim to situate himself in the cosmos, he spells out the following:

> Stephen Dedalus
> Class of elements
> Clongowes Wood College
> Sallins
> County Kildare
> Ireland
> Europe
> The world
> The universe.

He also comes to terms with the fact that he is only in the class of elements. He knows very little. He lacks experience and is baffled by many unanswered questions. Taking his little knowledge into account, he speaks little, listens and reads much. He can say nothing in the family Christmas party because he has nothing to say. Clongowes Wood is also a place of conflict for years before the college is ever built. Historically:

> Clongowes Wood College (Silva de Clongow) was originally a medieval castle built on the alluvial plain about a mile north of Clane near Sallins in County Kildare.... It was held for generations by the great

> territorial family of the Eustaces and its importance as a stronghold can only be realised if it is understood that it was one of the outposts of the Pale (a double ditch of six feet high above ground at one side or part which mireth next to Irishmen. (Gorman 23)

Identification with Clongowes is not particularly disturbing him at this time. But it is a place of fierce conflicts and stronghold for the subjugation of the Irish people. Its people are accustomed to conflict and the like. The picture at the Christmas party spells a Clongowes temperament. Consciously or not, Stephen picks this temperament and braves it through, against the odds, to pave his fated way in art.

In an attempt at self-realization, Stephen considers a new set of grounds wherein to situate himself. He says:

> Stephen Dedalus is my name,
> Ireland is my nation.
> Clongowes is my dwellingplace
> And heaven my expectation. (*Portrait* 16)

This is an attempt to situate himself within the confines of time and hopes for the future, based on his Catholic religion. If he must get to heaven, he must as well stick to the rules. He tries to, but finds he cannot. When he throws off his Roman Catholicism he does it consciously, for there was a time he consciously was a part of it.

As he goes with his father to sell the family property, he resituates himself again as follows: I am Stephen Dedalus. I am walking beside my father whose name is Simon Dedalus. We are in Cork, in Ireland. Cork is a city. Our room is in the Victoria Hotel. Victoria and Stephen and Simon. Simon and Stephen and Victoria. Names (*Portrait* 92).

When he is sick in school, he does not write to his father but writes to his mother. His letter, whether he sends it or not reads:

> Dear Mother,
>
> I am sick. I want to go home. Please come and take me home. I am in the infirmary.
>
> Your fond son,
> Stephen

He knows where he stands according to his needs and which of his parents to relate to, at what time. The circumstances under which he writes this letter also bring us to see where Stephen places himself in relation to eternity at this time. He is sure that if he should die he goes to heaven, with six angels at his back, two to sing, two to pray and two to carry his soul away.

These are his childhood imaginations, which he discards as he grows up. Death and dying no longer appear to him with such glory later on in the text. He is perhaps already affected by the general situation wherein there is "the loss of religious certitude, of belief in an outer life, in heaven or hell, and the consciousness of an immutable void beyond life, the nothingness of death" (Quentin Bell 215).

More than ever before, he has to come to terms with his sensual needs, seeing that they are as part of him as his brain. Pressured against his moral upbringing, he goes out to satisfy his sexual needs. It is forbidden to do this, but it is being true to his body system. He knows only two kinds of women, the virgin and whore. The virgin is not to be touched since, with the picture of the Holy Virgin Mary in his head, he dares not defile virginity. Like Joyce he goes out for the whore: "Prostitutes gave Joyce all his early sexual experience. So far as we know, he had no sexual experience of any kind with girls who were not prostitutes, until Nora" (O'Bien 18).

Stephen does not come to terms with his artistic vision until he is in the university. He knows he has studied and read enough to stand the intellectual frame of his day. Anthony Burgess notes that until he reaches university age, he says little, in which case the talk is mostly left to his parents, teachers and school mates. But when he has achieved the stage of free flight, he is almost unnaturally eloquent (Here Comes 20).

He also does not come to his vision until he has waved aside all the other voices that call him to other concerns, which are not art or art-related. There are the demands of his father urging him to be a gentleman and of his masters urging him to be a good catholic above all things. There is also another voice urging him to be strong and manly and healthy.

When the movement toward national revival begins to be felt in college, he hears another voice bidding him to be true to his country and help to raise up its fallen language and tradition. The world around him expects that he should raise up his father's fallen state by his labours. As a leading student and secretary in the gymnasium, his school comrades want him to be a decent fellow, to shield others from blame or to beg them off and to do his best to get free days for the school (*Portrait* 84). Joyce tells us that these other voices sound hollow to Stephen, and that he gives them an ear only for a time. He is happy only when he is far from them, beyond their call.

Having come to experience and self-realization, Stephen can now establish his artistic vision. Along the pathway of his vision, we meet him in the following mood: "A vague dissatisfaction grew up within him as he looked on the quays and on the river and on the lowering skies" (*Portrait* 66). There is the creative urge which presses hard on him and he must define it so that he sets out on a clear path. He wants to meet in the real world the unsubstantial image, which his soul so constantly beholds. He does not know where to seek it or how, but a premonition, which leads him on, tells him that this image would, without any overt act of his, encounter him. They would meet quietly as if they had known each other and had made their tryst, perhaps at one of the gates or in some more secret place (*Portrait* 65).

The stirrings of his vision are a thing of the soul; emotions, mind, volition. He feels it creep within him, sometimes making him moody, sometimes excited and elevated. At this juncture, he cannot yet give a tangible mental grasp to it. By premonition, this time a faculty of the spirit, he knows that artistic vision is personal and so he will be alone when he meets it. The other elements necessary for the meeting of his vision are darkness and silence. This leaves the impression that it is going to be something of a sacred moment.

The encounter with his vision is anticipated to be a moment of transfiguration and supreme tenderness in which he would be transfigured.[1] He imagines that he would fade to something impalpable under her [vision] eyes, then in a moment he would be transfigured. Vision here is given a female character, perhaps for the tenderness he imagines for the encounter. We also know that the thought of an idealized female has always led him to a moment of artistic creation. In his mind, a symbolic association between art and sex is established and as Levin says, it helps him to decide his later conflict between art and religion (Levin 20-21).

The encounter, he expects, should create an invigorating, emboldening and experiential effect: "Weakness and timidity and inexperience would fall from him" (*Portrait* 65). For the time being, his intuition is sharper than his mind and by it he receives a foreknowledge of the future, all of which are private and remote from the humanity around him. Joyce says:

> A tender premonition touched him of the tryst he had then looked forward to and, in spite of the horrible reality which lay between his hope of then and now, of the holy encounter he had then imagined at which weakness and timidity and inexperience were to fall from him. (*Portrait* 99)

Now that he is very close to his vision becoming palpable, "nothing moved him or spoke to him from the real world unless he heard in it an echo of the infuriated cries within him" (*Portrait* 92). He would wonder away to remote places and for company prefer phantasmal comrades. When not with these, he prefers the company of subversive writers. All leisure which his school life leaves him is spent in the company of these writers whose gibes and violence of speech set up ferment in his brain before they pass out in his crude writings (*Portrait* 78).

The more he tries his hand at writing, the more the word and the vision caper before his eyes. As these prance before him he is shocked to find in the outer world a trace of what he has up to then deemed a brutish and individual malady of his own mind. His recent monstrous reveries come thronging into his memory. They spring up before him, suddenly and furiously, out of mere words (*Portrait* 90).

The vision is getting more real, more externalised and Stephen begins to catch a mental glimpse of what hitherto is only felt: "The verse passed from his lips and the inarticulate cries and the unspoken brutal words rushed forth from his brain to force a passage" (*Portrait* 99). Furthermore:

> He had soon given in to them and allowed them to sweep across and abase his intellect, wondering always where they came from, from what den of monstrous images, and always weak and humble towards others, restless and sickened of himself when they had swept over him. (*Portrait* 90)

Going to the university opens to him a new intellectual sphere and the emancipation needed to accommodate his vision. Free from the direct censorious eye of the priests and their religious expectations for him, free from being prefect of Our Blessed Lady's Sodality, Joyce tells us: "University! So he had passed beyond the challenge of the sentries who had stood as guardians of his boyhood and had sought to keep him among them that he might be subject to them and serve their ends" (*Portrait* 165).

Under the pull of the end he is born to serve, he escapes from the church. Since his vision is not earthly, he begins to hear musical voices in the direction of his calling. The music leaps, "upwards a tone and downwards a diminished fourth, upwards a tone, and downwards a major third, like triple branching flames leaping fitfully" (*Portrait* 165).

He calls the musical voices he hears an elfin prelude, endless and formless. He seems to hear wild creatures racing from under the boughs and the grasses. Their feet, like the feet of hares and rabbits, of harts and hinds and antelopes passing in pattering tumult over his mind. Furthermore, he hears sounds like the sound of rain tapping upon the leaves.

After these mysterious musical voices and passing creatures, he immediately thinks of Newman, and a line from him. Soon, the musical voices move from without to being heard inside of him. He hears a confused music within him as of memories and names which he is almost conscious of but cannot capture even for an instant. From the confused music, "there fell always one long drawn calling note, piercing like a star the dusk of silence. Again! Again! Again! A voice from beyond the world was calling—hello, Stephanos!" (*Portrait* 167).

Premonitions of his free flight appear to him in the form of moving clouds:

> He raised his eyes towards the slowdrifting clouds, dappled and seaborne. They were voyaging across the deserts of the sky, a host of nomads on the march, voyaging high over Ireland, westward bound. The Europe they had come from lay down there beyond the Irish sea, Europe of strange tongues and valleyed and woodbegirt and citadelled and of entrenched and marshalled races. (*Portrait* 165)

More than ever before, his strange name is pronouncedly prophetic. This comes out more vividly in the passage that follows:

> Now, at the name of the fabulous artificer, he seemed to hear the noise of fabulous waves and to see a winged form flying above the waves and slowly climbing the air...a hawklike man flying sunward across the sea, a prophecy of the end he had been born to serve and had been following through the mists of childhood and boyhood, a symbol of the artist forging anew in his workshop out of the sluggish matter of the earth a new soaring imperishable being? (*Portrait* 169)

A full identification with the old artificer produces an experience of transcendence, an astral transportation, a conversion in him. Richard Taylor in *Understanding the Elements of Literature*, points out that the act of artistic creation is the most highly priced of all human activities, and that it is directly influenced and inspired by the supernatural which speaks through the imagination of the artist (30). In line with this thinking, we are told of a spirit that passes through Stephen's limbs, moves him to ecstasy and keeps his soul in flight:

> His soul was soaring in an air beyond the world and the body he knew was purified in a breath and delivered of incertitude and made radiant and commingled with the element of the spirit. An ecstasy of flight made radiant his eyes and wild his breath and tremulous and wild and radiant his windswept limbs. (*Portrait* 169)

With this experience, he is born again into artistic adulthood. The boyhood experience he has metamorphosed out of is spurned. Henceforth, he creates proudly out of the freedom and power of his soul like the mature artist, with a new wild life singing in his veins. The experience has imparted to him a great sense of the beautiful, and heightened his powers of apprehension and appreciation. The wading girl, almost an apparition, is seen with an artistic keenness hitherto unknown to him. In the vision of the wading girl, he sees a girl standing in midstream, alone and still, gazing out to sea. To him she seems like one whom magic has changed into the likeness of a strange and beautiful seabird. Her long slender bare legs look as delicate as those of a crane. Her thighs, full and soft-hued as ivory, are bared almost to the hips where the white fringes of her drawers are like feathers of soft white down. Her slate-blue skirts are kilted around her waist and dovetailed behind her. Her bosom looks to him soft and slight, like the breast of some dark-plumaged dove. But her long fair hair is girlish and her face carries with it the wonder of mortal beauty (*Portrait* 171).

The vision of the image of this girl passes into his soul for ever with no word breaking the holy silence of his ecstasy, as Joyce calls it. Furthermore:

> Her eyes had called him and his soul had leaped at the call. To live, to err, to fall, to triumph, to recreate life out of life! A wild angel had appeared to him, an angel of mortal youth and beauty, an envoy from the fair courts of life, to throw open before him in an instant of ecstasy the gates of all the ways of error and glory. (*Portrait* 172)

A sense of the aesthetic is born, and hence his aesthetic theory. He begins to forge out an aesthetic theory for himself. He feels that the spirit of beauty has folded him round like a mantle. With the priest in a philosophical conversation, they both discover that there is an art in the lighting of a fire. They discover that art falls in one of two groups; the useful arts and the liberal arts. Lighting a fire is a useful art, they agree. In the lighting of a fire, the object of the artist remains the creation of the beautiful (*Portrait* 185).

Stephen further discovers that there exists another form of art which he calls the improper arts, because they excite a kinetic feeling, for example, desire and loathing. He finds that the pornographic or didactic are improper arts because they excite a kinetic emotion. On the other hand, he says, "Beauty expressed by an artist cannot awaken in us an emotion which is kinetic or a sensation which is purely physical" (*Portrait* 185). Rather, "it awakens, or ought to awaken, or induces, or ought to induce, an esthetic stasis, an ideal pity or an ideal terror, a stasis called forth, prolonged" (*Portrait* 206).

Stephen is greatly influenced by Aquinas and quotes him for most of the time. His own aesthetic theory can be called applied Aquinas. According to Aquinas, when the apprehension pleases, then the thing is beautiful. But what is beautiful to one may not be to another. To this Stephen says that though the same object may not be beautiful to all people, all people who admire a beautiful object find in it certain relations which satisfy and coincide with the stages of all aesthetic apprehension.

According to Stephen, "art is the human disposition of sensible or intelligible matter for an esthetic end" (*Portrait* 207). The artist tries to "express from the gross earth, or what it brings forth, from sound and shape and colour which are the prison gates of our soul, an image of the beauty we have come to understand—that is art" (*Portrait* 207).

This said, he distinguishes three art forms; another classification different from what he comes to with the priest. There are the lyrical form, the epical form and the dramatic form of art. In the lyrical form, the artist presents his image in immediate relation to himself. In the epic form he presents it in relation to himself and to others, whereas he presents his image in immediate relation to others in the dramatic form of art.

The dramatic form of art is life purified and projected from human imagination. In this form, the artist's personality refines itself out of existence and impersonalises itself. The artist of this form, like the God of creation, remains within or behind or beyond or above his handiwork, invisible, refined out of existence, indifferent, paring his fingernails (*Portrait* 215).

When he has gone through his conversion experience into an artist, has worked out his aesthetic theory and set on composing according to his theory, he sees himself as "a priest of eternal imagination, transmuting the daily bread of existence to the radiant body of everliving life" (*Portrait* 221).

Note

1. He must be likening this to the bliss of the experience Peter, James and John have with Jesus in the Mountain of Transfiguration. But whereas they are many, in his turn, he is alone.

Works Cited

Bell, Quentin. *Virginia Woolf: A Biography*. New York: Harcourt Brace Jovanovich, 1972.

Burgess, Anthony. "Here Comes Everybody: An Introduction to James Joyce for the Ordinary Reader." London: Faber and Faber, 1965.

Dewey, John. *Art As Experience*. New York: Capricorn Books, 1958.

Gorman, Herbert. *James Joyce*. New York: Rinehart and Company Inc., 1948.

Hoffman, Scott Paris, Elizabeth Hall, and Robert Schell. *Developmental Psychology Today*. Auckland Bogota: McGraw Hill Inc., 1988.

Levin, Harry. *James Joyce: A Critical Introduction*. New York: New Directions, 1960.

Litz, Walton A. "Lawrence, Pound, and Early Modernism." *D.H. Lawrence: A Centenary Consideration*. Eds. Peter Balbert and Phillip L. Marcus. Ithaca: Cornell University Press, 1985, 15-28.

O'Bien, Darcy. "Some Psychological Determinants of Joyce's View of Love and Sex." New Light on Joyce from the Dublin Symposium. Ed. Fritz Senn. Bloomington: Indiana Uni. Press, 1972, 15- 27.

Peake, C.H. *James Joyce: The Citizen and the Artist*. London: Edward Arnold, 1977.

Plekhanov, G. *Art and Social Life*. London: Lawrence and Wishart, 1953.

Schutte, William. *M. Joyce and Shakespeare: A Study in Ulysses*, New Haven: Yale University Press, 1957.

Smidt, Kristian. *James Joyce and the Cultic Use of Fiction*, Oslo: Oslo University Press, 1959.

Taylor, Richard. *Understanding the Elements of Literature*. London: Macmillan Press Ltd., 1981.

13

As You Like It, in Amazing Location

Manju Dutta Gupta

As in other comedies of Shakespeare, the sense of place is more important in *As You Like It* than the sense of time. The play has the most multiple focuses. The Forest of Arden is a place of repose which Shakespeare chose after the dire period of his history plays.[1]

When we approach the question of location in *As You Like It*, the query of time cannot, however, be ignored. Time is concentrated and expanded in *Othello*, and that the dramatist played trick on his audience in the play, is evident to any critic, who has reflected on the action of the play. In *As You Like It*, seasonal references, such as, day, age, harvest, hour, tomorrow, twelve, month, year, yesterday and so on suggest the subject of time which runs all through the play.

In Rosalind's first meeting with Orlando in the Forest of Arden, Rosalind takes 'time' for her topic—A fragment of the dialogue between Rosalind and Orlando may be presented:

> **Rosalind:** I pray you, what is't o'clock?
> **Orlando:** You should ask me what time o' day; there's no clock in forest.
> **Rosalind:** Then there is no lover in the forest.
>
> (Act III, Sc II)

Rosalind's speech works. Orlando asks where she lives and gives her a chance to find a way into a second subject, i.e. 'courtship' and that leads to love and to the sickness of love. With a little help from Orlando, Rosalind gets to her overwhelming subject, 'Orlando'.

Was *As You Like It*, written in haste? In the exposition scene, Orlando gives Adam a long account of events. By the use of coincidence, Shakespeare has wisely made it easier to get the plot moving. While narrating the incident of Duke Senior's banishment, Charles admits this as 'old news'. Celia expresses her feeling, when she says that she was too young to value Rosalind when her father was banished, but now she knew her. (I-III). This is clear hint from the dramatist that Duke Senior with his co-mates and brothers was spending considerable time in exile. Jacques was merry to meet a motley fool in the Forest (III-IV). Duke Senior took interest in the fool. Touchstone was a young courtier in Duke Frederick's court. That is why Duke Senior came to know him in the Forest. These are meagre points but are able to contribute to the understanding of the action, as it moves from court to forest, and withdrawing again to the court life. Time is like a thread tying up the episodes towards the finale.

Orlando's first meeting with Duke Senior in Act II-VII is marked by his suggestive comments. He affirms that Duke Senior with his companions was neglecting the creeping hours of time under the shade of 'melancholy boughs'. Why do the boughs appear melancholy to Orlando? Now he was far from Oliver's malice. Of course, his future was uncertain and that strain might have caused sadness when Orlando first reached the Forest of Arden.

The sense of place is important in *As You Like It*, and a comparison with *A Midsummer Night's Dream* and *The Tempest* comes to our mind. In all these comedies, discovery of truth is made through errors and mistakes. As a story of flowers and young lovers and dreams, *A Midsummer Night's Dream* is unique as a play. Everyone is moonstruck in the moonlit wood, everyone is touched by magic. It is not merely the fairies magic but magic of Shakespeare over words which enchants all. There were troubles in the meantime. But at midnight, which is 'almost fairy time'. The whole household goes to bed, leaving Puck and the fairies to place a blessing on three bridal couples and they encircled the play with a garland of poetry as the Dream ends. *The Tempest* as a story of magic and monster, set in a distant sea is enchanting. The play tells of what happened in the island when beauty by nonsense and innocence and terror clashed for a time and then lulled into a final peace. As in a comedy, blissful and delighted, location is rewarding, a tragedy would demand a strange situation, an alarming arrangement in the plot so as to bring about the doom.

In *Othello*, Act II begins with a storm which Shakespeare did not find in the source. The storm takes on undreamed of meanings. The Turks were drowned in the storm. The Venetians were apparently safe, but its tumult swept away the most beloved pair on earth. In Act II, III, Iago in order to serve his monstrous design gets Cassio drunk, knowing well that Cassio had unhappy brains for drinking. Cassio's unwillingness to drink was foregone, for three lads were invited by Iago to drink to the health of the black Othello, the Governor of Cyprus. The three gallants, with swelling spirits (names not mentioned) form an element of menace in the play. The situation is invested with dread and mystery: Three unknown men and a door form an image of an undefined fear. This moment of unknown fear has been produced by the utmost economy of words.

As far as the background of Shakespeare's plays is concerned, the reader's best guide is his imagination. The atmosphere of willing make believe, made it possible for Shakespeare to conquer time and space in his plays. Shakespeare wrote the setting into the lines. At this point we may quote a few lines from Allardyce Nicoll's *British Drama*, where he has given an elaborate discussion of Elizabethan Theatre. He writes: "The main stage was bare, backed by a facade broken by two or more doors, through which the actors made their entrances and exits. In general, no attempt was made to localize the place of the action by means of scenery...a small tree could, if necessary, stand for a forest...while the carrying on of a flaring torch might suggest in the warmth of a June sun the darkness of night."[2]

The naturalistic mode of writing a play in the nineteenth century required that the properties and furnishing were as exact as possible on the stage. When Andre Antoine, the practical leader of Naturalism in France produced *Old Heidelberg*, he bought the interior of a student's from Heidelberg and transferred it to the stage. The stage was overloaded and such a restless impression was made that one had to make an effort to forget the reality of the scene in order to grasp the truth of the play. In this context, Donald Clive Stuart's comment may be cited. His opinion is: "There is no valid objection to a photographic reproduction of environment on the stage, provided it expresses the inner spirit of the play as well as the outward form of the place."[3] The naturalists' methods and results were not always successful. It is interesting to note that when censorship forbade the production of Tolstoy's *Power of Darkness* (1886) on the Russian stage, Antoine produced it in 1888 with success in Paris. The play was destined to be one of the important influences in to the revolution of dramatic art.

Samuel Beckett's *Breath* takes few seconds in faint light on the stage, littered with miscellaneous rubbish, brief cry could be heard. Silence prevails for few seconds. Cry recorded, important that two cries are identical, switching on and off, strictly synchronized light and breath. Breath amplified in recording.

In Samuel Beckett's "*Not I*", the stage is in darkness but for the Mouth. Some powerful images in *Waiting for Godot* prompt serious thought. In the opening act, the bare tree, perhaps a 'willow' and its sudden sprouting with leaves is a mysterious sign. The tree on the scenery remains as elusive as ever. With the awareness of life's absurdity, it is intensely felt, that Nature shares in the problematical experiences of life.

U.K. premiere presented Arnold Wesker's *Love Letters on Blue Paper* by the National Theatre on its Cottesloe stage on 15 February 1978, directed by Arnold Wesker. At the dramatist's wish, all Sonia's Letters were recorded and put through speakers around the auditorium to give the effect of Sonia's voice speaking gently to each member of the audience. A composite set was on the stage. Some partitioned rooms were set side by side. Sonia walks into the kitchen, fills her kettle in the sink (sound of water could heard): She puts the kettle on the gas. Her tired gait is noticed. She takes clothes from the washing machine and hangs dazzling white sheets and pillow slip on clothes-line in the garden adjacent to the rooms. This realism, however, was no restraint in accepting the most profound, essential and the poetry of the play.

It would not be out of place, to give a brief account of a British production of *As You Like It* some time in the winter of 1961-62 in Calcutta at National Library campus. The play was staged on the green lawn of the library. The players acted with a huge trunk of a tree in the background. No stage was built on the green lawn. There were no curtains and no doors for the players to enter and exit. Huge spotlights were used to light the performing area. Characters appeared from the surrounding darkness and perhaps they used the cottages on the fringe of the campus of the library as their green rooms. The two-storied auditorium built of bamboo was a novel structure. People without tickets enjoyed the play by peeping through the bamboos. There was an Indian actor in the cast. Audrey rarely stood still on the ground, she seemed to be restless all the time. Plump, rosy-cheeked, simple Audrey's gestural language gave delightful reading to the text and reinforced the other texts that constructed the play in performance. In fact, the codified language of theater came to life in Audrey's role.

In *As You Like It* appeared, a courageous younger brother misused by an elder brother, a usurping younger brother misused the daughter of an exiled elder brother. Even a pre-critical reader would not fail to apprehend the vicious impulse of power-loving people in life.

A more peaceful scene however, lay outside the walls of the usurper's troubled city. In a forest as sylvan as Oberon's, the banished Duke as weary as Henry VI found his fortune in misfortune:

> Now, my co-mates and brothers in exile,
> Hath not old custom made this life more sweet.
> Than that of painted pomp? (II.1.1-3)

Henry VI in disguise was captured by two keepers in a forest in the north of England and was sent to London and imprisonment,—he lamented the world of grief and woe:

> O God! methinks it were a happy life
> To be no better than a homely swain,
> To sit upon a hill as I do now.
> To carve out dials quaintly, point by point. (II.V.22-25)

To the Forest of Arden, unknown to one another, drifted, like the lover's of the *A Midsummer Night's Dream*, Orlando and Rosalind. Like the Forest of Oberon, the Forest of Arden soon heard the murmur of a lonely lover:

Orlando: O Rosalind! These trees shall be my books,
And in their barks my thoughts I'll, character,
That every eye which in this forest looks,
Shall see thy virtue witness'd everywhere.
Run, run, Orlando: carve on every tree
The fair, the chaste and unexpressive she.

(III.II.5-10)

In response, the trees of the forest whisper the sighs of Rosalind extolled in these lines:

> O coz, coz, my pretty little coz, that thou didst know how many fathoms deep I am in love! But it cannot be sounded. My affection hath an unknown bottom, like the Bay of Portugal.

(IV-1.195-98)

In this quiet woodland, a sylvan lover entreats a less devoted mistress:

> Silvius: Sweet Phebe do not scorn me, do not.
> Phebe, say that you love me not, but say not so in bitterness.

(III.VI. 1-3)

The pangs of these lovers might have been appeased by the art of an Oberon. Luckily known to Orlando was a boy of the forest who had been tutored by his uncle who was a magician. The boy seemed to be a spirit from fairy land destined to order the affairs of the forest. The boyish looking elf turned out, however, to be something other than he appeared.

Disguise is thoroughly in keeping with twin themes of dissimulation and deception in Shakespeare's plays. A situation in which a boy actor impersonates a woman, who pretends to be a boy, creates its own problems of credibility. The contrast between mind and face was a moral commonplace at Shakespeare's time. The powerful motif of inner reality against outward appearance is a characteristic feature in Shakespeare's plays. This important thread runs through *As You Like It.* Known to Celia by the name of Rosalind, she continued to conceal herself to put things right till the end. To Phebe, she pretended to be the youth she was not, to Orlando to be the girl she was, and at last concocted plans to unite three pairs of true lovers like a fairy king.

The Forest is not a fairy land, for there is struggle for existence. Duke Senior talks of killing a venison, but was disturbed with the thought of killing native burghers in their own confines. Jacques pierced through the country, city, court and of their life in the forest, swearing that they were mere usurpers, tyrants. The killing of a deer is a simple image but it can form part in a larger pattern of life.

A pattern of increasing parallels and contrast between the Forest and The Court develops in *As You Like It.* In the play speculation about nature, human nature and human destiny intensifies into a passionate dialectic.

A highly modern dramatic approach can be traced in *A Midsummer Night's Dream*, Act IV-I. Five mortals (in the last thirty lines of the scene) spent the night in the wood under the spell of Oberon and Puck. The mortals speak of their experience, as if it had been a dream. Which is dream and which is real ever fascinated Shakespeare. The point of my observation is that Bottom as an audience was able to distinguish between dream and reality. His waking experience has estranged him from his trance-like state. Audience questions the truth of what it has seen and thus sharpens the rational level of the play.

The reader and the spectator enjoy the luxury of finding Shakespeare's play responding to modern values and modern critical method. To Brecht, an actor's task was to put himself 'at a distance' from the character he was portraying in order to arouse an enquiring response in the theatre-spectator. In the play, Touchstone is never emotionally involved in any circumstance. Touchstone is critique of country and court alike. Enjoying the liberty of a court fool, he could express his views with sceptical humour and that he alienated himself from his surroundings made him a distinct character.

To my mind, the last word on Touchstone cannot be said. It is true, we would not have known a delicate side in Touchstone's character unless we heard from Celia. "He'll go along o'er the wide world with me" (1.111.135). Celia rightly thought that Touchstone's presence was needed in the Forest of Arden, an unknown locality fraught with dangers for the princesses. Celia-Touchstone relationship did not develop as a theme in the play, for, as for as Shakespeare and most of his contemporaries were concerned, this relationship could not have developed in the natural order of things. But a glance cast on the hidden romantic mood of Touchstone could be of delight to modern reader/spectator.

That Rosalind was confined and weakened in the court was clear from her speech when she told Orlando, while giving him a chain from her neck:

> Gentleman, wear this for me; one out of suits with fortune,
> That could give more but that her hand lacks means.
>
> (1.11.235-237)

In this state, Rosalind was wary in choosing her language to communicate. In the early part of the play, Rosalind was once impatient with Celia for she asked her to be merry. In few words, she expressed her unhappiness. To learn to remember any extraordinary pleasure, she should first forget her banished father.

A victim of patriarchal mode, when the word of basis banishment was imposed on Rosalind, she was dignified in her speech with Duke Frederick, but insisted on knowing the nature of her fault. It is likely, anxiety was a primary ontological feeling with Rosalind in the court. She needed freedom which she received in the Forest of Arden. Freedom is prominent in Kierkegaard, the greatest of the existentialists. To him, to exist and to be free are almost synonymous expressions. Freedom which is metaphysical and even mystical in the language of philosophers was prime with Rosalind who found immense joy in the forest. She knew, her father was in the forest and at the same time learnt that Orlando was also in the forest and loved her. Rosalind rose in brilliant conversation in this new life. Released from patriarchal structure, in a changed locality, Rosalind's language formed her individual subjectivity. Chris Weedon postulates: "Language is the place where actual and possible forms of social organization and their social and political consequences are defined and contested."[4] For structuralist theory the common factor in the analysis of social organization, social meanings power and individual consciousness is language. This theory assures that subjectivity is socially produced. We may return briefly to the points that Rosalind acknowledges the feeling of being a different person in a different situation and between two discourses her struggle is manifested. Her language served as a challenge to the melancholy humour of Jacques. Phebe was madly in love with Ganymede. Rosalind's sharp reaction to her letter is problematical. She expresses her displeasure with words:

> 'Why, she defies me,
> Like Turk to Christian'
>
> (111.111.32)

To Rosalind, the words in the letter were Ethiop words, blacker in their effect, than in their countenance. To Orlando, she seemed like a spirit, who could conjure magic by her charming youthful qualities. During her courtship in masquerade, her arguments could be open to constant re-reading and reinterpretation.

For endless times, the audience would like to witness the most beautiful and bright heroine on the stage, who once relegated to the margins of power, took upon herself the right to self-determination. Language is central to the process in *As You Like It*.

Marilyn French believes language to be the theme in *Love's Labour's Lost*. She writes: "In *Love's Labour's Lost*, Shakespeare makes events revocable not so much through disguise—although that is an element—but by focusing on language as theme, on language that embodies the inconstancy of the characters."[5]

It may not be out of place here to mention the name of "Levine Teerline, (a Flemist painter) who was invited to England by Henry VIII and retained as court painter by his three successors—Edward VI, Mary I & Elizabeth I was one of a number of Flemish women artists...strong has attributed the first frontal majestic images of the Queen, the image on the Great Seal and numerous documents, to drawings by Teerline." Shakespeare, we may assume was aware of all that was happening around him. One may also assume that all the experience of the poet went into the making of characters like Rosalind, who were remarkable for their independence and initiative.

The Forest of Arden is not merely a backdrop for the characters to act their roles against. Shakespeare used the forest as one of the principal subjects, even though the theme of romantic love absorbed the audience. With the arrival of the courtiers, it is likely, that the unstained happiness of the forest would gather specks of dust on it. We do not search for imperial relations in the forest. A colonial power has not been imposed on the forest—the import is different, the centrality of empowerment is on the mental level.

As You Like It is basically about right values and good life and this is symbolized in the character of Corin. He is simple, dignified and sensible. Like Phebe, Audrey spurs her local lover, William, in favour of an attractive courtier. Audrey's absence from the forest is hopelessly irreparable. Some parts of the forest perhaps heaved with William's sigh. He received awkward treatment from Touchstone. Will Phebe have a complete sense of fulfilment in future with Silvius?

Hymen bars confusion in Act V-IV for he was to conclude with the wedlock hymen. Duke Frederick was converted, Duke Senior regained his crown, and Orlando's lands were restored. Jacques arrives to bid farewell for he was not for dancing measure. He would stay in the forest, at the abandoned love of Duke Senior to know his philosophy. He would learn from the usurping Duke who had put on a religious life. Duke Senior would return ho his former honour. Continuity of life is signified in the Duke's returning to the court.

Duke Senior was 'colonized' by happiness at this moment. He proceeded to begin the rites, which he trusted would end in free delights. He did not perusade Jacques to return with him to the court. The hidden forces in his character could have opened vision of heaven to Jacques.

To my mind, the conclusion of *As You Like It* is played on two levels. There was happiness for majority of the characters and some endured unhappiness. The audience has to live through each experience. There are clash of colours in the 'happy' ending of the play. The 'melancholy bough' is like a sign which remains in our imagination. This feature reminds me of Vincent Van Gogh's painting of broad landscapes with threatening skies. Juxtaposition of colours is an important mark in Picasso's paintings.

I would like to quote a brief passage from *The Life and Times of Claude Monet*, the great impressionist painter. This attempt can be taken as a pre-saying to what I am trying to express. Derrida, in fact, suggests that in reworking, the structure preface text becomes open at both ends. Commenting on the inter—inscribing of 'readers' 'writers' he remarks: "The text has no stable identity, no stable origin, no stable end. Each act of reading the text is a preface to the next."[6] To the critic, Edmund Swinglehurst, Monet, famous for his spacious and colourful paintings of his lily pond, opened a window into another kind of vision. He writes: 'Once more, Monet found himself in financial trouble. He was not deflected from his artistic purpose, however, which he had once summarized for an American student as being to paint, not the objects, but the colours...throughout the 1870s, he contributed to the

Impressionist exhibitions...in which he included the superb Gare Saint—Lagare series.... This group of paintings, which inspired the praise of Emile Zola, seeks to capture the effects produced by smoke and sunlight at the Paris railway station."[7]

In the colonial paradigm, Caliban was finally sent back to his cell, perhaps for routine work. Ariel was promised freedom. A blemish has thus been set on the playwright's dream. In actual life, there are tolerance, forgiveness, forget fullness,— but the audience in *The Tempest* is deprived of enjoying this humane side in Prospero's character.

In Kalidas's *Shakuntala*, the ashrama is enriched by a garden and a forest and these are enriched by lotus of immense beauty and purity. The delicate persuasion of the King Suka, mango and sirish can be felt in every sequence of the play. When Shakuntala started for her husband's palace, to their surprise, the hermit boys found silk, jewels and golden ornaments clinging to the branches of fairy trees. When Shakuntala met with the curse of non-recognition, we could imagine what sadness overpowered the forest, which normally bloomed with lotus.

After the courtiers left for the city, did a sense of emptiness turn the Forest of Arden, could a melancholy sigh be heard ever since?

References

1. All references to Shakespeare's work in this essay are to *The Complete Works* ed. Peter Alexander (Collins London and Glasgow, 1960).
2. Allardyce Nicoll, *British Drama* 5th edition (George G. Harrap & Co. Ltd., London, 1969) 69.
3. Donald Clive Stuart, *The Development of Dramatic Art* (Dover Publications, New York, 1960) 550.
4. Chris Weedon, *Feminist Practice and Post Structuralist Theory*, (Blackwell 1992) 21.
5. Marilyn French, Shakespeare's *Division of Experience* (ABACUS 1981) 93. It is interesting to note that in feminist and humanist subject language is central to the discourse since it is in a new or reclaimed language that radical feminists hope to recapture their terrestrial womanhood.

6. Whitney Chadwick, 'Domestic Genres and Women Painters in 'Northern Europe', *Women, Art and Society* (Thames and Hudson Ltd., London, 1994) 105-06.
7. Jacques Derrida, *Of Grammatology*, trans. by Gayatri Chakravorty Spivak (Motilal Banarasidas Publishers Pvt. Ltd., Delhi, 1994) XII.

14

Gerard Manley Hopkins: The Poet and the Priest: A Study of *The Windhover*

Nandini Sahu and *Padmini Sahu*

Gerard Manley Hopkins (1844-1889) is a poet of distinction. Though the assortment of his work is slender, his outstanding creativity both in theme and *modus operandi* of writing is enormous. His admirers, readers, critics and scholars see him in the height of Shakespeare, Donne, Eliot and Yeats. They appreciate him as 'the first modern poet', 'a major poet', and above all, 'a remarkable technical inventor'.[1] But these rosy appreciations are not without spiky disparagements. A good number of his readers and critics label him "a difficult", "an obscure" and "an odd"[2] poet and his experimentation in contemporary poetry is damned as merely creative licentiousness. In fact, the flaw of his style of writing is pointed out by those who seek a constant literary etiquette in his poetry and are grown to be prejudiced of its dearth. And those who brand his poetry as 'difficult', 'ambiguous', 'odd' and 'obscure' are the advocates of the faith that poetry ought to be straight away graspable. But in the cutting test of censure, materializes the real poetic faculty and craftsmanship of Hopkins. His method of writing, metaphysical interpretations and astonishing thoughts personified in his poems have been the invariable browsing soil of the critics. But the orb of controversy is—Hopkins is more a poet than priest or more a priest than poet. Does religious conviction compose Hopkins as a poet? Or does it condense the range, the potency, the class of his art? This less grazed meadow is yet to draw the vital notice of Hopkins's readers and stimulates one to bring the matter to lime light and clear up the controversy. The object of this reading is to deliberate the poet and the priest in Hopkins with particular allusion to his poem, *'The Windhover'*, the poet's masterpiece. In order to carry out the object of this study, the poet's career and his other poems have been partially dealt here, but the focus is mainly on *'The Windhover'*.

Born in 1844, Hopkins turned into a Jesuit Priest in 1868 and put aside the writing of poetry, "as not belonging to my profession...unless it were by the wish of my superiors"[3]. For seven years, he maintained a poetic silence. This period of his abandonment of poetry is marked by his internal divergence between a poet and priest. His poetic silence terminated in 1875 with his *'The Wreck of the Deutschland'*. This epoch of profound religious barrenness which mystics term as the "dark night of the soul"[4] prepared a platform for his divine accomplishment. This mood of divine termination is expressed in his "terrible sonnets"[5] written between 1885 and 1889. This is aptly been in his letters to Robert Bridges: "What verses I had written before I became a Jesuit (i.e. 1868) and resolved to write no more, as not belonging to my profession...so for seven years. I wrote nothing but two or three little presentation pieces which occasion called for.... I had long had haunting in my ear the echo of new rhythm which now I realized on paper.... I do not say the idea is altogether new...but no one had professedly used it and made it the principle throughout, that I know of...however, I had to mark the stress...and a great many more oddness could but dismay an editor's eye, so that when I offered to our magazine *The Month*, they dared not print it."[6] And this echo of new rhythm is called the illustrious *Sprung Rhythm*. After that he sent his manuscript to Robert Bridges and Canon Dixon for publication. Robert Bridges published Hopkins's poems posthumously in 1918, long after his death in 1889. There is an unambiguous basis for the posthumous recognition of the lyrical mastermind. The technical intricacies of the Sprung Rhythm made his poems a prohibited constituency for the reviewers. The intensive reading of his English poetic text was pioneered in the twenties by I.A. Richards and William Empson as it is a technique that is appropriate to intimately textured poems like those of Hopkins. Richards took the poem *The Windhover* in the American Magazine *The Dial* in 1926, and it was well accepted as a poem of fusion of intellectual power and passion by the critics like Geoffrey Grigson and F.R. Leavis.

After Hopkins became a priest, he developed a very singular style of his own. His world was now changed with the splendour of God. And for this change from the poet to a priest, he has suffered many charges by the critics. Bridges had shown a deep distaste for his mysticism and religious outlook. As he writes: "Most of his poems are religious, and marked with catholic theology and almost all are injured by a natural eccentricity, a love for subtlety and uncommonness."[7] Eliot has sturdily condemned Hopkins that by writing devotional poetry Hopkins confines his poetic spirit. I.A. Richards is of the opinion that the poet in Hopkins is often subjugated and subdued by the priest: "The conflict between sensualism and asceticism which lie behind all Hopkins's better poems with temporarily reserved through a stoic acceptance of sacrifice. And asceticism fails to reach ecstasy and accepts the failure. All Hopkins's poems are in this sense the poems of defeat."[8]

But the poet is not muted by the priest in Hopkins's poems, if his poems are interpreted justifiably. Rather, they go via each other, they are harmonizing each other. His poems are homages to God's glory, but they are the compliments of the senses. So his sombreness does not essentially curtail his poetic spirit. As a poet, by nature he was an idealist and a sensualist. His early verse was rich in Keatsian sensuous charm and he elevated himself to immensity by pertaining to great causes as freedom and faith. In his poems like *'Pied Beauty'*, *'The Windhover'* and *'The Starlit Night'*, the poetic strength comes from a fundamental wakefulness of the objective magnificence of the earth. That awareness in sensualism is revealed in original metaphors such as "mealed with yellow shallows", "piece-bright—paling, "daylight's dauphin", "a stallion stalwart", "very violet-sweet", and many others of their kind in his poetry. The route from a sensualist to a celebrant is clearly evident in his poems. In '*The Windhover*', the objective catalogues of images are direct and concise in the dedication, '*to Christ, Our Lord.*'

Hopkins is a poet—a religious poet. The notion of spiritual love is articulated in most of his poems. The best of this convention is '*Pied Beauty*', a simple and beautiful piece where Hopkins celebrates the eternal love:

"Glory by to God for dappled things."

In this poem, all Hopkins's love for the mottled, dappled, spotted—symbol of the distinctive, of life's multitudinous—is brought in concert, given dignity and composure in the last two lines:

"He fathers—forth whose beauty is past change: Praise him".

Though the main idea is the Praise of Him, but Hopkins's poetic talent is pronounced in the use of rich imagery and rhythm like:

"for skies of couple—colour as a brindled cow;
...Landscape plotted and pieced—fold, fallow, and plough"

His poem, 'Hurrahing in Harvest'—perhaps the most purely blissful of all his poems—ends with an astonishing image which amends the moment of understanding into a clean physical activity when the beholder all of a sudden realizes that Christ is the resource of the world's beauty:

"The heart rears wings bold and
bolder and hurls for Him,
O half hurls earth for Him,
Off under his feet"

The poet in Hopkins awakens a holy sentiment in his heart after watching the starlit night.

Besides being a Jesuit Priest, Hopkins was a insightful poet enthralled by language and rhythm and a fervently dedicated patron of colour, form and elements of the world of nature. He got contentment from moods of the natural world, linked with an insightful wisdom of natural magnificence as a mirror image of celestial reality. The claims of religion and the obligations of his religious occupation were dominant no doubt, but his artistic interests emphasized themselves with a tender energy, and it was not constantly easy for him to resolve his religious vocation with his poetic genius. Hopkins celebrates this disposition in his famous sonnet 'The Windhover' which he composed in 1877 and himself said that it was the best thing that he has ever written.

'The Windhover', more than any other poem, shows pure *Sprung Rhythm* working with spirit, vocabulary and grammar, vividness and meticulousness of thoughts, and the array of indulgence with great spiritual intensity and convolution. The best way of accepting and appreciating this poem is to follow the printed words while reciting it. The amazing wavering progress of the opening of *'The Windhover'* is typical of Hopkins's rhythmic effect. In the first two lines the strong assonance in 'caught' is echoed and repeated in:

"...I caught this morning morning's
minion, king-dom of daylight's dauphin,
dapple-dawn-drawn Falcon,
in his riding"

In the next two lines, the vowels of 'level', 'rolling' are echoed in 'air', 'high' and 'rein'. The free use of alliteration, in phrases like 'daylight's dauphin', 'morning's minion', 'dapple-dawn-drawn', 'wimpling wing', 'steady air and striding' add to the musical effect more vigorously. The inquisitive plummeting effect of this rhythm reproduces efficiently the growing movement of the bird. *'The Windhover'* has been variously explicated by the critics. The dialogue about this sonnet opened in 1926 by I.A. Richard. The reflection seems to be that the elated flying of the bird stirs the poet's heart. The expression 'in hiding' connotes the poet as a priest, with his heart veiled from mortal things in the service of God. In the amalgamation of beauty, strength and glory which the poet sees in the bird, there is a motif of the beauty. This strength and glory of Christ, he addresses as "My Chevalier". It is risky to see this persona in Christ as Christ usually stands for humility and suffering. But it is "no wonder" that Christ's humanity and suffering are bound up with beauty and glory. To Hopkins, "sheer plod" can make the ploughshare shine as it cuts its furrow, and a black coat in fire can fall over and break and reveal the hot interior, its "gold-vermillion" gashes suggesting both beauty and pride and Christ's sore and anguish.

The sonnet 'The Windhover' displays the same pattern of thought—an evolution from the tangible loveliness of nature portrayed in the octave, to its divine meaning or analogue in the sestet. The plan is simple, but the execution is complex which is the peculiarity with Hopkins. The poem is built upon two intermingled—a falcon in the vastness of morning and a plough-share in the furrow. These two images are associated to a third and more imperative theme that familiarizes us with its sub-title, the allegiance, "*To Christ Our Lord*". But these objective metaphors do not revolutionize their distinctiveness while they contemplate on this important theme and also become apparent for it. The poem works upon the opposites. The vigorous bodily beauty of the bird is compared with his serene spiritual renunciation. In the octave, the light of the daybreak and the actions of the bird are set against the shadows and the stagnation oblique in the poet's own state, "my heart in hiding". In the sunset, a new expressive reaction is recommended by pretty diverse kinds of light and movement. Here, the dappled dawn of the opening is compared with the diluted sheen of the plough and the "Gash" of the fallen embers. Similarly, the splendour of the birds journey contrasts with the "sheer plod" of the ploughman falling in the fire. On the emotional area, the antagonism is between the poet's primary ecstasy in the complete magnificence of the bird, his appreciation and desire of its mastery in its own constituent, his alarm about it as the emblem of the victory of the risen Christ, and his ultimate recognition that his vicinity must be surrendered that stands for Christ's sacrifice and resurrection.

From the very beginning, the poet seizes the spectacle of the Falcon flying high and extroverted in the early morning sky and reacts with a rupture of intense enchantment. The faction of this opening is one of raising emotions. There is a progression of the stress in the words 'morning', 'morning's', 'minion'. The recess between the stress discrepancies accentuates the sequence from the chronological 'morning' to the domineering personification, 'morning's'. The intense result is noticeably palpable in the words like 'minion', 'dauphin', the chivalric words. 'Minion' means lover, 'dauphin' brings the idea of 'majesty', the 'riding' suggests the stature of the 'chevalier', and implements the suggestion in 'dauphin' of the Falcon's authority and control of its empire. The Falcon is seen as a diminutive sun, blinking so high up that he is seen as a 'daylight's dauphin'. The Falcon stands for Christ. But thc whole panorama is illustrated in the idiom of the substantial world. The progress of the bird is a balanced hovering, the bird rises 'striding/High there' and 'rung upon the rein of a wimpling wing'. Another physical image, the wide area of a skating 'edge' portrays the open vowels in 'sweeps smooth on a bow band'. The energy and elegance of the bird is summed up in:

> "the hurl and gliding
> Rebuffed the big wind."

Two interpretations are possible for the phrase 'dapple-dawn-drawn-Falcon". Secluded, it may appear that the Falcon is drawn alongside the dappled dawn, but this is too stagnant and motionless. The most reasonable elucidation can be that the Falcon is 'dawn-drawn' as a majestic favorite of God is fascinated to His royal presence. Though he may overpower the sky, he is himself drawn out by the daylight. The bird appears subsequently as a young horse walking briskly, but the falcon's grasp is fascinating. And the final idea is of the 'steady air'—submissive air. This emphasis on the Falcon's pre-eminence and power is delicate further when his long whirling slither emerges to have 'rebuffed the big wind'.

The expression 'rung' stands for the exact hawking term for unfolding a divine ascend. That creates a brilliant illustration of the Falcon's invigorating voyage, the power of the bird heaving beside the curl of its ascend would give exactly the feeling of being held on an operational 'rein'. This expresses the idea of "controlled freedom".[9] To Hopkins, man's actions are predisposed by God that man is on running 'rein'. The Falcon's wing is described as 'wimpling' because of the manner in which the feathers emerge in gratifying folds when seen from below. "In his ecstasy" again suggests the great effort in relation to the Christian knight. As the bird scuffles against the wind, he appears to celebrate his might as does the knight in his encounter against malevolence. It is as though the hero can find his accurate power and point, as if his valour is pinched from the energy of resistance.

Relinquishing the glamour of a peripheral life of quest, the poet transmits its eminence of gallantry to the inner being, the inner realization. Henceforth, it has been the bird itself that governs the poet's thought—"the achieve of the mastery of the thing". Now, the bird develops into something out of the ordinary to him. His thoughts turn innermost to his own effort and objective. The bird is seen as the image of Christian speculation. But the spectacle awakens the poet, "my heart in hiding, stirred for a bird". But hiding from what? I.A. Richards correctly points out that the poet's heart is "in hiding from life...has chosen a safer way".[10] The intensely stimulating pounding of his spirit is itself a category of 'ecstasy', a being caught up in the course of revelation. This stirring purpose of God's supplementary elegance in response to the natural magnificence is a common thing in Hopkins's poetry. In fact, it is the essential theme of 'The Windhover'.

From this scrutiny, one proceeds to the further important themes in the sestet. The sestet opens:

> "Brute beauty and velour and act,
> O, air, pride, plum, here, Buckle!"

Hopkins calls on the qualities of the bird that have keyed up his appreciation and stimulated a 'heart in hiding'. The appreciation and elucidation of the sestet depends upon the implication of 'buckle' and 'chevalier', in different ways deduced by critics. However, the word 'buckle' is to draw together or to button up to the poet's heart the beauty and grace, 'pride' and 'plumage'. The next implication may be the antiquated sense of the exploration for accomplishment. The most suitable meaning of 'buckle' is to crinkle, to disintegrate as Elizabeth Schneider argues "This material world, so abstracted—'brute, beauty, velour and act, O, air, pride, plum here Buckle' and as it collapses before the poet's vision, the fire of Christ 'breaks' through, 'a billion times told lovelier, more dangerous.'"[11]

The priest does never eclipse the poet in him. Hopkins discards neither the nature's exquisiteness of the bird, nor the aesthetic enchantment that he unearths in them. Rather they are the foundation of insight and force behind his creativity. They must not be shorn of; they must not be hassled thinking the priest does the unconditional surrender to God's will. In all this, there is no cause for a revelation, "no wonder of it". The premier Christian superiority in him should be struck out of conflict. It is the 'sheer plod', the sheer effort involved in driving the ploughshare through the zillion that makes it shine, as does spiritual culmination to sharpen Hopkins's creative talent. So also do 'blue-beck embers' smack their brightest fire, 'gold vermillion', means blood colour, they split from the self-consuming heat of the fire and gash and gall themselves alongside the external world. The laceration and power of these words evoke the fighting spirit of the falcon and the knight. Again, it may noted that this comparison is not expressed for the inside anguish of a "terrible pathos"[12] though Bridges has created that axiom for Hopkins's poetry. Rather, it is the spirit of radical fanaticism and absolute enchantment that makes the sonnet alive. The image "gash gold vermillion" speaks of the torment of Christ whose wounds gawk blood-red in the effort for salvation yet garner like gold because of His mysterious glory. This might also elucidate the pitch of deep love in "ah, my dear"—words from the territory of mysticism. In the delineation of contemplation, '*The Windhover*' is uncomplicated and the emotions are exacting. Its convolution lies in the embellishment of the illustration entwined with ornately echoing patterns of resonance but the two counterpoints are rather two sets of opposites. The first is the antagonism of the substance and the spiritual united by the 'dauphin'. The second pair of opposites emerge in magnificence and fright that run through the poem without any resolution. They are articulated through the suggestion of power in the 'mastery' of the bird and the 'lovelier' and more 'dangerous' flames of Christ.

The different facets of Hopkins's poetry are his lyrical patterns, his outlandish metaphors, his natural world, his exposed *Sprung Rhythm* and his 'Inscape' and 'Instress'. His poetry has often been charged of being ambiguous and odd because of intractable enigma in his metrical experimentation. But the more the poems are studied, the clearer the idiosyncrasies become crucial to his aim and accomplishment. They are always calculated, premeditated, they are not blemishes. F.R. Leavis argues against the allege of obscurity to him: "Rather he had positive uses for ambiguity, and he presumed to expect the readers' prolonged and repeated intellectual effort."[13] This quantifies to his far-reaching inventiveness. Obscurity, quaintness, confusion and complicatedness occur not from bizarre ideas or metaphysical interpretations but from the poet's resolve to make music. Hopkins himself has adequate justification against the charge of being incomprehensible in his letters to his friend Robert Bridges. He urges his readers to read his verses aloud to get the music out of it:

> "...but take breath and read it with ears as I always wish to be read, and my verse becomes alright"[14] (February, 1879).

It is the desire to be divergent that pushes for him to write in his own way, as he mentions in one of his letters to Robert Bridges:

> "No doubt my poetry errs in the side of oddness. I hope in theme to have a more balanced and Miltonic style. But as air, melody is what strikes me most of all in music and design in painting, so design, pattern or what I am in the habit of calling 'inscape' is what I above all aim at poetry. Now it is the virtue of design,

> pattern or inscape to be distinctive and it is the voice of distinctive to become queer. This voice I cannot have escaped."[15]

Hopkins has achieved a mechanical triumph in poetry that is the accomplishment of sprit. He uses English language as a living thing. He belongs to the School of Shakespeare, Donne, Eliot and Yeats as opposed to Spencer, Milton and Tennyson in his use of the words and images. His words and phrases are events, sounds, ideas and images that must be read with the ear. His tempo has a dramatic force. He is most creative in his technical innovation *Sprung Rhythm*. He writes in a letter to Robert Bridges about the reason of inventing such a new technique: "Why do I employ *Sprung Rhythm* at all? Because it is the nearest to the rhythm of prose, that is the native and natural rhythm of speech, the least forces, the most rhetorical and emphatic of all possible rhythms combining as it seems to me, opposite and one would have thought, incompatible excellences, markedness of rhythm that is rhythm's self—and naturalness of expression.... My verse is less to be read than heard, as I have told you before, it is oratorical that is the rhythm is so (21st August, 1879)."[16] At this point, Hopkins seems to be next to Wordsworth as he defends Sprung Rhythms principally because it is the closer to the rhythms of prose that is the native rhythm of the tongue. But put into practice, he wished for a metaphorical delivery of his poems. Hopkins's poetry is written, as some critics have commented, in a language of stimulation, as did Shakespeare and Milton. Like these poets he uses the whole property of the language by entertaining alliteration, internal rhyme, assonance, and dissonance, the words being his apparatus. Hopkins's poetry in comparison with Shakespeare's would further clarify the point:

> "Down in dim woods in diamond delves!
> the elves-eyes!"
>
> (*The Starlit Night*)
>
> "I caught this morning morning's minion,
> Kingdom of daylight's dauphin,
> Dapple-dawn-drawn Falcon, in his riding."
>
> (*The Windhover*)

"Back beauty, keep it beauty
beauty, beauty...."

(*The Landen Echo*)

These Hopkinsean lines resemble Shakespeare's
"...bloody, bawdy, villain!
Remorseless, treacherous, lecherous
kindless villain!"

(*Hamlet, 11, ii*)

"Reputation! Reputation! Iago...
my Reputation."

(*Othello*)

"...cabin'd, cribb'd confined."

(*Macbeth, 111 iv*)

Gerard Manley Hopkins, however, remains very much realistic in his experiments in making verse. Hopkins's notes are, like a painter's, not mere efforts at pictorial writing. They are word aerobics prompted by the intelligence aimed at illumination of the five senses. And his keen surveillance and sensibility led to a dramatic development in his poetry. Hopkins understood that poetry called for a language divergent from that of a prose, a language prosperous in implication, both to the wits and intellect. His lexis is drawn from many sources—ancient, idiomatic, archaic and vernacular words, all being used dramatically. In the *Sprung Rhythm*, the scrutiny runs on from the commencement of a stanza to the end and all the stanzas in one long twist. This is the design of a bold syntactical firmness. The basic code of his effort to break away from the rigorously conservative patterns is that—each foot contains one stress probably, but not inevitably, pursued by any number of unstressed syllables. Hopkins's workmanship and his premeditated craftsmanship lie in his experimentation. So far as sonnet is concerned, the trendsetter in Victorian period was Hopkins. "Hopkins's experiments with the sonnets are extremely interesting and he made something new in the form."[17]

Nature and the landscapes is another important feature of Hopkins's poetry. Hopkins's poetry is rich in nature imagery.

A luxurious love of nature, based on a infinitesimal surveillance, is found in most of Hopkins's poetry. To Hopkins, the beauty of nature articulates God. It is the materialization of this conviction that released Hopkins from a self-imposed refraining from poetry. His concept is that "Man was created to praise reverence and serve God, Our Lord."[18] Hopkins's concept of Nature reminds us of that of Wordsworth. His poetical works commemorate the nurturing influence of beauty and terror eternally represented in the natural phenomenon. As he writes in some of his famous poems:

"But huge and mighty forms; that do not live
like living men, moved slowly through the mind
By day, and were a trouble to my dreams."

(*The Stolen Boat*, 11, 38-44)

"The anchor of my purest thoughts, the nurse,
the guide, the guardian of my heart, and soul
of all my moral being."

(*Tintern Abbey*, 111-113)

Hopkins's concept of nature being the reflection of God's grandeur comes close to that of Ted Hughes. In Ted Hughes also, the beauty and dread of nature is a mirror image of the beauty and terror of its Creator. Hughes, in his poem '*Hawk Roosting*', describes the thoughts operating through the mind of a hawk resting on his perch. In '*Hawk Roosting*', the Hawk views himself as the 'Lord of Creation'. Like an authoritarian tyrant, he occupies a world where there are no real choices and he kills wherever he pleases, 'because it is all mine'.

"It took the whole of creation
To produce my foot, my each feather,
Now I hold creation in my foot."

(*Hawk Roosting*)

To judge Hopkins as a poet of Nature will unquestionably find some resemblance of Hopkins with Meredith, the close contemporary to him. Hopkins comes a few years after the nineteenth century poets like Thomas Hardy, Henry James, Tennyson and Browning when the methodical minds were slowly extroverting themselves into nature. Fanatical feelings declined to an effortless accepted sentiment, poets and painters modified themselves by intriguing only the choicest details of nature. But Hopkins comes after them more intellectual and more ardent. He does not take only the select details of nature. He does not make allegorical waves towards nature, no signal of a wing for the yellow cloud or no notch of a thumb for the rainbow. To Hopkins, the unequivocal entity is more weird or the clouds are like ants' eggs in the unwrapped nest. They are on the whole, dissimilar with Tennyson's clouds in water colour. Such a perception burdens him with more systematic knowledge as Geoffrey Grigson calls Hopkins's poetry as a "passionate science".[19] He describes natural things with the maximum gracefulness, potency and astuteness. The momentous fact of his poems is that they have a sense of passionate compassion that tells between Hopkins and other English poets. Passionate Science is acceptable also as a portrayal of his own commotion since Hopkins endeavours to be a transformed kind of poet. He does not want to incriminate his world with any magnificence of his own quixotic plan. The God of Hopkins is not inside Nature, but He is under the world's splendour. After he became a priest, nature became to him a statement of God's glory, electrified with the majesty of God. Stars sat like flames in the air, pied beauty was fathered forth by God he admired, the kestrel stood to gale with pride and valour and act and fire.

Hopkins's astonishing power of surveillance, his exploration of idiosyncratic beauty, for momentous aspect of prototype in the natural world found their passage in his *Journal*. For this beauty of pattern, he coined the word 'inscape' and for the powerful feeling it puts forth on him, the word 'instress'. Trees, flowers, the sky, clouds, stars, glaciers, pictures, all have their own inscapes. "All the world is full of inscape", he writes, after admiring the beams of a great barn: "I thought how sadly the beauty of inscape was unknown and buried away from simple people and yet how near at hand it was if they had eyes to see it and it could be called out everywhere again." [20] To Hopkins, the splendour of nature is a faint flash of the splendour of Christ. Quite a good deal of resonance of '*The Windhover*' comes from simplicity of theme, clarity of structure, and directness of movement. But the final effect is of an intricately designed poem. It demands an unremitting scholarly endeavour from the readers. '*The Windhover*' can be treated as an austere poem in view of its homage to the beauty and terror, pride and modesty of Christ. The poetic force warbles out from a vital awareness of the objective beauty of the Falcon. The priest Hopkins is responsible to create a sensitivity in the poet Hopkins to write poetry, nourishing his sensitive, poetic imagination.

Works Cited

Palgrave's *Golden Treasury,* London: Macmıllan, 1875.

Complete Works of William Shakespeare, Wordsworth Editions Ltd., 1996.

References

1. I.A. Richards, *Gerard Manley Hopkins, Poems, A Casebook*, ed. Margaret Bottrall, London: The Macmillan Press Ltd., 1975, 66.
2. *Ibid.*, 68.
3. *Ibid.*, 70.
4. C.C. Abbott (Ed.), *Letters of Gerard Manley Hopkins*. London: Oxford University Press, 1935, 102.
5. *Ibid.*, 39.
6. *Ibid.*, 68.
7. *Gerard Manley Hopkins, Poems, A Casebook*, 41.
8. *Ibid.*, 73.
9. Quoted by Elizabeth Drew, *Poetry: A Modern Guide to its Understanding and Enjoyment*. New York: Dell Publishing Co., INC, 1959, 249.
10. I.A. Richards, *Gerard Manley Hopkins, A Casebook*, 73.
11. Elisabeth Schnedier, '*The Windhover*': *Gerard Manley Hopkins, A Casebook*, 184.
12. Quoted by Dennis Ward, '*The Windhover, To Christ Our Lord*'; *Gerard Manley Hopkins, A Casebook*, 142.
13. F.R. Leavis, "Gerard Manley Hopkins", *New Bearings in English Poetry*, London: Penguin Books Ltd., 1937, 134.

14. *Ibid.*, 88.
15. *Ibid.*, 66.
16. *Ibid.*, 46.
17. Lees, F.N., "Gerard Manley Hopkins" *The Pelican Guide to English Literature* 6, from Dickens to Hardy. Ed. Boris Ford Harmondsworth. Middlesex England: Penguin Books Ltd., 1958, 372.
18. Quoted by H.L.B. Mody, *Literary Appreciation, A Practical Guide to the Understanding and Enjoyment of Literature in English*. London: Oxford University Press, 1935, 91.
19. Geoffrey Grigson, *Gerard Manley Hopkins*. London: Longman, Green and Company, 1955, 5.
20. *The Letters of Gerard Manley Hopkins*, 50.

15

D.H. Lawrence: Cosmic Symbolism in *Sons and Lovers*

Vinita Singh

> "You mustn't look in my novel for the old stable ego of the character. There is another ego...."
>
> D.H. Lawrence

The three major novels of D.H. Lawrence—*Sons and Lovers, The Rainbow* and *Women in Love*—written in quick succession, depict a surge of creative energy unique in the history of fiction. His first two novels, *The White Peacock* and *The Trespassers*, for all their promise, remain prentice-work. Ford Madox Hueffer, his first publisher, put him under a self-imposed discipline of realism and form that resulted in his first major achievement, *Sons and Lovers*. But even before Henry James' curt dismissal of the novel as "hanging in the dusty rear of naturalism", Lawrence was busy making a "new raid upon the inarticulate". *The Wedding Ring*, begun immediately after *Sons and Lovers* took final shape as two magnificent novels, *The Rainbow* and *Women in Love*. The emergence of psycho-analysis and the discovery of the Russian novel, particularly of Dostoevsky, conspired towards the disintegration of the static character and the triumph of the symbolic mode and now Lawrence finds his most natural form of expression in symbolism.

In Lawrence's major novels, the symbolical aspect is much more important than the psychological. For him no explanations of symbols are final. In writing about Melville's *Moby Dick*, he makes the point explicit:

> "You can't give a great symbol a 'meaning'. Symbols are organic units of consciousness with a life of their own, and you can never explain them away...; A symbol has a life of its own, 'which cannot be explained away or exhausted. It is a mode of thought whose relevance and power have their sources in the unconscious'."

Primarily, in his novels, Lawrence is concerned with a body of darkness located within the self, a darkness which the light of consciousness is unable to penetrate. To present the realm of human consciousness, Lawrence develops the symbolic mode which helps in revealing the unconscious states through which his characters pass in the progression from *Sons and Lovers* to *Lady Chatterley's Lover*.

From *Rainbow* onwards, symbolism becomes an inevitable tool of expressing Lawrence's sensuous mysticism and his novels now are triumphs in the symbolic mode. Yet, symbols abound in *Sons and Lovers* too, and are its integral part. The cosmic symbols particularly the flower symbol are a favourite of Lawrence, occurring repeatedly in his novels as well as tales, especially in *Sons and Lovers*.

Lawrence uses cosmic symbolism of trees, flowers, darkness, light, sun, moon, etc. and *Sons and Lovers* is as rich in floral symbolism as *The White Peacock* is in the bird symbolism and *The Trespassers* in the sea symbolism. From the very beginning of the novel we find the enactment of the flower symbolism, in abundance. Walter Morel's conflict has been vividly presented through appropriate symbols. Towards the end of the first chapter entitled "The Early Married Life of the Morels" Mrs. Morel is described while pregnant with Paul as wandering deliriously in the garden. She, being the victim of Morel's drunkenness, is driven out of the house. Her life is always guided by the life-force which forces her from all sides to nature. Though she is rebellious of this life-force, the perfume of the pollen-filled lilies makes her gasp with fear. Ultimately she returns, arouses Morel from his drunken sleep and he lets her in. In the bedroom mirror she sees that her face is smeared with the yellow dust of the lilies. "Both mother and unborn child", Spilka says, "have been developed by the powerful dark forces of life, and the dust becomes a kiss of benediction for them both, the confirmation of their vitality. The symbols of "moonlight", "lilies" are suggestive of a vast torrential force-magnificent and inhuman and infinite. The lily is symbolic of vital individuality. The same flower reappears in Aaron's rod. This symbolism is not decorative but quite functional like the imagery of the metaphysical poets. It is the embodiment of felt experience which ironically suggests the bond which Mrs. Morel has established with the child "within her" and starts living an aloof life from her husband who mistreats her and never understands her feelings. From the very infancy, Paul is shown united with his mother against his father. Hence, Lawrence has used the symbolic enactment as the appropriate action to objectify the moment of inner revelation. Ghent rightly says that Lawrence found spontaneous identification between image and meaning, between real things and what they symbolize. Again, when Paul is a young boy Mrs. Morel accepts the flowers which he brings for her as "a woman accepting a love-taken". Flowers, thus, play dominant symbolic role in revealing the attitude of the characters. The entire novel is saturated with their presence, and Paul and his three sweethearts are judged, again and again, by their attitude towards them, or more accurately, by their relations with them. The attitude and characters of three loves—spiritual (Miriam), Oedipal (Mrs. Morel) and possessive (Clara)—have been vividly presented through floral symbolism. Miriam's is a deadly bloodless communion with flowers and therefore she loves Paul as he loves flowers. One night Paul, in a moment of emotional struggle, goes out into the garden which is full of "the scent of Madonna lilies":

> "He went across the bed of pinks, whose keen perfume came sharply across the rocking, heavy scent of the lilies, and stood alongside the white barrier of flowers. They flagged all loose, as if they were

> panting. The scent made him drunk. He went down to the field to watch the moon sink under.
>
> The moon slid quite quickly downwards, growing more flushed. Behind him the great flowers leaned as if they were calling. And then, like a shock, he caught another perfume, something raw and coarse. Hunting round, he found the purple iris, touched their fleshy throats and their dark, grasping hands. At any rate, he had found something. They stood stiff in the darkness. Their scent was brutal. The moon was melting down upon crest of the hill. It was gone; all was dark. The corncrake called still."

The flowers, here, stand for "otherness" which establish an existence of their own as separate and strange selves and the iris rudely insistent in their scent. Paul senses this reality and beings to realize his independent life and puts himself into relation with himself. The word "something" suggests Paul's realization of his own alien reality and thus he returns to his mother, breaking off with Miriam.

Once Miriam, Paul and Clara come to an open field, the "clusters of strong flowers" excite Miriam. Out of excitement she gazes at Paul. Their eyes meet, they achieve communion of souls but Clara sulks. Paul and Miriam start picking flowers:

> "Miriam plucked the flowers lovingly, lingering over them. He always seemed to her too quick, and almost scientific. Yet his bunches had a natural beauty more than hers. He loved them, but as if they were his and he had a right to them. She had more reverence for them: they held something she had not."

This floral symbolism makes the characters and attitudes of Miriam and Paul clearer. Paul has got a strong hold on life as flowers have on life. His contact with the "God-stuff" is spontaneous and direct; he, too, is alive and organic, and the flowers are his to take. But just opposite to him is negative, sacrificial, spiritual Miriam who "wheedles the soul out of things". She kills life and has no right to it. According to Spilka, what is wrong for her is actually right for him, since life kindles life and death kills it—which is the essence of

Lawrentian communion. Clara comments that flowers should not be picked because the picking kills them. As she is separated from her husband like the flowers, she too wants to remain proud in her isolation—not to be "picked" by any man. Paul, on the other hand, believes that life belongs to the living and comes to the argument pointing at the pagan flower dance. In the meantime he "scattered a handful of cowslips on her (Clara's) hair and neck". Later on, "he gathered up the flowers he had sprinkled on her". Spilka maintains that because of this pagan ritual, Paul and Clara now engage in their first warm, spirited conversation—about a patch of bluebells poised in fear at the edge of the wood, like a man about to go outward into life, or like a woman about to enter the dark woods of love...on the deeper level, the poised flowers hint at one of Lawrence's favourite major themes—that western man, living too much in the open spaces of the mind, must sooner or later confront the darker depths of emotion. And the key to all this revelation is how to pick flowers: "Miriam, with false reverence, Paul with love, like a lover: and Clara not at all—but at least she respects the life in them." Paul scatters the flowers of life in Clara's hair and puts the flowers of death in Miriam's arms.

Sons and Lovers, consequently, is rich in revealing the minds of the characters through the symbolism of flowers. One evening Miriam insists on showing Paul a wild rose-bush she has discovered: "They were going to have a communion together—something that trilled her, something holy." "When they reach the bush Paul is disquieted and pained by her attitude, for the natural beauty of the rose is not enough for her; for "there was a cool scent of ivory roses—a white, virgin scent". This is indicative of the whole cold relationship. Again, it is Miriam's blindness to certain features of life which so antagonizes Mrs. Morel towards her. The two women are obviously of different temperaments; for example, three or four pages after the rose-bush episode, the mother becomes full of enthusiasm over some "glories of the snow" which she finds in her garden. The "joy", "elation" and the excitement which she shows when she discovers the flowers contrast markedly with the cloying sentimentality of Miriam's attitude towards the wild-roses. Thus, Mrs. Morel is understandably hostile towards the girl who becomes the centre of her son's artistic life and whose main fulfilment seems to lie in "mothering" or caring for his soul and mind. Later on, Miriam's "spirituality" becomes intolerable to Paul who sees the true nature of her character in yet another flower-episode in the chapter, "Defeat of Miriam", where she shows him some daffodils, going on to her knees before them, and taking one, "caressing it with her mouth and cheeks and brow". Her enthusiasm for the daffodils is still cloying and in contrast, Clara is willing to accept him as a lover and she is much more practical and realistic about life. Therefore, Paul gives "many scarlet carnation petals, like splashed drops of blood" to Clara. The importance of these flower symbolisms is, in this way, "not simply pictorial, although it could well be that there is a certain artificiality and awkwardness in the contrived use of every flower to carry some symbolic overtones of meaning; the technique is not always as masterly in this novel as it is to be in the following novels and in the short stories.

In the entire novel, there is a fine "poetic evocation of scenes, environments and atmospheres". In Lawrence's novels nature is never a dark background as in Hardy's fiction, rather, it is an upward surging like music, poetry, religion. Lawrence moves to nature not as a Wordsworthian alternative but as life force dark gods, sex, destructiveness, weapons of the unconscious or primitive instincts which can be used against machinery and industrial civilization. He uses symbols drawn from nature in abundance. These symbols seem to function as integral strands in the web of emotional tensions. They are seldom used in the Elizabethan sense, as mere omens of supernatural pleasure or displeasure; instead they seem to express some close relationship between man and nature. *Sons and Lovers* is an excellent novel which evokes the feeling of the immediacy and richness of the natural background and hence of life itself. Symbols taken from nature reveal as well as suggest the feelings of the characters; for example, Paul hates the ash tree which is symbolic of masculine control. He associates the ash tree with his father. The shrieking of the wind-swept ash tree symbolizes "the anguish of the home discord" to the children. They hear the loud shouts of the father coming home drunk and then the banging of Morel's fist on table and sharp cries which are finally "drowned in a piercing medley of shrieks and cries from the great, wind-swept ash tree.... The wind came through the tree fiercer and fiercer". Lawrence presents the same experience in his poem *Discord in Childhood.* Again, while Paul and Clara are on love-making the reference to "the Trent" symbolises their love turning mechanical. The Trent performs a double function: first it is an image of power and vitality and then, in a shadowy way, it becomes an image of perversity and mechanism 'so that the black water ran not far from his face and it gave a little thrill'. Lawrence, thus, expresses human emotions in terms of natural objects. Even the scenes are handled to embody and suggest symbolically the passionate desire for life that is quite imprisoned in the character. His use of the countryside and natural objects is twofold—first, to particularise the special circumstances of Eastwood whose effect is cumulative through the novel; second, as a source of imagery and symbolism to convey extremely delicate and intangible emotional attitudes. It is a poetic use of language where intellect is at the tip of these senses.

To suggest the dichotomy between reason and emotion, Lawrence uses a double rhythm in this novel, thesis thrusting against antithesis, lion against unicorn, darkness against light. Darkness is associated with the father while "light" with the mother who is symbolic of unconscious and conscious hold of life, one through the senses, and the other through the reason. Light is more often associated with women than with men. Again, the symbolism of darkness is suggestive of the phallic reality which is the correlative of passionate life assertion, strong as the thrust of the grass stems in the field where Paul and Clara make love and in the dynamics of the wheeling stars. Lawrence believes that darkness covers half of rhythm of the day, the darkness of the unconscious, half of the rhythm of the mind and the darkness of death half of the rhythm of life.

To him man is renewed to himself by accepting the dark. Sometimes the symbolism of darkness provides tragic dignity; for example, William's coffin is brought through the darkness of the night. Here darkness appears as the mystery, the darkness of death. Ghent holds that no other modern writer besides Rilke and Mann has tried so sincerely to bring death into relationship with life as Lawrence did, and each under the assumption that life, to know itself creatively, must know its relationship with death. When William's coffin comes home from darkness to light it suggests the darkness of the unconscious and the light of consciousness; the usurpation of one by the other is a perversion of both. Besides, sun is used as a symbol of the source of life and the moon as the symbol of non-being. When Paul is born, Mrs. Morel holds Paul, her unwanted baby, up to the sun as symbolic of ritual renunciation; sun stands for God of life, energy and vitality. After a violent quarrel with his wife Morel cuts the forehead of his wife with the drawer which he flings at her. Mrs. Morel is holding Paul on her lap and when she averts her face from Morel's stumbling concern, blood drips from the wound on the baby's hair. Morel, too, remains fascinated as the blood soaks through the scalp. His "manhood breaks" because of the symbolic sealing of the blood-tie between Mrs. Morel and Paul. Later on, Paul as a young lad gazes at the blood-red moon which arouses his first sexual passion. "In each case", Spilka observes, "the relation between man and nature is direct and vital and sun, blood, and moon are more 'integral' than symbolic". The symbolism merges with the inner meaning of the novel; it never remains symbolic merely as ornamentation. Life and death, too, have been used as two poles of the reality. Thus, throughout the novel, we sense the sensation of life, an extraordinary sense of that life in other: not only in people, but in plants and animals and even in constellation. So far as the story of a provincial upbringing with the tensions between parent and child is concerned, the novel is nearer to Arnold Bennett's *Clayhanger*. But its poetic beauty, extreme honesty and simplicity place it on a higher level. This gift of Lawrence makes Leavis declare, "Lawrence is incomparably the greatest creative writer in English of our time...; one of the greatest

English writer of any time." It is characteristic of Lawrence, the intuitive writer, that he can get inside the skin of an animal and tell...in the most convincing detail how it felt and how dimly, inhumanly it thought. In this novel Lawrence appears first and foremost a poet, feeling his thought like a poet, clothing his intuitions in the actuality of the world, and making them live in the guise of people and things. Lawrence's style, thus, smells of life, his words bear the imprint of experience. The naturalist first part is balanced by the analysis of emotions in the second part.

From *Sons and Lovers* onwards, symbolism for Lawrence is no longer an esthetic exercise—it becomes part of his prophetic vision. In *The Rainbow* and *Women in Love*, Lawrence is in active reaction against naturalism—a reaction assisted by the impact of the three powerful forces active during the time—the emergence of psychoanalysis, the new theories of expressionism in art and the discovery of the Russian Novel. His interest is now diverted from the external to the internal, from the visual to the analytical, from the realistic to the romantic. All this leads to a complete repudiation of the 'state character' and 'rigid form' in fiction and the wholehearted adoption of the symbolic mode—infusing into his novels the intensity of poetry, with the meaning lying in the symbol.

Works Cited

Beal, Anthony. (Ed.) *Selected Literary Criticism.* The Viking Press, New York: 1956.

Lawrence, D.H. *Sons and Lovers*. Penguin, 1960.

Lawrence, D.H. Spilka, Mark (Ed.) Prentice-Hall, Inc. 1963.

Leavis, F.R. *D.H. Lawrence: Novelist*. Penguin Books.

Moore, H.T. (Ed.) *The Collected Letters of D.H. Lawrence,* Heinnemann, 1965.

Moynahan, Julian. *The Deed of Life*. Princeton University Press, 1963.

Sinha, Radha Krishna. *Literary Influences on D.H. Lawrence.* Chanakya Publications, 1985.

Spilka, Mark. *The Love Ethic of D.H. Lawrence*. Bloomington: Indiana University Press, 1957.

16

Macbeth and Lady Macbeth: A Case Study in Management*

Arindam Das

To correlate or not to correlate Management theories and Shakespeare studies is a dilemma that has been, during recent times, positively resolved. As a corporate executive, one may cautiously long for the odd head to roll, for the plans of probable competitors to be spectacularly foiled, for his/her role as aggressive and assertive leader to be accredited and lauded by all. Putting aside exaggerated fantasies, however, the more conservative manager in one may also estimate that the profession of managing is for the eight-to-five daily grind and that Shakespearean drama is perhaps better suited for the special evening at the theater. This is sorely underestimating the potential influence of the great Bard. If we consider *Hamlet,* it is but a poignant case of an over-sensitive young executive who fails to climb up the corporate ladder because of his incapacity to make decisions. Or *Julius Caesar*, which at its heart is nothing less of an attempt at an antagonistic takeover by disgruntled stockholders. Or *King Lear*, a warning to all executives of family businesses, the perils of divestiture,

---

* The paper was presented at the World Shakespeare Conference: International Shakespeare Scholars' Meet (held by Shakespeare Society of Eastern India in collaboration with Tagore Gandhi Institute for Cultural Studies and Service Learning), Kolkata 2006-2007.

unplanned retirement and barriers of proper flow of communication.

Recent authors like Paul Corrigan (*Shakespeare on Management: Leadership Lessons for Today's Managers*, London: Kogan Page, 1999), Jay M. Shafritz (*Shakespeare on Management: Wise Business Counsel from the Bard*, New York: Carol, 1992), John O. Whitney and Tina Parker (*Power Plays: Shakespeare's Lessons in Leadership and Management*, New York: Simon and Schuster, 2001), Robert A. Brower (*Fictions of Business: Insights on Management from Great Literature*, New York: John Wiley and Sons, Inc., 1998), Richard Oliver (*Inspirational Leadership: Henry V and the Muse of Fire: Timeless Insights from Shakespeare's Greatest Leader*, Rollinsford New Hampshire: Spiro Press, 2003), and Norman R. Augustine and Kenneth L. Adelman (*Shakespeare in Charge: The Bard's Guide to Leading and Succeeding on the Business Stage*, New York: Hyperion Press, 1999) had essentially focused and relevantly highlighted the comprehensibility of Management leadership skills through the analysis of Shakespeare's protagonists. In the following paper, I propose to encompass these concepts of leadership qualities and move yet further to explicate certain basic hardcore theories of Management and Organizational Behavior through the study of the Shakespeare's *Macbeth*.

Jay M. Shaftritz remarkably observed: "Remember what Prince Philip is supposed to have said, 'A man [or woman] can be forgiven a lot if he [or she] can quote Shakespeare in an economic crisis'."[1] Yet quoting Shakespeare in Management classes or board-room meetings or analyzing his plays with a corporate edge is no mere ostentation; far from being a matter of ivory tower there is a definite practical purpose. Macbeth and his spouse's inordinate ambition to build up an empire and the consequent failure in doing so is a pertinent example of the dos and don'ts in a business environ. Further the strategies adopted by the duo, politics of leadership, the intricacies involved in an individual's pursuit and execution of power and authority, the attitude which the characters display, their interpersonal and intra-personal dealings, the lack of proper and effective 'board-room' tactics and a total negation of C.S.R. (Corporate Social Responsibility) helps to illustrate the various aspects, doctrines and theories of management.

1. Managerial Skills: How much did the 'butcher'-like King and his 'fiend'-like queen have it?

Essentially speaking there are three key skills for the business administrators as was identified by Robert L. Katz which are Technical Skill, Human Skill and Conceptual Skill (1974, 90-102).

A. Technical Skill: "It is the knowledge and the proficiency in activities involving methods, process, and procedures. Thus, it involves working with tools and specific techniques. For example, mechanics work with tools, and their supervisors should have the ability to teach them how to use these tools" (Harold and Weihrich 1998, 6-7). Macbeth in his supervisory level as an efficient general makes a flamboyant display of his technical skill. As reported by the bleeding Captain Macbeth "with his brandished steel,/ which smok'd with bloody execution,/ Like valor's minion, carved out his passage" (1984, 7). Yet the same Macbeth aspiring for the top level management as the king of Scotland blunders the nitty-gritty of handling a dagger after the assassination of Duncan. Macbeth, horror-stricken and thus psychologically topsy-turvyed, unlike the proposed plan brings back the blood-drenched dagger with him. At the end, though Macbeth tries to reassert the initial technical zest: "But swords I smile at, weapons laugh to scorn" (1984, 157), yet he is decapitated by a better technical player Macduff. Whereas on the other hand though Lady Macbeth confronts her lack of technical mastery in handling a dagger, her reason being that of Duncan resembling her father in looks, yet it was she who goes back to the chamber of murdered Duncan to lay the dagger beside him. She further connived the appropriate time to ring the bell for Macbeth after making the requisites for the murder of Duncan ready.

B. Human Skill/Soft Skill: "It is the ability to work with people; it is cooperative effort; it is team work; it is the creation of an environment in which people feel secure and free to express their opinions" (Harold and Weihrich 1998, 6). In the initial sections of the play, Macbeth makes attempt towards associative group dynamics, but then they are mere attempts which in turn is rendered futile. He throws a banquet in honor of the king but fails to do the needful though being a host and even quits the merry-making group at the dining table. This sheer lack displaying team dynamics is thoroughly chided by Lady Macbeth: "He (Duncan) has almost supp'd. Why have you left the chamber" (1984, 40). Moreover, in the Banquet, scene, Macbeth divulges his total interpersonal incompetence. The ghost of Banquo appalls Macbeth and he is so very shaken with it that he becomes cabin'd, cribb'd and confin'd to his own sole self. Dr. S.C. Sengupta makes a clarified comment in this context: "The sight shakes him violently and Lady Macbeth has to exorcize all her powers in order to be able to cope with the situation. She does her best to tackle it, but she cannot stop Macbeth's compromising disclosures.... Lady Macbeth does her best to keep up appearances, but the strain it involves leaves her totally exhausted. The banquet ends abruptly, for she has to dismiss the guests hastily at last" (1998, 176). Though Macbeth thoroughly blunders his soft skills, yet Lady Macbeth puts in her best effort towards a crisis management. Even earlier Lady Macbeth exhibited her refined interpersonal skill in the welcoming of Duncan in the absence of the actual host Macbeth. Far from mere sycophancy her words were the proper welcome for a king borne in her eyes, hands and tongue: "Your servants ever/ Have theirs, themselves and what is theirs, in compt,/ To make their audit at your highness' pleasure,/ Still to return your own" (1984, 17). Indeed she never slacked in her presentation skills. But the same lady, who was supposed to have well-known the nitti-gritties of the corporate etiquette, gaffes in the 'discovery scene'. At Macduff's public declaration that the royal king has been murdered, Lady Macbeth blurted out off guard: "Woe alas! What! In our house"? (1984, 29).

C. Conceptual Skill: "It is the ability to see the 'big picture', to recognize the significant elements in a situation, and to understand the relationships among he elements"

(Harold and Weihrich 1998, 6). The other way of putting it is that a manager must have the cerebral acumen to analyze and diagnose complex situation. Managers ought to target problems, prove themselves as sound decision-makers, correct the problem, weigh all alternatives and select the best one. Macbeth in his famous soliloquy—"If it were done, when 'tis done, then it were well/ It were done quickly: (1984, 36) attempts to do the very same thing. He conjures the big picture but not without the pros and cons. He analyses the varied shortcomings of such an Icarian ambition in becoming a king. He targets the problem, but yet lacks the holistic approach in doing so. He addresses the practical part of it and intentionally pooh-poohs (as his language reveals) the intrinsic ethical part. No wonder there is but only one shortcoming which he ultimately concludes, that bars him from assassinating Duncan: "I have no spur/ to prick the side of my intent," (1984, 40). Macbeth thus becomes resolute: "We will proceed no further in this business" (1984, 40). Yet such a decision made with such narrow an overview is doomed to not to hold too long.

Even Lady Macbeth encountered a problem and was required to display a sound judgement of decision-making. Macbeth she analyzed was too lily-livered, sentimental and mawkish to attempt the regicide. The milk of human kindness was brimming in his ethos. Yet such a view revealing Macbeth falls insufficient. Dr. S.C. Sengupta soundly observes: "How accurately she anticipates the recoiling of Macbeth. With insight knowledge she lays bares his character. But it is only the surface of his mind that she can expose; she has no understanding of its deeper reaches out of which the scruples well up. It is significant that she is a blind, as he himself is, to the real reason of his vacillations" (1998, 120).

Thus both the characters are not fully accurate with their managerial skills and this they fail to comprehend or knowingly overlook. Thus when the tragedy ensues then they themselves are the lynchpin cause for it.

2. Five Steps of Managerial Functions. How Effective were the Protagonists?

In early twentieth century, a French Industrialist Henri Fayol wrote that all managers perform five management functions: plan, organize, command, coordinate and control (*Industrial and General Administration.* Paris: Dunod, 1916). The recent Management studies have condensed them down to: planning, organizing, staffing, leading and controlling.

A. Planning: "The Planning function encompasses defining an organization's goals, establishing an overall strategy for achieving those goals, and developing a comprehensive hierarchy of plans to integrate and coordinate activities" (Robbins 2003, 2). But what makes an analytical Plan to a real Plan is a decision-making. Both Macbeth and Lady Macbeth chalk out their plan of how to materialize the regicide:

> "We fail!
> But screw your courage to the sticking-place,
> And we'll not fail. When Duncan is asleep—
> Whereto the rather shall his day's hard journey
> Soundly invite him—his two chamberlains
> Will I with wine and wassail so convince
> That memory, the warder of the brain,
> Shall be a fume, and the receipt of reason
> A limbeck only: when in swinish sleep
> Their drenched natures lie as in a death,
> What cannot you and I perform upon
> The unguarded Duncan? What not put upon
> His spongy officers, who shall bear the guilt
> Of our great quell"? (1984: 43)

To this Macbeth further adds his innovativeness: "Will it not be received,/ When we have mark'd with blood those sleepy two/ Of his own chamber and used their very daggers,/ That they have done't?" (1984, 44). They thus arrive to a concrete decision both seeming "settled, and bend up/ Each corporeal agent to this terrible feet" (44, 1984).

B. Organizing: "It includes the determination of what tasks are to be done, who is to do them, how the tasks are to be grouped, who reports to whom, and where decisions are to be made" (Robbins 2003, 2). Not only is their aforementioned plan organized but while executing it out, they make further improvements on it. Lady Macbeth doing the needful of her part of job rings the bell for Macbeth's posset which in actuality is a signal bell stating the fact that the stage of murder is all set. But when the supposedly well knit planning and organization is almost at a jeopardy with the sudden awakening of Donalbain and Malcolm; and Macbeth's forgetting of putting aside the blood stained dagger with the murdered Duncan; and Macbeth's conscience stricken ravings at the act, Lady Macbeth intervenes with an aggressiveness of a consummate corporate leader. She rebukes Macbeth's infirmity of purpose:

> Infirm of purpose!
> Give me the daggers: the sleeping and the dead
> Are but as pictures: 'tis the eye of childhood
> That fears a painted devil. If he do bleed,
> I'll gild the faces of the grooms withal;
> For it must seem their guilt. (1984, 55)

With her re-entrance, they find a hard knocking on at the south entry gate and Lady Macbeth decides that they shall need to move indoors to get themselves dressed and even to clean their hands, for the discovery of the murder shall make the guests call upon them.

C. **Staffing:** "It involves filling and keeping filled, the position in the organization structure. This is done by identifying workforce requirements; inventorying the people available; and recruiting, selecting, placing, promoting, appraising, planning the carriers of, compensating, and training or otherwise developing both candidates and current jobholders to accomplish their tasks effectively and efficiently" (Robbins 2003, 23). This staffing part is essentially done by Lady Macbeth in recruiting and selecting Macbeth himself for the heinous deed:

> Hie thee hither,
> That I may pour my spirits in thine ear;
> And chastise with the valour of my tongue

All that impedes thee from the golden round,
Which fate and metaphysical aid doth seem
To have thee crown'd withal" (1984, 13)

She plans his career as the King of Scotland and helps to promote him thus. She trains him to maintain a veneer, a facade-to be a serpent under the garb of a flower. Macbeth also attempts to do the staffing with Banquo by meeting him out the career opportunity of a better future: "If you shall cleave to my consent, when 'tis,/ It shall make honour for you" (1984, 22). But Banquo resolutely chooses to remain free of any obligation from Macbeth or be a consort to his scheme. Macbeth reveals his élan for staffing in his recruitment of three murderers for Banquo and Fleance.

D. Leading: This "includes motivating employees, directing others, selecting the most effective communication channels, and resolving conflicts" (Robbins 2003, 3). It is at this point where both protagonists fail miserably. As a royal employer, instead of motivating employees, they go ahead to assassinate them and their family. The communication channels between each other fail miserably at the end. Further, Macbeth chooses the most equivocatory type of communication—the quasi-veracious weird sisters to trust his life upon. Each fail to resolve the conflict within them self. Their minds remain full of scorpions, which leads one to self-annihilate and the other to opt for an almost-suicide. Thus Shakespeare's Macbeth like most of his tragedies, is less about leaders and more about failed leaders.

E. Controlling: This is the final function of a manager/ leader. "To ensure that things are going as they should, management must monitor the organization's performance. Actual performance must be compared with the previously set goals. If there are any significant deviations, it's management's job to get the organization back on track. This monitoring, comparing, and potential correcting is what is meant by controlling function" (Robbins 2003, 3). But Macbeth proves thoroughly unqualified in any control be it over his revolting men, jeopardized country or shudder-shaken self. The frame of things has fallen disjoint for him everywhere. He requests the Royal doctor to scrutinize the syndromes of the malfunctioning circumstances of Scotland but himself remains knowingly blind of the whys and wherefores.

3. Theories of Motivation: "All our nights and days to come give solely sovereign sway and masterdom"

A. Maslow's "Hierarchy of Needs" (Maslow, Abraham. *Motivation and Personality*, New York: Harper & Row, 1954): This is one of the early and popular theories of Motivation. Maslow hypothesized that within every human being there exists a hierarchy of five needs. These are:

1. Physiological: Includes hunger, thirst, shelter, sex, and other bodily needs.
2. Safety: Includes security and protection from physical and emotional harm.
3. Social: Includes affection, belongingness, acceptance, and friendship.
4. Esteem: Includes internal esteem factors such as status, recognition, and attention.
5. Self-actualization: The drive to become what one is capable of becoming; includes growth, achieving one's potential, and self-fulfilment. (Robbins, 156, 2003)

If in the initial phase of the play, Lady Macbeth acts as an agent, who gears up Macbeth through her dynamics of motivation, then she does not orderly climb the ladder of Maslow's hierarchy of needs. She whets the latent self-actualization dreams of Macbeth, conjuring the golden round in front of his eyes, overlooking the basic physiological needs of the person. Sleep and good feast, which according to Wilson Knight is the positive life themes in Macbeth[2], something Macbeth so desperately longs for and something that remains an ever eluding factor to the hero is never addressed by Lady Macbeth:

> Methought I heard a voice cry 'Sleep no more!
> Macbeth does murder sleep', the innocent sleep,
> Sleep that knits up the ravell'd sleeve of care,

The death of each day's life, sore labour's bath,
Balm of hurt minds, great nature's second course,
Chief nourisher in life's feast,.... (1984, 24)

When Macbeth trembles in the fact that his entire essence has been rendered incarnadine through the bloody deed, his emotional equilibrium having gone for a Tsunamical toss, Lady Macbeth fail to provide a gratification for his emotional safety needs. She rather spurns the entire matter:

Why, worthy thane,
You do unbend your noble strength, to think
So brainsickly of things. Go get some water,
And wash this filthy witness from your hand. (1984, 25)

Further, there is no cessation of the physical threat that looms large over Macbeth, though having self-actualized himself he has to climb down the ladder for his safety needs: "To be thus is nothing; But to be safely thus.—Our fears in Banquo/ Stick deep;" (1984: 35). Macbeth's acknowledgement of the fact that he is almost ostracized from societal belongingness, friends and peers reveals his lack of fulfilment in social realm:

I have lived long enough: my way of life
Is fall'n into the sear, the yellow leaf;
And that which should accompany old age,
As honour, love, obedience, troops of friends,
I must not look to have; but, in their stead,
Curses, not loud but deep, mouth-honour, breath,
Which the poor heart would fain deny, and dare not.
(1984: 73-74)

This very speech also hints the fact that the withered state is not only with regards to an emaciated body, but even to a deciduous heart, which in turn insinuates a proper respect earned for the self. Macbeth's esteem needs are further not fulfilled in failing to earn the proper respect and recognition as a king—all but remains sycophancy and mouth-honouring.

B. Herzberg's "Two-Factor Theory" (Herzberg, F., Mausner, B. and Snyderman, B.B. *The Motivation to Work*. John Wiley, New York: 1959): This theory proposed by the psychologist Fredrick Herzberg is also known as Motivation-Hygiene Theory. The analysis of his experiment revealed the fact that that unhappiness or dissatisfaction of an employee was related to the environment in which people were working. On the contrary, feelings of happiness or satisfaction were related to their jobs. Thus, hygiene/maintenance/environmental factors, extrinsic to the job, are necessary not to provide satisfaction but an absence of the same will lead to dissatisfaction. Hence, these were labeled 'dissatisfiers'. On the other hand, motivational factors are intrinsic parts of the job. Any increase in these factors will satisfy the employees and help to improve performance. But decrease in these factors will not cause dissatisfaction. Therefore, based on personality, there could either be a "motivation seeker" or a "maintenance seeker". In relation to Macbeth, he is both. His urge for esteem and self-actualization makes him a motivation seeker; whereas physiological, safety and social needs make him a maintenance seeker. An absence of the hygiene factors makes him dissatisfied with his job. But if Macbeth continues with the same is because: "I am in blood/ Stepp'd in so far that, should I wade no more,/ Returning were as tedious as go o'er:" (1984, 47).

C. **Alderfer's "ERG Theory"** (Alderfer, Clayton P., *Existence, Relatedness, and Growth; Human Needs in Organizational Settings*. New York: Free Press, 1972): Clayton P. Alderfer of Yale University has reworked Maslow's need hierarchy to align it more closely to the empirical research. His revised need hierarchy is labeled ERG Theory. According to him, there are three groups of core needs: Existence (E), Relatedness (R) and Growth (G). The existence need group is equated with Maslow's physiological and safety needs. The relatedness need group is equated with social need and external components of Maslow's esteem classification. Finally, the growth need is inclusive of Maslow's self-actualization. Besides substituting three needs for five, the ERG theory demonstrates that "(1) more than one need may be operative at the same time, and (2) if the gratification of a higher level need is stifled, the desire to satisfy a lower-level need increases" (Robbins,

2003, 161). Thus it is when the interpersonal relationships and social communions—an aspect of the relatedness—are impeding in the life of Macbeth than he thinks of unperturbed sleep.

D. McClelland's Theory of Needs (McClelland, David Clarence. *The Achieving Society*. Princeton, NJ: Van Nostrand, 1961): David McClelland of Harvard University and his associates identified three types of human needs, namely the need for achievement (n Ach), the need for affiliation (n Aff) and the need for power (n Pow). People with achievement motive take calculated risks, set moderate goals, want immediate and precise feedback, they are not merely matcrially motivated, are highly dedicated and take personal responsibility in solving problems. People with power motive always desire to influence and control people. It is the ability to manipulate and control the activities of others to suit one's own objectives. People with a high need for power seek position of leadership. They are outspoken, forceful and demanding. The people with the need for affiliation motive "reflects a desire to interact socially with people. Persons with a high need for affiliation usually desire pleasure from being loved and tend to avoid the pain of being rejected. They are concerned with maintaining pleasant social relationships. Social relationship takes precedence over task accomplishment for such persons. They are motivated by jobs that demand frequent interaction with co-workers. Such people are not likely to succeed well at tasks that force them to work in isolation" (Harold and Weihrich 1998, 5.30-5.31). Lady Macbeth indubitably is a character in need of power. She influences Macbeth to behave in a way in which Macbeth might not have behaved otherwise. On the other hand Macbeth starts as achievement oriented manager. He weighs too much of practical pros and cons, relying on the great virtue of "If". Pertinently did Stephen P. Robbins observe: "They (High Achievers) like to set goals that require stretching themselves a little. When there is an approximately equal chance of success or failure, there is the optimum opportunity to experience feelings of accomplishment and satisfaction from their efforts" (2003, 162). Indeed he is an over-stretcher being well aware that such vaunting ambition might lead him to "dishonor and wretchedness instead of glory and felicity".[3] But Macbeth's ultimate need is the need for affiliation. He yearns for friendship, camaraderie, love, trust and admiration.

E. Adam's "Equity Theory" [Adams, J.S. "Inequality in Social Exchange" in *Advances in Experimental Psychology*, L. Berkowitz (ed.). New York: Academic Press, 1965, 267-99): The theory was formulated by J. Stacy Adams of the United States in 1965. The theory is based on the assumption that members of an organization expect justice, balance and fairness in treatment by their employers. There are two main variables in this theory—inputs and outcome. Inputs are the contributions which an individual perceives that he puts into his job. Outcomes are the rewards which the individual receives from the organization and from his job. Inputs include the employee's training, experience, special knowledge, personal characteristics, etc. Outcomes consist of pay, promotion, recognition, status, fringe benefits, etc.

Inputs and outcomes are thus important elements in the exchange relationship between the organization and its members. When the individual feels that the outcomes he receives from the organization are fair in terms of his inputs he is satisfied and motivated. The individual also compares his input outcome ratio with the input-output ratio of other members of his level or status in the organization. If the individual feels that his ratio is equal to that of others, there is equity. He feels satisfied and motivated. If the ratio is significantly less in comparison with those of others, the individual feels underpaid and frustrated. If the ratio is significantly more, the individual feels overpaid and guilty. He is likely to reduce/increase his input of effort to create equity. To say otherwise:

Equity = Self outcomes/Self inputs = Other's outcomes/ Other's inputs

Taking Macbeth's point into consideration, not that there is much disparity between his inputs and his outcomes, for he is crowned with success in the most literal sense, but what makes him dissatisfies is Banquo's present privileged position, between Banquo's outcome/input ratios:

> then prophet like
> They hail'd him father to a line of kings:
> Upon my head they placed a fruitless crown,
> And put a barren sceptre in my gripe,
> Thence to be wrench'd with an unlineal hand,
> No son of mine succeeding. If 't be so,
> For Banquo's issue have I filled my mind;
> For them the gracious Duncan have I murder'd;
> Put rancours in the vessel of my peace
> Only for them; and mine eternal jewel
> Given to the common enemy of man,
> To make them kings, the seed of Banquo kings!
> Rather than so, come fate into the list.
> And champion me to the utterance! (1984, 75)

F. Vroom's "Expectancy Theory" (Vroom, Victor. *Work and Motivation*. New York: John Wiley, 1964): By far, one of the most widely accepted theory of motivation is Vroom's Expectancy Theory. Expectancy theory argues that the strength of a tendency to act in a certain way depends on the strength of an expectation that will be followed by a given outcome and on the attractiveness of that outcome on the individual. The theory, therefore, focuses on three relationships:

1. Effort-performance relationship. The probability perceived by the individual that exerting a given amount of effort will lead to performance.
2. Performance-reward relationship. The degree to which the individual believes that performing at a particular level will lead to the attainment of a desired outcome.
3. Rewards-personal goals relationship. The degree to which organizational rewards satisfy an individual's personal goals or needs and the attractiveness of those potential rewards for the individual. (Robbins 2003, 171)

These are variously dubbed by Vroom as *Expectancy*, *Instrumentality* and *Valence*. According to Vroom, Motivation/Force is an outcome of the sum total of the above three.

Macbeth, the Thane of Glamis with his efforts in the battlefield, became the highest performing general of all—"Bellona's Bridegroom". This brought unto him Organizational rewards, he was crowned Thane of Cawdor. But his Personal goals were yet to be satisfied for he wanted to be crowned the King. This dissatisfaction led him to gear up his efforts in being the murderer of Duncan—the ultimate audacious performance. This in lieu brought him the 'Golden Round'. But yet his personal goals were far from being satisfied. Macbeth, who efforted, performed and was rewarded by a personal satisfaction that quenched his Icarian ambition of being a king, realized to his chagrin that all has been labored in vain. Quenching his dark and deep desires he has lost his eternal jewel, like the farmer who hanged himself in expectation of plenty:

> To-morrow, and to-morrow, and to-morrow,
> Creeps in this petty pace from day-to-day
> To the last syllable of recorded time,
> And all our yesterdays have lighted fools
> The way to dusty death. Out, out, brief candle!
> Life's but a walking shadow, a poor player
> That struts and frets his hour upon the stage
> And then is heard no more: it is a tale
> Told by an idiot, full of sound and fury,
> Signifying nothing. (1984, 77)

G. McGregor's "Theory X and Theory Y" (McGregor, Douglas. *The Human Side of Enterprise*. New York: McGraw-Hill, 1960): Douglas McGregor proposed two distinct views of human beings: one basically negative, labeled Theory X, and the other basically positive, labeled Theory Y. After viewing the way in which managers dealt with employees, McGregor concluded that a manager's view of the nature of human beings is based on certain grouping of assumptions and that he or she tends to mould his or her behaviour toward employees according to these assumptions:

Under Theory X, the four assumptions held by managers are:

1. Employees inherently dislike work and, whenever possible, will attempt to avoid it.
2. Since employees dislike work, they must be coerced, controlled, or threatened with punishment to achieve goals.
3. Employees will avoid responsibilities and seek formal direction whenever possible.
4. Most workers place security above all other factors associated with work and will display little ambition.

In contrast to these negative views about the nature of human views, about the nature of human beings, McGregor listed the four positive assumptions that he called Theory Y:

1. Employees can view work as being as natural as rest or play.
2. People will exercise self-direction and self-control if they are committed to the objectives.
3. The average person can learn to accept, even seek, responsibility.
4. The ability to make innovative decisions is widely dispersed throughout the population and is not necessarily the sole province of those in management positions. (Robbins 2003, 157)

Lady Macbeth's use of the dynamics of persuasion conforms to both the above stated theories. Lady Macbeth's initial assumption of Macbeth's infirm-of-purpose kind of nature essentially arises of her assessment of Macbeth's character from the Theory X angel:

> Yet do I fear thy nature;
> It is too full o' the milk of human kindness
> To catch the nearest way: thou wouldst be great;
> Art not without ambition, but without

The illness should attend it: what thou wouldst highly.
That wouldst thou holily; wouldst not play false,
And yet wouldst wrongly win: thou'ldst have, great Glamis,
That which cries 'Thus thou must do, if thou have it;
And that which rather thou dost fear to do
Than wishest should be undone.' Hie thee hither,
That I may pour my spirits in thine ear;
And chastise with the valour of my tongue
All that impedes thee fro the golden round,
Which fate and metaphysical aid doth seem
To have thee crown'd withal. (1984, 13)

But while persuading Macbeth, Lady Macbeth in concurrence to theory Y rightly assumes that Macbeth is ambitious, he has all the will to attain the highest recognition, he could self-direct himself and even self Motivate. She uses the royal 'We' which future-hints to an involvement in decision-making. From autocratic leadership she shifts into democratic leadership:

Art thou afeard
To be the same in thine own act and valour
As thou art in desire? Wouldst thou have that
Which thou esteem'st the ornament of life,
And live a coward in thine own esteem,
Letting 'I dare not' wait upon 'I would,'
Like the poor cat i' the adage?...
Be so much more the man. Nor time nor place
Did then adhere, and yet you would make both:
They have made themselves, and that their
fitness now
Does unmake you...
We fail!
But screw your courage to the sticking-place,
And we'll not fail. (1984, 19-20)

4. Corporate Social Responsibility: "The Water of Macbeth's land" never casted, her disease never found.

In his seminal book *Social Responsibilities of the Businessman* (New York: Harper & Row, 1953), Howard, R. Bowen suggested that execution of business, its policies and operations, must have a positive impact on society. Macbeth's failure as an entrepreneur primarily lies in his scrupleless, compunctionless, ethicless and self-centric megalomaniac enterprises. Macbeth failed to understand that his social involvement would rather enhance his power and influence, as was the case in Duncan's.

Thus, Macbeth and Lady Macbeth from the Management perspective remains failed leaders, with potentials high but realizations infirm and improper.

Notes

1. As quoted by Jason Cattrell of the New Route Theatre Company, 'Shakespeare Business Advisor' in The British Theatre Guide in <http://www.britishtheatreguide.info/articles/130102.htm> accessed on 12 January 2009.
2. Knight, G. Wilson, 'The Milk of Concord: An Essay on Life Themes in Macbeth'. The Wheel of Fire, London: Oxford UP, 1930.
3. G.K. Hunter as quoted in Kenneth Muir ed. *Macbeth, The Arden Shakespeare*, 1984, 40.

Works Cited

Koontz, Harold and Heinz Weihrich. *Essentials of Management*. Fifth Edn. New Delhi: Tata McGraw-Hill, 1998.

Katz, R.L. "Skills of an Effective Administrator", *Harvard Business Review*, September-October, 1974.

Robbins, P. Stephen. *Organizational Behaviour*. Ninth Edition. New Delhi: Prentice-Hall of India Pvt. Ltd., 2003.

Shakespeare, William. *Macbeth*. Ed. by S.C. Sengupta. Kolkata: A. Mukherjee & Co. Pvt. Ltd., 1998.

17

Dreams, Nightmares and *The Ancient Mariner*

Nishi Pulugurtha

The Rime of the Ancient Mariner, Christabel, and *Kubla Khan* depend on striking images for their effect. Coleridge's aim was, as he writes in the *Biographia Literaria*, to take supernatural "incidents and agents" and convey them with "dramatic truth" as would "naturally accompany such situations, supposing them real"[1] and to effect "for the imagination that willing suspension of disbelief for the moment which constitutes poetic faith".[2]

In his lectures on Shakespeare, Coleridge says:

> ...he [the poet] acquires the right and privilege of using time and space as they exist in the imagination, obedient only to the laws which the imagination acts by.[3]

In another notebook entry of 1805, Coleridge asserts the superiority of mind over nature:

> In looking at the objects of nature while I am thinking, as at yonder moon dim glimmering thro' the dewy window-pane, I seem rather to be seeing, as it were *asking*, a symbolical language for something within me that already and forever exists, than observing anything new.[4]

The *Biographia* passage makes Coleridge's interest in the psychological and imaginative clear.

On his voyage to Malta in 1804, alone like the Mariner and haunted by guilt and misery, Coleridge identified himself closely with the Ancient Mariner. A notebook entry of this time reveals an important comment on the nature of poetry.

> Poetry a rationalized dream dealing [? about?] to manifold Forms our own Feelings, that never perhaps were attached by us consciously to our own personal Selves—What is the Lear, the Othello, but a divine dream/ all Shakespeare, and nothing Shakespeare.—O there are Truths below the Surface in the subject of Sympathy....[5]

Coleridge recognizes the identity of feeling and form. This entry reveals Coleridge's awareness of the unconscious and of the similarity between artistic creation and dreams.

The Rime of the Ancient Mariner is a poem that is chiefly concerned with the problem of the existence of evil, the spiritual barrenness that comes after sinning and the wandering of a soul whose redemption is partial. In a notebook entry, Coleridge writes, "Wandering Jew/ a romance".[6] Wordsworth provided much of the subject of the poem. Coleridge and Wordsworth, as is well-known, began the poem, as a joint effort in November 1797, to provide the money for a walking tour in Somerset. Wordsworth wrote many years later,

> Much of the greatest part of the story was Mr Coleridge's invention; but certain parts I suggested; for example, some crime was to be committed which should bring upon the Old Navigator, as Coleridge afterwards delighted to call him, the spectral persecution, as a consequence of that crime and his own wanderings.... 'Suppose', said I, 'you represent him as having killed one of these birds on entering the South Sea, and that the tutelary spirits of these regions take upon them to avenge the crime'. The incident was thought fit for the purpose, and adopted accordingly. I also suggested the navigation of the ship by the dead men.... We began the composition together, on that to me memorable evening.... As we endeavoured to proceed conjointly...,

> our respective manners proved so widely different that it would have been quite presumptuous in me to do anything but separate from an undertaking upon which I could only have been a clog.[7]

Coleridge's notebook entries of this time show clearly that he was involved deeply in a conflict between Faith and Reason, God and Nature, mechanistic and transcendental explanations of the universe, much of which are reflected in *The Rime of the Ancient Mariner*. In a letter to his brother George (March 10, 1798), Coleridge writes of his awareness of evil and the incongruity between it and the pantheistic belief that love of Nature leads ultimately to love for all creation.

> Of guilt I say nothing; but I believe most steadfastly in original Sin; that from our mother's wombs, our understandings are darkened.... And for this inherent depravity, I believe, that the *Spirit* of the Gospel is the sole cure—but permit me to add, that I look for the *spirit* of the Gospel 'neither in the mountain, nor at Jerusalem'.[8]

The need for the Gospel to overcome the sinful nature of the will sheds light on the evil impulse of the Mariner when he shot the Albatross:

> Ah! well a-day! what evil looks
> Had I from old and young!
> Instead of the cross, the Albatross
> About my neck was hung.[9]

In the same letter, Coleridge describes the power of poetry,

> ...to elevate the imagination and set the affections in right tone by the beauty of the inanimate impregnated, as with a living soul, by the presence of Life.[10]

The Rime of the Ancient Mariner reveals some connection between nature and the soul of man. Nature, in the poem, does not seem benevolent or capable of destroying evil. However, the concepts of Original Sin and the power of the Gospel to heal are present in the poem. Coleridge builds the human experience of the poem around the depression and the sense of isolation which the Mariner describes in Part IV. The Mariner is isolated to a great degree,

> Alone, alone, all, all alone,
> Alone on the wide wide sea.[11]

Not only is he isolated physically but socially as well.

> And never a saint took pity on
> My soul in agony.[12]

The ordinary world has been depleted of its beauty:

> The many men, so beautiful!
> And they all dead did lie[13],

and the Mariner is left alone with worthless, disgusting things:

> And a thousand thousand slimy things
> Lived on; and so did I.[14]

There is a sense of guilt also. When he tried to pray:

> I looked to heaven, and tried to pray;
> But or ever a prayer had gusht,
> A wicked whisper came, and made
> My heart as dry as dust.[15]

The feeling is one of the drying away of energy, of weakness:

> For the sky and the sea, and the sea and the sky
> Lay like a load on my weary eye,
> And the dead were at my feet.[16]

This is the central experience of the Mariner and comes in the middle of the poem. What follows from here is the recovery and the aftermath.

Coleridge was interested in the depiction of nightmare states of the mind and used some of his own experiences in shaping the Mariner's. His interest in the nature of the Mariner's suffering continued even after the publication of the poem in 1798. An awareness of his own dreams and nightmares and an interest in psychological states of the mind possibly led to the revisions of the poem. Most of the revisions pertain to the third section of the poem, the appearance of the spectre ship. Coleridge's feelings of isolation and depression intensified towards the end of 1803 and on the voyage to

Malta in 1804, as his notebook entries of the time reveal, he associated himself with the Ancient Mariner.[17]

The journey to Malta was one of Coleridge's many escapes from the reality of life. Marital discord, disillusionment in his love for Sara Hutchinson, a feeling of the waning of his poetic powers—all added to his isolation and hence an identification with his creation on the becalmed sea. A number of observations made on this voyage were later incorporated into the revised version of the poem. In May 1804, he referred to the object of the sailor's superstition—"...the Star, that dogged the Crescent".[18] Coleridge altered this phrase to "the star-dogged Moon".[19] He saw the "...Light of the Compass & rudder man's Lamp reflected with forms on the Main Sail",[20] which anticipates the line "The steersman's face by his lamp gleamed white".[21]

Most of Coleridge's revisions of the poem contain some significant indications of his knowledge and understanding of nightmares. On the voyage to Malta, confined to his cabin by sea-sickness, Coleridge writes what death by drowning would be like.

> Sleeps, these Horrors, these frightful Dreams of Despair when the sense of individual Existence is full and lively only <for one> to feel oneself powerless, crushed *in* by every power—a stifling boding, one abject miserable Wretch/ yet hopeless, yet struggling, removed from all touch of Life, deprived of all notion of Death/ strange mixture of Fear and Death.[22]

"Nightmare Life-in-Death," a later incorporation into the poem, is a reworking of the phrase "ever-living Death". In a letter of 1796 to Thomas Poole, Coleridge writes of Charles Lloyd who was living with him as suffering from "a kind of Night-mair".

> He falls all at once into a kind of Night-mair: and all the Realities round him mingle with, and form part of the strange Dream. All his voluntary powers are suspended; but he perceives everything and hears everything, and whatever he perceives and hears he perverts into the substance of his delirious Vision.[23]

Coleridge carefully distinguishes between a dream and a nightmare. A nightmare is:

> a state not of Sleep but of Stupor of the outward organs of Sense.... This stupor seems occasioned by some painful sensation, of unknown locality...which withdrawing the attention to itself from its sense of other realities present makes us asleep to them indeed but otherwise awake....[24]

During a nightmare, "the true inward Creatix" creates its own forms which seem to be real because:

> the power of Reason being in good measure awake, most generally presents to us all the accompanying images...very nearly as they existed the moment before.... In short, this night-mair is not properly *a Dream*; but a species of Reverie, akin to Somnambulism, during which the Understanding and Moral Sense are awake tho' more or less confused, and over the Terrors of which the Reason can exert no influence....[25]

The Rime of the Ancient Mariner had a subtitle in the second edition of the *Lyrical Ballads*—"A Poet's Reverie"—at the insistence of Wordsworth. The events of the poem are seen through the eyes of the Mariner. However, the Mariner does not comprehend the seriousness of his situation and our view of him. He commits a heinous crime against the "One Life" and hence, has to undergo the trials and tribulations to restore the harmony. The first version of the poem just reported the killing of the bird by the Mariner.

These lines of 1798:

> Listen Stranger! Storm and Wind,
> A Wind and Tempest strong!
> For days and weeks it play'd us freaks-
> Like chaff we drove along.
>
> Listen Stranger! Mist and Snow,
> And it grew wondrous cauld;
> And Ice mast high came floating by
> As green as Emerauld.[26]

were later expanded to:

And now the STORM-BLAST came, and he
Was tyrannous and strong:
He struck with his o'ertaking wings,
And chased us south along.

With sloping masts and dripping prow,
As he who pursued with yell and blow
Still treads the shadow of his foe,
And forward bends his head,
The ship drove fast, loud roared the blast,
And southward aye we fled.[27]

Coleridge was concerned with questions of moral evil and guilt. During 1803-1806, when he made a number of revisions to the poem, there are a number of notebook entries that have a bearing on the poem. "The Pains of Sleep", composed in 1803, is a poem that records three nights of bad dreams:

But yester-night I prayed aloud
In anguish and in agony,
Up-starting from the fiendish crowd
Of shapes and thoughts that tortured me:
Fantastic passions! Maddening brawl!

And shame and terror over all!
Deeds to be hid which were not hid,
Which all confused I could not know
Whether I suffered, or I did:
For all seemed guilt, remorse, or woe,
My own or others still the same
Life-stifling fear, soul-stifling shame.[28]

The fears of guilt, the doubts as to whether he is a suffering victim or an active agent of evil, the startling and horrifying effects of nightmarish figures are reminiscent of the Mariner's experiences.

The Mariner's act reveals a lack of thinking on his part about its significance and consequences. In the passage in *The Statesman's Manual* that explains the origin of evil, Coleridge says:

> in its utmost abstraction and consequent state of reprobation, the will becomes satanic pride and rebellious self-idolatry in the relations of the spirit to itself, and remorsely despotism relatively to others... in short, by the fearful resolve to find in itself alone the one absolute motive of action, under which all other motives from within and from without must be either subordinated or crushed.[29]

Both, *The Rime of the Ancient Mariner* and *Christabel* are concerned with individuals who have been separated from the main course of life, either by faults of their own or inadvertently. The ties that bind them to the general course of life are ruptured and what characterizes their state is deprivation. This for Coleridge is the tragedy of the human condition; in particular, it is his own personal tragedy.

Throughout his life, Coleridge was always seeking for an anchor, someone on whom he could rely and depend on. Images of women figure prominently in Coleridge's supernatural poems. In *The Rime of the Ancient Mariner,* Nightmare Life-in-Death is a representative both of life and death.

A characteristic feature of Coleridge's poetry is his interest in states of the mind. Personal experiences and introspection are an important feature of his work and form a bridge between his philosophical speculations and the more personal reflections. The prime concern of Coleridge's poetry was an attempt to discover a mode of knowing and feeling. Psychology forms the basis of much of Coleridge's criticism and permeates his work. His poems testify to his great interest in dreams and nightmares. Together with a deep-seated psychological interest in the inner recesses of the human mind was an interest in political ideals, a feeling for human relationships, nature and love.

Coleridge revised his poems over a period of years and his revisions are rooted in awareness of his problems and in psychological states of the mind. The various revisions of the poems at different times clearly reveal changes in the way he viewed the events and characters in the poems often in relation to the incidents of his own life. The revisions of *The Rime of the Ancient Mariner,* the Argument and the gloss contribute to an understanding of the poem and all its nuances with the poet as guide, leading the reader along. *The Argument of the 1798 Lyrical Ballads* version restricts the focus of the poem geographically. It tells how a ship after having crossed the Equator is driven by storms towards the South Pole and of the strange incident that took place. *The Argument in the 1800 Lyrical Ballads* version, however, makes a reference to the deed and its consequence. In this version the geographical details are omitted. The gloss of the *The Rime of the Ancient Mariner* acts as a commentary on the events of the poem and is an obvious indication of the poet's intrusion into the framework of the poem. The gloss was added in 1815-1816, when a collected edition of Coleridge's poems was being prepared, and was first published in the *Sibylline Leaves* (1817). Even before the reader gets to the poem, he is faced with a way of reading it. This is part of Coleridge's strategy to be in control of everything, circumscribing the reader's response. The Argument and gloss seem to deny an independent elaboration of the poems. The revisions create new levels of narrative which force different reading experiences, each time one that Coleridge would have wanted his readers to have. This conscious strategy of being in control of the reading experience can be linked to the absence of control in his life. Coleridge's poetry presents the poet turning away from externality to his individual life, to understand and explore his psyche.

Whatever the changes his philosophy underwent, one thing that remained constant was his belief in the unity of things, the presence of a single principle, what later on he referred to as the "one Life". This theme is predominant in his poetry and criticism. It is a part of the personal need to establish an inner wholeness. It is what the Ancient Mariner has lost in killing the Albatross, and for which he must do penance as long as he lives.

References

1. *Biographia Literaria*, II, 5. ed. Shawcross. 2 vols. Oxford: Oxford University Press, 1907, rpt. 1968.
2. *Ibid.*, p. 6.

3. Samuel Taylor Coleridge, *Shakespearean Criticism*, ed. Thomas Middleton Raysor. 2 vols. London: J.M. Dent & Sons Ltd., 1960, vol. I, p. 176.
4. *The Notebooks of Samuel Taylor Coleridge* (Henceforth referred to as *CNB*), ed. Kathleen Coburn. 3 volumes. Vol. 1. New York: Pantheon Books Inc., 1957. vols. 2, 3. London: Routledge & Kegan Paul, 1962, 1973, vol. II, 2546.
5. *CNB*, II, 2086.
6. *Ibid*., I, 45.
7. Quoted by John Livingstone Lowes, *The Road to Xanadu: A Study in the Ways of the Imagination*, London: Constable, 1951, 222-23.
8. *Collected Letters of Samuel Taylor Coleridge* (henceforth referred to as *CL*), ed. Earl Leslie Griggs. 6 vols. Oxford: Clarendon Press, 1956-1971. Vol. I, 396.
9. *The Works of Samuel Taylor Coleridge* (Henceforth referred to as *PW*), Hertfordshire: Wordsworth Poetry Library, Wordsworth Editions Ltd., 1994, 191, ll. 139-42.
10. *CL*., 397.
11. *PW*, 196, ll. 232-33.
12. *Ibid*., ll. 234-35.
13. *Ibid*., ll. 236-37.
14. *Ibid*., 197, ll. 238-39.
15. *Ibid*., ll. 244-47.
16. *Ibid*., ll. 250-52.
17. *CNB*, II, 1996.
18. *Ibid*., 2060.
19. PW, 196, l. 212
20. *Ibid*., 2001.
21. PW, 195, l. 207
22. *CNB*, II, 2078.
23. *CL*, I, 257.
24. *CNB*, III, 4046.
25. *Ibid*.
26. *PW*, 188.
27. PW, 188, ll. 41-50.
28. *Ibid*., 187-88, ll. 14-17, 25-32.
29. Appendix C, 65.

18

The House as Sign in *Sons and Lovers*

Bristi Basu

The word was made flesh

John 1: 14

D.H. Lawrence chooses to begin the original Foreword (1913) to his third novel with these heavily loaded words from the Gospel of St. John and employs the advantage of the plethora of meanings of this cryptically orchestrated apophthegm in the execution of what was to become his passport to the canon. Finding himself at the cross roads of the well grounded Victorian narrative tradition with its apparent complacency and the avant-garde Modernist (self-reflexive) narrative stance, Lawrence prepared to launch a surreptitious attack on the sense and sensibility of his readers.

The Maxim when turned around could be equally assimilated in the structuring of the test. In this interface of varied and divergent movements of ideas, an intricate pattern of sensory images emerge to enmesh with the fabric of the text. They remain as watermarks on the text and tantalize the readers. This elusive nature of the images and the signals they send out, their effortless transition from the conventional notions of signifiers and signified appear to be the markers of Lawrence's innovative style and pave the way for the novel's success. He capitalizes on the ideational fluidity of the 'teens in Europe and infuses this spirit of flux into *Sons and Lovers* with élan.

This paper endeavours to study two groups of sensory images as they occur in the text and show how they transcend the peripheries of what one understands by the term 'word' which describes an object/ 'concept', to become the 'object' and even more beyond, to achieve a merger of the two. The text derives its charge from simulating the enactment of a contest—the contest between the conflicts that the various characters go through in course of the novel in which the reader vicariously participates and the clues or aids that the text provides for the reader to resist the vicarious participation in order to maintain one's identity. This contest manifests itself as the text's effort to catch the 'word' the 'flesh', the character and the reader in a vortex of changeable significations and to drag them into a realm of excess of meanings. The act of reading *Sons and Lovers*, then comprises taking a plunge into the text, getting soaked in the innumerable swirls caused by the streams of significations that pass the reader by, and finally the laborious task of extricating oneself from this temptation of abundance to arrive at a position of equanimity and if possible the Miltonic state of rest where there is calm of mind when all passion is spent. However, keeping with the spirit of his times Lawrence resorts to irony in order that the reader can maintain a well marked out notion of the self.

For those who want to resist getting caught in this mazy layout of the novel, the best place to start engaging with the text would be the beginning—"the Bottoms". Is the Bottoms really the beginning? It actually "succeeded to Hell Row" (18)[1]. The semantic association with the word "Bottom" crowd in and jostle with each other for priority. Bottoms is not the first, Bottoms is low but not the lowest. 'Bottoms' is hardly a name one would associate with human habitation. As a matter of fact it has a matter ominous ring to it. The reader's misgivings are heightened because 'Bottoms' is preceded by the Squares—"great quadrangles of dwellings"—which has or palpable Foucauldian connection with a prison house. A person is a site not only for punishment but also for isolation. The description of the Squares which stood on the hillside of Bestwood sends very different vibes when compared with what

Bestwood Village would have appeared to be. A similar tone of difference runs through the descriptions of Hell Row and Bottoms when read in tandem; and the Bottoms was erected on the site of Hell Row.

After reading a couple of paragraphs of the text, the reader starts making other associations with the name Bottoms. The signified slips under the signifier and becomes the signifier, since the Bottoms is the mine-workers' lodgings, who erected it? Carston Waite and Co., of course. They meant business... and profit and a minimum of fuss:[2]

The Bottoms consisted of six blocks of miners' dwellings two rows of three, like the dots on a blank—six domino and twelve houses in a block. This double row of dwellings sat at the foot of the rather sharp slope from Bestwood, and looked out from the attic windows at least on the slow climb of the valleys towards Selby. (19)

It was erected "(to) accommodate the regiments of mines" (19). The word regiment has a military origin and has ultimately evolved out of the Latin regere (to rule). The Bottoms does not visibly resemble the Benthamite panopticon or barracks where regiments of soldiers are housed, but the overtones of rule, discipline and order act as innuendoes especially when related to the Squares.

A detached cosmetic appraisal of the houses grout gardens, fragrant flora, title porches, privet hedges and dormer windows—which conjures images of comfort and contentment are immediately cut through by contrapuntal images of the dwelling room, which is the kitchen mainly, situated at the back of the house, overlooking scrubby backyard, and ash pits. The prettier parts—"the uninhabited parlours of all the colliers' wives" (19)—stands in sharp contrast with the alleys, where the inhabitants—men, women and children—are actually found.

The text makes no bones of the fact that Mrs. Morel was not eager to "descend" (19) to the Bottoms from Bestwood. Another slippage of the signified occurs when the reader endorses the linguistic code and participates in the play off between the opposed semantic associations involving 'bottom' and 'best'. Mrs. Moral feels that she has to compromise on her standard of living and (prudish) sense of class when she is left with no alternative but to come down to live in the Bottoms. She ekes out an extra sixpence from her coffers towards rent to uphold her "superiority in station" (19) by having an extra patch of garden and only one neighbour. While gregariousness is a far cry for Mrs. Morel, the already prickly interpersonal relationship between the Moral spouses takes a turn for the worse in the Bottoms. Morel's going away to the wakes by himself and Mrs. Morel's evaluation of his action only under scores this erosion, Mrs. Morel has young children and her life is primarily bound to her home and she in turn identifies with it. The isolation of the Bottoms rubs on to her and permeates into her children especially into Paul her favourite, who would be born here and would grow up essentially to be a loner on a quest which would often obfuscated by his bonding with his mother.

The string of associations which starts as the architectural traits of the Bottoms is juxtaposed with the human condition of the Morel family, carries on to its logical conclusion as the signified slides under the signifier at different levels viz., lexical to the semantic, to the social, to the emotional and finally, to create a psychological condition in the novel. It is difficult not to notice the relationship between the word and the object which merges with the word progressively making ground for further connections.

The associations between the Morels and their house take on newer dimensions as they change, their lodgings once more (Ch 4, 74). The new wind swept house stands on the brow of a hill overlooking the valley unlike the one in the Bottoms which was situated at the foot of the hill from Bestwood and looked out to the rising hill. This house with a view has a huge ash (tree) standing in front that shrieks in the wind. The very mention of the word ash takes the reader back to the image of the ash pits in the Bottoms although he/she is aware that the ash here in a tree which can endure strong guest of wind.

The onomatoposic quality of the sound 'ash' creates a sound pattern which, as Saussure would argue is the reader's "psychological impression of the sound"[3] and the wind blows through the tree and makes it shriek. The ash pit as signifier, by association signifies dullness, boredom and inaction. However the ash (tree) as signifier by association signifies action and turmoil as the word shriek would suggest. The shrieking tree is music to Morel's ears. "It sends me to sleep" (74), he comments. The act of sleeping by implication disjoins Morel from the children's reaction to the sound of the ash. They simply hate it. Paul finds the noise almost 'demoniacal" (74). Lawrence uses a conventional Romantic trope,[4] pathetic fallacy, to draw a parallel between the tree tormented by wind and the children tormented by fear and anguish. This is another typical instance of what one might call double slippage:

> Shriek—tree tormented by wind—children tormented by fear/anguish
>
> (Signifier)—(Signified) Slippage (Signifier)—(Signified)
>
> (Signifier)—(Signified) Slippage—(Signifier)—(Signified)

The text reads:

> This terror came in from the shrieking of the tree and the anguish of the home discord. (74)

The slippages lead to such intense associations that the order in which the signifier and signified are arranged become immaterial:

> He heard the booming shouts of his father, come home nearly drunk then the sharp replies of his mother, then the bang, bang of his father's first on the table, and the nasty shout as the man's voice got higher. And then the whole was drowned in a piercing medley of shrieks and cries from the great, windswept ash-tree. (74)

The agony which the children suffer gets focused around violence.

> He might hit their mother again there was a feeling of horror, a kind of bristling in the drinkness and a sense of flood. (74)

Another link is set up between the earlier episodes (Ch 2) where Morel in an inebriated state flings a table drawer at Mrs. Morel making her bleed. The sheer immensity of the agony is expressed by interpolating two other sensory images, one visual—darkness and the other experiential—silence. The text cashes in on a sense of limitlessness that is attached to both these words. Dragging on the description of agony would tantamount to dalliance. Silence—induced by an abrupt drop in the noises outside and inside the house—adds to the poignancy of the agony. Darkness prevails.[5] Fear, anxiety and suffering in their varied facets become staple to the novel:

> From her the feeling was transmitted to the other children she never suffered alone anymore; the children suffered with her. (75)

The transmission of suffering from mother to children and further on to all those people who become intimate with the Morels, especially with Paul, sets, the psychological tone of *Sons and Lovers*. The shadows of discord and the shrieks of anguish that enumerate from the Morel lodgings are the psychological manifestations of the merger of the signifier and the signified leading to newer orders of significations. As the signified slips under the signifier, the definition of 'word' and 'object' get modified by association. Meaning is heaped upon meaning and the result is an excess of meaning. The text is left open ended. Paul Morel as well as the reader is left alone to grapple with this overflowing sense of excess.

References

D.H. Lawrence, *Sons and Lovers* (Calcutta: Rupa and Company, 1981), 18. All subsequent references to the text will follow the edition.

For a discussion on the Bottoms from a social perspective, refer to Graham Holderness, "Language and Social context in *Sons and Lovers*" cited in *Sons and Lovers: Contemporary Critical Essays*, ed. Rick Rylance (Hampshire and London: Macmillan Press Limited, 1996), 136-37.

Ferdinand de Saussure, "Nature of the Linguistic Sign" cited in *Modern Criticism and Theory: A Reader*, ed., David Lodge (New York: Longman Inc, 1988), 10.

'The Wind came through the tree fiercer and fiercer. All the cords of the great harp hummed, whistled and shrieked' (74). Readers cannot resist establishing a link with the Coleridgeam expression "Mad Lutanist" from his Dejection: An Ode".

Dorothy Van Ghent in her essay 'On Sons and Lovers' cited in *Sons and Lovers: A Case Book,* ed. Gamini Salgado (Hampshire and London: Macmillan Press Ltd., 1969), 128-29 discusses the implications of darkness in this novel.

19

Of Human Bondage: Fact-Fiction Interface

Reena Mitra

The literary career of William Somerset Maugham (1874-1965) which began with the publication of his first novel *Liza of Lambeth* in 1897 was remarkable in that it had the rare distinction of spanning a period of over half a century and earned for the author, an eminence and stature by virtue of which he stood tall among his contemporaries. He established his sovereignty in four distinct genres of creative expression, namely, the novel, the short-story, the stage play and the sound film. His versatility extended further to the publication of travelogues and of autobiography, to the enunciation of critical observations in literature and personal evaluations of religious and philosophical tenets.

Maugham, who spent five years as a medical student at St. Thomas's Hospital in London, did not regard that time stretch as misspent; rather, in his autobiographical work, *The Summing Up* (1938), he declares, "I do not know a better training for a writer than to spend some years in the medical profession." He attributed to this training the clinical attitude that he was able to cultivate, an attitude that became an integral part of his personality and characterized his approach to life. This dispassionate way of looking at things which *The Cambridge Guide to English Literature* refers to as "his merciless, anti-romantic powers of observation"[1] is closely related to the religious and philosophical views fostered by Maugham to foreground what is commonly known as cosmopolitanism. It is a cosmopolitan society that feeds his fiction. In *The Summing Up,* referring to his travels, he says that he always kept his eyes open for characters, oddness and personality and that his material for his works was drawn from a diversity of sources and a multiplicity of standards and morals and hence no general conclusion can be drawn from it. Each discrete fact that he draws upon is impressive in its own way and furnishes Maugham with matter to be utilized for his fictional art but this art is only narrative in nature and never judgemental.

Maugham's novel, *Of Human Bondage,* provides a very close parallel to the incidents in the author's own life but it is by no means an autobiography; it is, at best, an autobiographical novel. The writer himself endorses this categorization of the novel in *The Summing Up* where he asserts that *Of Human Bondage* is "not an autobiography, but an autobiographical novel; fact and fiction are inextricably mingled".[2]

Some of Maugham's novels like *Of Human Bondage* (1915), *Cakes and Ale* (1930) and *The Razor's Edge* (1944) have been immensely popular but the one that really made a mark was the first of these which is the most autobiographical of them all and had provided emotional release to the writer as he had poured out his woes and experiences on paper. The psychological catharsis effected by the writing of this work was as pacifying as the sublimation accomplished by Bennett's *Clay Hanger* and Well's *Love and Lewisham.*

Of Human Bondage, set in early twentieth century England, has a Naturalistic plot which presents the story of a young man's search for a way of life founded on common sense and bolstered by the scientific discipline and rationalistic approach he had inculcated in his early years of existence. It is a record of the thoughts and actions of an embittered and befuddled boy—a tale narrated with the considered wisdom of a creative writer who had been subjected to some of the same confused emotions in his own youth. Maugham conveys to us that the events and the situations depicted have been drawn from his own experience as well as those of his friends. Some instances, however, are solely products of his creative imagination and are certainly not grounded in real life incidents.

The personal element in *Of Human Bondage*, which charts the life and adventures of a young man in 'Blackstable' and 'Tercanbury' (fictionalized versions of Whitstable and Canterbury where Maugham lived during his childhood and later years, respectively) has been a matter of great interest and curiosity to readers the world over but one needs to be wary in trying to identify the protagonist with the author himself for Philip Carey's adventures are not a precise transcript of the latter's ordeals and encounters in life. Though Maugham acknowledges the fact that many incidents in Philip's early years are based on occurrences and episodes that transpired in his own life, the book remains a novel and none must be beguiled into believing that everything that happens in the book documents the life of the author.

Despite all the misery and suffering that *Of Human Bondage* depicts the emergence of the protagonist from hurtful insecurity to spiritual liberation and maturity is positive in spirit and his eventual realization that life has no meaning like that of his creator, Maugham, enables him to come to terms with existence.

Of Human Bondage tells the story of Philip Carey's life from his birth till the time he is thirty years old. The novel opens with the death of his widowed mother and his adoption as a diffident boy with a club-foot by his uncle, the Vicar of Blackstable. Philip is sent to a good school but he revolts and protests against the ecclesiastical career that his uncle tries to force on him. He pursues painting in Paris till he is convinced of his lack of genius in the art. Subsequently, after struggling against poverty and an irrational passion for an unscrupulous and despicable girl, Mildred, he settles down as a doctor and marries another girl, Sally Athelny, who is much younger than himself and, though he cares for her, she does not arouse in him the kind of passionate love he had once felt for Mildred.

The earlier chapters of *Of Human Bondage* are dispassionately, unemotionally and simply written and have a cheerless and dismal ring about them. The opening chapter delineates bleakly a predicament in which a mother on the verge of death sees her young son for the last time. In Chapter V, it is heart-rending to see this ill-fated woman have her photographs taken—"she wanted her son to know what she looked like at the end". This episode was lifted from the life of the author who had on his bedside table a photograph of his charming mother taken in 1882. Right till the end of the book, there are numerous incidents extracted from Maugham's life. The minutiae of activities in the hospital and Philip's encounters in the Out Patient's Department are unmistakably transcribed from his personal experiences. The protagonist's visions of journeying to the Far East, to countries like Malaya, Siam, China and India and other distant destinations are very similar to Maugham's own. This drawing of parallels between the writer and his character is done with greater conviction after being acquainted with Maugham's own admission that the model he has used for his characters is Somerset Maugham. In the novel under consideration, we witness a man who is conscious of and affected by the unwarranted agony and inexplicable cruelty in the world around, assuming scepticism, cynicism, and distrust as his weapons and rejecting sentimentalism which most men adopt as a measure of security and as a guard against the unfeeling world. *Of Human Bondage* is the author's austere recollection of his loneliness and frustration in youth and of his firm belief in the doctrine of self-reliance for faith in God or religion he had shed early in life. There is an incident in Philip's childhood which is probably referred to in *The Summing Up* (Section 65) when the author says that in *Of Human Bondage*, he tried to project his own loss of religious faith through the portrayal of the central character. Philip observes that his uncle believes literally in the wisdom of the proverb "faith can remove mountains". He naively prays for his club-foot to disappear before the start of the new school session. On that specific day, he wakes up hoping to find himself cured but nothing of the kind seems to have happened. At breakfast time, he asks for an explanation in a veiled manner and the vicar responds by stating that the failure to remove the mountain must be due to absence of faith. Philip sardonically retorts, "I suppose no one ever has enough faith".

An important point to be marked regarding *Of Human Bondage* is that towards the end, the novel swerves sharply away from the course of Maugham's life. Maugham did not marry till about twenty years after he qualified as a doctor and till he attained distinction as a playwright. Also, he did not marry an uneducated girl like Sally but a qualified and eligible career woman. Significantly, when he wrote *Of Human Bondage* he was still unmarried.

Coming now to the "novelistic" part of *Of Human Bondage*, the divergences of Philip's life from Maugham's are many and strengthen the belief in the element of "fiction" in the work. Generally, in the early part of the novel some of the minor factual differences between the experiences of Philip and Maugham remain undistorted and verifiable: Mrs. Maugham, the novelist's mother, died in 1882, Philip's mother in 1885; Mrs. Maugham died in Paris, Mrs. Carey in London; in the novel the father is shown to have died first. As already mentioned earlier, Whitstable becomes Blackstable and Canterbury becomes Tercanbury. Maugham's aunt died when he was still pursuing his course in Medicine and her husband, the Vicar, married again three years before his death in 1897.

A parallel may also be instituted between the physical abnormalities of the novel's protagonist and his creator. Maugham never had a club-foot like Philip did, but the agony and embarrassment caused by his stammer was often as traumatic as the distress caused by a more conspicuous and physically perceptible deformity. Philip grew from the simplicity and naivety of his childhood to the grating and grinding awareness of the derision he was subjected to on account of his club-foot. An excerpt from Chapter XIII of the novel tells us, "Philip passed from the innocence of childhood to bitter consciousness of himself by the ridicule which the club-foot had excited." A similar sense of humiliation was often occasioned by Maugham's stammer, but this stutter in the novel is substituted by a more obvious physical deformity, a club-foot. This alternative chosen by the author is also a conscious effort to fictionalize facts. The moving incident of Philip's prayer to be rid of his deformity is drawn directly from Maugham's own experience of his stammer not disappearing despite his fervent belief in the unlimited powers of God, the Almighty. It is this unfulfilled hope that led to his first religious disillusionment in life.

The record of Philip's stimulating year at Heidelberg in Germany is closely autobiographical. For Maugham, too, as for Philip, it had been an exciting year of growing up like his protagonist, and again, Maugham had not been very sure about his choice of profession when he returned from Germany in 1892. After having undergone a short spell of training for becoming a chartered accountant he decided to join the medical school at the age of eighteen; Philip was much older when he started his studies in Medicine. Though not a very bright student, Maugham never failed like Philip did and he completed his course in five years at the age of twenty-three.

Miss Wilkinson's character is based on an Alsatian friend of Maugham's uncle and the model for Fanny Price, the governess was a plaintive and pitiable girl he was acquainted with in Paris in 1904. A question that still remains to be answered is who was the original for Mildred in real life? The intensity of the portrayal and the incisively graphic description of the character is evidence of the fact that she was certainly not a figment of his imagination. The Mildred tale only vaguely and remotely echoes what Maugham had experienced in his youth. The latter vehemently states that the Mildred incidents are all primarily fabricated. The only one that replicates an experience of Maugham is the one in which Philip finances Mildred's and Griffith's trip to Oxford. Maugham, too, had once given five pounds to his rival in love. However, whether Mildred's character is inspired by a real life person or is largely fictional is immaterial for she remains a fully realized individual who is unforgettable and has come alive in the novel as one of the most detestable women characters in British fiction.

Another blend of fact and fiction is evident in the observation that unlike Philip, Maugham never pursued a course in painting in Paris although he did live there sometime during the early years of the century. Maugham, however, never experienced such extreme indigence. The character of Cronshaw was suggested by an idiosyncratic and capricious poet called Aleister Crowley; Cronshaw conveys Maugham's message that life should be lived for aesthetic pleasure and each experience only adds a motif to the complexity of the pattern of existence.

Of Human Bondage, then, is neither an unalloyed autobiography nor a work of pure fiction stemming from the author's creative imagination. It is a work that makes the best of the interaction and reciprocity between the two genres of literature, autobiography and fiction. Autobiography here becomes a mode of literature and lends verisimilitude to the narrative which though drawing profusely from the writer's own experiences in life gains in credulity and vitality as a piece of fictional art.

References

1. Ian Ousby, ed., *The Cambridge Guide to Literature in English* (Cambridge: Cambridge University Press, 1988, rpt. 1991).
2. Cited in John Brophy, *Somerset Maugham* (Essex: Longmans, Green & Co., 1952, rpt. 1958).

20

Shakespeare: The Bard Par Excellence

Vandana Datta

There should be no exaggeration in saying that the Elizabethan age is predominantly an age of poetry. Even drama for which this age is well-known, produced the finest poetry of its times and it did so, because of the predominance of Shakespeare. He was decidedly first and foremost a poet. Not to talk of the sonnets and the long poems, his plays—comedies as well as tragedies—are also full of the gems of poetry. If we undertake a journey of the plays of Shakespeare from the beginning to the end, we'll find language put to varied uses—ellipses, puns, metaphors. Perhaps, Shakespeare enjoyed nothing more than playing with language. No summary can do justice to the variety of Shakespeare's poetic effects. Since it is beyond the scope of this paper to analyze all of Shakespeare's plays to go into the nuances of his poetic genius, some of them have been selected here for concentrated study.

When Shakespeare began writing, the English theatre was dominated by Marlowe. It was in his hands that the Elizabethan imagination was concretized on the English stage. His 'mighty line', the resounding blank verse echoed the colonial aspirations of the English people and brought new life to the English theatre. Will, determination and self-confidence that knew no limits found expression in eloquent verse. The intoxication with power is amply manifest in these lines from *Tamburlaine:* 'Is it not passing brave to be a King,/ And ride in triumph through Persepolis?' Equally highly charged are the passionate lines that describe the emotional condition of Faustus in compelling imagery:

> Curst be the parents that engendered me:
> No Faustus, curse thyself, curse Lucifer,
> That hath deprived thee of the joys of heaven.
>
> *The clock striketh twelve.*
>
> O it strikes, it strikes: now body turn to air,
> Or Lucifer will bear thee quickly to hell.
>
> *Thunder and lightening.*
>
> O soul, be changed into little water drops,
> And fall into the Ocean, ne'er to be found.
> Thunder, and enter devils.
> My God, my God, looke not so fierce at me. (Act V, sc. iii, *ll* 184-90)[1]

There is flexibility in the tempo as it corresponds to the rise and fall in the emotion. It is this great blank verse that Shakespeare inherited from Marlowe and made it his own.

The first account of Shakespeare's pre-eminence as a dramatist is by Meres in his *Palladis Tamiab*, 1598:

> "As Plautus and Seneca are accounted the best for comedy and tragedy among the Latins, so Shakespeare among the English is the most excellent in both kinds for the stage...."[2]

With the taste for drama formed by Marlowe, it was quite natural for Shakespeare to begin in the prevailing fashion. He did so with *Titus Andronicus*. Modelled on Kyd's *The Spanish Tragedy*, it is a play full of horrors, its theme being the revenge of Tamora, the Queen of Goths, on Titus Andronicus and his retaliation. Titus and his daughter are shockingly mutilated by Tamora's device, and the Roman, in retaliation, having killed the Queen's two sons, bakes their heads and serves them up to their mother in a Thysetean banquet. Though the action is highly improbable, the play does reveal the genius of the playwright. It is a better structured play than those of Marlowe. In matters of style, it is Marlowian—the extravagant, bombastic blank verse abounding in classical allusion is very much there:

Now by the burning tapers of the sky,
That shone so brightly when this boy was got,
He dies upon my scimitar's sharp point
That touches this my first-born son and heir!
I tell you, younglings, not Enceladus,
With all his threatening band of Typhon's brood,
Nor great Alcides, nor the god of war,
Shall seize this prey out of his father's hands.

(Act IV, sc. ii, *ll* 89-96)[3]

But the play also demonstrates that, Shakespeare possesses something that Marlowe lacked—the intensity of emotion, the power of pathos. This is Titus talking about his dumb and mutilated daughter:

It was my deer; and he that wounded her
Hath hurt me more than had he killed me dead:
For now I stand as one upon a rock
Environed with a wilderness of sea,
Who marks the waxing tide grow wave by wave,
Expecting ever when some envious surge
Will in his brinish bowels swallow him.
This way to death my wretched sons are gone;
Here stands my other son, a banished man,
And here my brother, weeping at my woes:
But that which gives my soul the greatest spurn,
Is dear Lavinia, dearer than my soul.

It is these speeches in blank verse that pave the way for the great soliloquies of *Hamlet* or for the speech of Brutus in *Julius Caeser*, to name a few. In *Titus Andronicus*, as also in the other early plays, mostly comedies, we see tendencies that blossom to their fullest in the mature plays. Comedies are meant to be in a lighter vein. The bombastic style of Marlowe makes way for playful thought and feeling. The regular simplicity of blank verse is heightened by the metrical harmony:

Swift as a shadow, short as any dream;
Brief as the lightening in the collied night,

That, in a spleen, unfolds both heaven and earth,
And ere a man hath power to say "Behold"!
The jaws of darkness do devour it up:
So quick bright things come to confusion.

There is ingenious verbal wit in formal and regular metrical patterns, as in *Love's Labour's Lost:*

If she be made of white and red,
Her faults will ne'er be known;
For blushing cheeks by faults are bred,
And fears by pale white shown.
Then if she fear, or be to blame,
By this you shall not know;
For still her cheeks possess the same
Which native she doth owe.

(Act. I, sc. ii, *ll* 95-102)

In these plays, Shakespeare's development as an artist lies in fusing the lyric with the dramatic. Fancy sometimes gets to play with unbridled freedom so that there is hardly any touch with reality. At the same time, pervading behind everything, there is an atmosphere of humanity and society. This helps in building scenes of delicate beauty—as the courtship scenes in *As You Like It:*

No, no, Orlando; men are April when they woo, December when they wed; maids are May when they are maids, but the sky changes when they are wives. I will be more jealous of thee than a Barbary cock-pigeon over his hen, more clamourous than a parrot against rain, more new-fangled than an ape, more giddy in my desires than a monkey. I will weep for nothing, like Diana in the fountain, and I'll do that when you are disposed to be merry; I will laugh like a hyen, and that when thou art inclin'd to sleep.

(Act IV, sc. i, *ll* 131-39)

These lines in simple prose—Shakespeare does sometimes indulge in prose, but mostly he keeps to blank verse—sparkle with the effulgence of wit and delicate humour and have a poetic quality because they are seeped in tender feelings. On the other hand there are the sombre, philosophical verses of Jacques seeped in wisdom:

All the world's a stage,
And all the men and women merely players;
They have their exits and entrances;
And one man in his time plays man parts,
His act being seven ages. At first the infant,...

(Act II, sc. vii, *ll* 140-45)

Again, it is the lyrical vein that lends to the scene between Viola and the Duke in *Twelfth Night*, a transcendent beauty:

Duke: ...
For women are as roses, whose fair flow'r
Being once displayed doth fall that very hour.
Viola: And so they are; alas, that they are so!
To die, even when they to perfection grow!

(Act II, sc. iv, *ll* 37-40)

Equally unforgettable is the garden scene in *The Merchant of Venice*. The images come alive:

Portia: ...
How far that little candle throws his beams!
So shines a good deed in a naughty world.
Nerissa: When the moon shone, we did not see the candle.
Portia: So doth the greater glory dim the less:
A substitute shines brightly as a king
Until a king be by, and then his state
Empties itself, as doth an inland brook
Into the main of waters.

(Act V, sc. i, *ll* 90-97)

The didactic strain in Portia's oft-quoted speech on the qualities of mercy does in no way undermine the smooth flow of the blank verse. Shakespeare has moved much beyond the end-stopped lines of Marlowe. It is not in a leap that Shakespeare achieved perfection. He began where Marlowe began, with the mainly end-stopped, rigid form of blank verse which in his short literary career Marlowe hardly outgrew.

Shakespeare experimented with rhythmic construction of the lines so that he came very close to perfection in the overflowing line, though there were still a number of end-stopped ones:

> ...It is twice blest:
>
> It blesseth him that gives and him that takes.
>
> 'Tis mightiest in the mightiest; it becomes
>
> The throned monarch better than his crown;...
>
> (Act IV, sc.i, *ll* 181-84)

A finer example can be had from *Romeo and Juliet*:

> ...Ah dear Juliet
> Why art thou yet so fair? Shall I believe
> That unsubstantial death is amorous,
> And that the lean abhorred monster keeps
> Thee here in dark to be his paramour?
> For fear of that I still will stay with thee,
> And never from this palace of dim night
> Depart again: here, here will I remain
> With worms that are thy chambermaids; O here
> Will I set up my everlasting rest,...
>
> (Act V, sc. iii, *ll* 102-10)

An even better one can be had from *Macbeth*:

> Thou hast it now, King, Cawdor, Glamis, all,
> As the weird women promised; and, I fear,
> Thou play'dst most foully for't; yet it was said,
> It should not stand in thy posterity.
>
> (Act iii, sc. i, *ll* 1-10)

Romeo's speech has long sentences spoken in a feverish state of emotion—the line overflowing into one another express this heightened condition of his. Banquo, on the other hand, is recapitulating past events—hence the short broken phrases with complete disregard of the end-pause. What Shakespeare aimed at is an utterance which is natural for the character in his/her situation. The young dramatist seems to be listening to a rhythm that his heart played, not to any rigid sound pattern. And so he could evolve a speech that came close to the impulses and emotions of the character. This is how Shylock speaks:

> 'Fair Sir, you spit on me on Wednesday last;
> You spurn'd me such a day; another time
> You called me dog; and for these courtesies
> I'll lend you thus much moneys.
>
> (Act I, sc. iii, *ll* 121-24)

The Elizabethan convention of regarding a Jew as villain is the starting point for Shakespeare too. But he humanizes his villain and seeks reasons for his villainy. The flow of the rhythm, the calculated pauses and breaks serve to bring out the accumulation of the indignant irony.

In this context, a masterpiece is the play *Othello* where the diction, the verse, the phrases play a great role in bringing out the contrast between Othello and Iago.[4] Their speeches are characterized by images which reveal the character of the speaker. Othello's lines possess pride, a high self-esteem, a clarity of thought and vision and sincerity:

> ...I fetch my life and being
> From men of royal siege; and my demerits
> May speak unbonneted to as proud a fortune
> As this that I have reached. For know, Iago,
> But that I love the gentle Desdemona,
> I would not my unhoused free condition
> Put into circumscription and confine
> For the sea's worth....
> ...
> My parts, my title, and my perfect soul,
> Shall manifest me rightly.
>
> (Act I, sc. ii, *ll* 21-28)

The sea is a metaphor that conveys Othello's internal experience. When this is placed alongside Iago's first address to Othello the contrast becomes clear:

> Though in the trade of war I have slain men,
> Yet do I hold it very stuff o' th' conscience
> To do no contrived murder.
>
> (Act I, sc. ii, *ll* 1-3)

Iago has already appeared in the first scene and made his hostility clear. The audience already familiar with his grossness immediately realizes that this is a picture that he is presenting to Othello. 'I am not what I am' he has said already and what he offers to Othello is just a 'show of service'.

Another distinct quality of Shakespeare's poetry is its metaphysical traits. A typical example is this lament of Richard II:

> I wasted time, and now doth time waste me;
> For now hath time made me his numbering clock;
> My thoughts are minutes and with sighs they jar
> Their watches on unto mine eyes, the outward watch,
> Whereto my finger, like a dial's point,
> Is pointing still, in cleansing them from tears.
> Now sir, the sound that tells what hour it is
> Are clamorous groans, which strike upon my heart
> Which is the bell: so sighs and tears and groans
> Show minutes, times and hours: but my time
> Runs posting on in Bolingbroke's proud joy,
> While I stand fooling here, his Jack o' the clock.

While it is true that the conceit has been stretched here out of proportion, the fact remains that Time is a favourite theme with Shakespeare. In the sonnets, he goes back to it again and again. The ravages of time and mutability and mortality are dealt with in a various ways. In his obsession with Time and also in the speech rhythm of his blank verse, he seems to be a precursor of the metaphysicals. L.C. Knights sees these similarities between him and Donne:

> 'Now "the problem of Time" is a metaphysical problem, and in various forms it is a preoccupation of some of the Metaphysical Poets. Moreover, between Shakespeare's mature verse and Donne's there are similarities which it is important to recognize—the immediacy, the images generating intense mental activity ("the intellect at the tip of the sense"), the exploiting of speech rhythm and idiom, and so on: a good deal of Mr. Eliot's account of Metaphysical Poetry applies equally—as he points out—to the

> blank verse of Shakespeare and other late Elizabethans."[5]

However, in the same breath, he distinguishes between the two: Shakespeare, he says is interested in 'experience and sensation' and not in 'speculative thought'. He makes 'finer experiences available for others, but they offer no resolution of metaphysical problems'.[6]

The theme of Time occurs in the plays too, but here there is 'no defiance, the conflict is resolved by the more or less explicit acceptance of mutability'.[7]

So much for *Othello*. As one moves to the other tragedies, one finds that there essential structure is poetic. At the height of his maturity, Shakespeare exploits the blank verse as though it were his handmaid. Smooth and pliable, it is the vehicle to express his vision of man, which includes immense possibilities, more so when the will of man is seen struggling towards a proposed end. There seems to be something lyrical about it. The feeling expressed in the cry in one of the sonnets—'Tired with all these, for restful death I cry' echoes through the anguish of Hamlet:

> Time's out of joint, O cursed spite!
> That I was born to set it right!

His soliloquies are the culmination of what Shakespeare could get out of blank verse. There is no need to repeat here the oft-quoted "To be or not to be...." What I choose to quote here is Ophelia's speech, decidedly one of the best in Shakespeare:

> O, what a noble mind is here o'erthrown!
> The courtier's, soldier's, scholar's, eye, tongue, sword;
> The expectancy and rose of the fair state,
> The glass of fashion and the mould of form,
> Th' observ'd of all observers—quite, quite down!
> And I, of ladies most deject and wretched,
> That suck'd the honey of his music vows,
> Now see that noble and most sovereign reason,
> Like sweet bells jangled, out of time and harsh;
> That unmatch'd form and feature of blown youth

Blasted with ecstasy. O woe is me
T' have seen what I have seen, see what I see.

(Act III, sc. i, *ll* 150-61)

The tragedy of Hamlet is primarily the wreck of a noble spirit. In the four great tragedies of Shakespeare, all the protagonists are in some way or the other responsible for the tragedy. Not Hamlet. He is not a participant in the rot that perpetuates in Denmark. But nobody suffers more than him. For he sees his world crushed and can do nothing about it. It is true that he postpones all action. But what action could restore his world to him? What revenge could restore his idealized image of his mother? Hence, the shattering effect on his sanity. This speech of Ophelia sums up what Hamlet was and what he has become. The images, the metaphors serve to delineate the various dimensions in which the tragedy has had its impact. The last sentence is shorn of all imagery and in bare words is able to convey the depth of Ophelia's grief.

In *King Lear,* the language matches the tone of the play. The first two acts are done in a violent mode. The feelings that dominate are passion, anger and wrath. The language has to match this and it does so very well:

Let it be so; thy truth then be thy dower!
For, by the sacred radiance of the sun,
The mysteries of Hecate and the night,
By all the operation of the orbs
From whom we do exist and cease to be,
Here I disclaim all my paternal care,
Propinquity and property of blood,
And as a stranger to my heart and me
Hold thee from this forever.

(Act I, sc. i, *ll* 107-15)

It is only in Act 4 that the picture changes. With Lear now to meet Cordelia, virtue takes the place of wrath, patience of anger and reason of passion. The language is calm and soothing—a balm to Lear's wounds:

O my dear father, restoration hang
Thy medicine on my lips, and let this kiss

Repair those violent harms that my two sisters
Have in thy reverence made!

(Act V, sc. vii, *ll* 25-28)

Macbeth is another superb example of Shakespeare's poetic genius. Not to be forgotten is the line that defines the objective correlative of Lady Macbeth's guilt:

Here's the smell of blood still:
all the perfumes of Arabia will not sweeten this little hand.

(Act V, sc. i, *ll* 49-50)

or again, Macbeth's conscience pricking him in this sleep-metaphor:

Methought I heard a voice cry 'Sleep no more!
Macbeth does murder sleep'—...

(Act II, sc. ii, *ll* 35-36)

Or again there is *Antony and Cleopatra* – a love story bound to be doomed, the only redeeming factor being poetry:

Eternity was in our lips and eyes,
Bliss in our brows' bent, none our parts so poor
But was a race of heaven. They are so still,
Or thou, the greatest soldier of the world,
Art turned the greatest liar.

(Act I, sc. iii, *ll* 35-39)

And these lines are nothing short of a masterstroke:

Peace, peace!
Dost thou not see my baby at my breast
That sucks the nurse asleep?

(Act V, sc. ii, *ll* 305-07)

The fact is that examples can be multiplied and multiplied. There is simply no end to illustrate the ways in which Shakespeare excelled as a poet. This paper is too small to do justice to his great talent. I, therefore, conclude with the words of Schlegel:

"...with the exception of a few witticisms now become unintelligible or foreign to the present taste, nothing could be taken away, nothing added, nothing otherwise arranged, without mutilating or disfiguring the perfect work."[8]

References

1. Christopher Marlowe, *Doctor Faustus*, Calcutta: OUP, 1980.
2. Quoted by W.J. Courthope, *A History of English Poetry*, Vol. IV, London: Macmillan, 1911, 54.
3. *The Complete Works of Shakespeare*, (by arrangement with Collins), Delhi: Rupa & Co., 1989. All extracts quoted in the paper are from this edition.
4. J.C. Maxwell, 'Shakespeare: The Middle Plays' in *The Age of Shakespeare*, 'A Guide To English Literature' Vol. 2, ed. Boris Ford, Great Britain: Penguin, 1956, 223-34.
5. L.C. Knights, 'Shakespeare's Sonnets' in *Elizabethan Poetry: Modern Essays in Criticism*, ed. Paul J. Alpers, London: OUP, 1967, 294-95.
6. *Ibid*., 295.
7. *Ibid*., 297.
8. Quoted by W.J. Courthope, *A History of English Poetry*, op. cit.

21

William Blake: A Symbolist with a Prophetic Vision

Sanghita Sen

Blake does not appear to be a true "*Romantic*" so far as his apparently eventless personal life and the age that he lived in are concerned. Among all Romantic poets the closest in age to him was William Wordsworth and the age difference has been 13 years. Dweller of quite an uninteresting and unadventurous life, Blake did not earn fame during his life time for his art. It is indeed difficult categorizing Blake's work in one homogeneous genre. However his influence on the poets of later ages proves paramount in terms of his treatment of traditional thematic binaries such as heaven and hell, knowledge and innocence, good and evil and external reality versus spiritual truth. The relevance of Blake's vision is of paramount importance even in the context of our contemporary world, as Northrop Frye rightly notes in the Preface of the 1969 edition of his seminal book *Fearful Symmetry*,

> that reactionary and radical forces alike are once more in the grip of the nihilistic psychosis that Blake described so powerful in *Jerusalem*, one of the most hopeful signs is the immensely increased sense of the urgency and immediacy of what Blake had to say.

A fervent dissenter against all conventional types of institutional oppression Blake zealously espouses gender as well as racial equality and that justice be made available to all.

Hayes (2004) points out that Blake's prophetic poems, viz. *The Marriage of Heaven and Hell* (c.1793), *America: A Prophesy* (1793), *Europe: A Prophesy* (1794), *Visions of the Daughters of Albion* (1793), *The Book of Urizen* (1794) and *Jerusalem* (1804) promise the restoration of a "a state of eternal bliss" after the apocalypse1. Blake, like Shelley, dreams of a millennium that renders justice to all despite differences and this dream is clearly articulated in *Jerusalem*,

> I will not cease from mental fight,
> Nor shall my sword sleep in my hand
> Till we have built Jerusalem
> In England's green and pleasant land.

The portrayal of feminine figures in his prophetic poems bears testimony to his resistance to the misogynous tradition that holds the woman responsible for the man's fall. In Blake the figure of Eve is not "just a woman but the Emanation" or a means to perceive the world. By portraying Eve in such light Blake not only recognizes "women's existence" in the world that is considered to be essentially androcentric but also acknowledges sexual power. A sympathetic stance for women's cause was made possible due his recognition of as well as resistance to the discriminatory practice that ran rampant in the society and potential of sexual power that was socially subdued seriously unlike most of his contemporaries. Such a stance makes him highly relevant in context of feminism and gender studies even today. Helen P. Bruder (1997) asserts that,

> Blake is of value to feminism not because he maintained an exemplary and unwavering feminist commitment but rather because he took sexual power seriously. (36)

His spirit of rebellion not only foregrounded issues pertaining to the women's question and sexual power but also posed a strong resistance to the contemporary elitist attitude to epistemology in general and to Art in particular that traditionally equated classical style with elevated style. Such an elitist and exclusionary stance attempting to keep art within the reach of people "classically educated" seems to have enervated many, including another great Romantic such as

John Keats. It was his constant effort to offer an opportunity of aesthetic pleasure to common people that redeems them, from the bondage of the mundane, through art making it available to them

> a Great Majority of Fellow Mortals who can Elucidate My Visions, and Particularly they have been Elucidated by Children, who have taken a greater delight in contemplating my Pictures than I even hoped. (23rd Aug. 1799—Blake's letter to Dr. Trusler, in Keynes, 1957, 793-94—Capitalization original)

This sense of resistance to the epistemological hegemony of his day that attempted to exclude the mass from the purview of artistic appreciation and the desire to make Art available to the common people may have prompted him to take recourse to popular religious imagery drawn from the Bible and "emblematic imagery of earlier centuries" (Bindman 1986) as a vehicle of his poetic communication and prophetic vision. His constant experiment with forms and medium is evident in his attempt to make art available to the common people. Personalising the connection between life and belief to penetrate into the secrets of the real world around us through poetry that bombard our day to day quotidian existence—to read the untold stories of our daily mundane existence and to hear the silenced voices as well as obliterated existence: when poetry is made to uphold the emotional response of the society and excavate the untold lives of forgotten presences and insignificant absences, what we get is William Blake. For some moments his poetry enables his readers to walk into someone else's shoes—cry their share of tears and suffer their share of pain—till the blissful state of elevation through poetry and art is achieved.

Stimulated by the contemporary socio-political issues, domestic encounters in his day to day experience his poetry reflects the "dark fusion of his mind" (Roberts 2008) in his depiction of secrets of human life and existence as part of a divine network inspired by "visions" that Blake saw since his early childhood (Bentley 2001). While his mundane unadventurous life may prejudice his readers to consider him as a *true Romantic*, his "visions," attachment to the past, viz. Italian Renaissance and Classical antiquity, aesthetic sensibilities, a great mastery over his art and concern for the suffering humanity certainly qualify him to be regarded as a most distinguished Romantic and prophetic visionary.

His prophetic vision, radical Imagination and the spirit of resistance may have its origin in his childhood exposure through his parents' faith in non-conformism to a symbolic religious language mat amalgamated sexual and religious imagery (Roberts 2008). We must remember here that his mother had been a member of the protestant Moravian Church that has its origin in the place now known as Czech Republic in her maiden days spent in Nottinghamshire. Bindman (1986) observes that,

> [i]t is impossible to miss in Blake's prophetic writings the combination of anti-Catholicism and apocalyptic imagery so characteristic of earlier Protestant polemic in northern countries. (712)

His characters and imagery creatively symbolize inspiration and represent his resistance to oppressive institutions such as the state, society and church.

An important part of Blakean aesthetic is the re-creation of the existing symbolic order to represent the "fusion" of Blake's inner self and prophetic vision. As Northrop Frye (1969) rightly observes that the artistic mind is "something in which the barrier between 'inside' and 'outside' dissolves" though the power to do so originates in the mind that is actively involved in the project because the "work of art is the product of this creative perception" (p. 85). That which is unperceivable by the common mind blurred by materialistic myopia can be clearly seen by such an illuminated mind. Art enables one to see "images as permanent living forms outside time and space" (*Ibid.*). Hence the mundane and apparently uninteresting details of common lives acquire the status of the poetic *representability* by the magic touch of Blake's poetic genius.

Blake fuses knowledge gained from his day to day encounter with life with his Imagination to create his poetic universe. For him no distinction exists between knowledge and art as it does in case of Plato. By virtue of its capability to illumine human mind and soul no knowledge is ever considered illegitimate by Blake no matter what it unfolds. Frye (1951) comments mat for Blake "both knowledge and art are recreation" though Plato distinguishes between the two by considering the knowledge as recollection and art as imitation. His representation of the realities and secrets of life emerges out of a wonderful blend of knowledge with Imagination. As Bindman (1986) points out that Plate 76, the frontis piece of the final chapter of *Jerusalem* that shows the Tree of Life to which the Christ figure is nailed is actually the Tree of Knowledge. He draws our attention to the painter poet's attempt to establish a connection between the Tree of Life and Human Imagination through such a depiction. This particular reception of knowledge and art as complementary to each other fits fine with his non-conformist stance. Blake, the master symbolist, devices and uses symbols to uphold his unique prophetic vision through his art that is a combination of visual forms and words.

"Blake does indeed seem to epitomize Symbolist doctrine" —Bidney (1987) observes. An avid advocate of the Spiritual, Blake believes in reality of visions and communicating with "symbolic essences"—magic, neo-platonic universe and the creation of his poetry depends much on this belief. He believes that Art's chief function lies in its capacity to "reveal the truth of the spiritual world by liberating the imagination" (Bowman 1951, 53). He considers the act of revealing the truth of the spiritual world to be the "great task" of an artist. Prompted by such a belief and aesthetic responsibility bestowed upon artists, he declares:—"I rest not from my great task!" His aesthetic conviction and intended representative role as a poet to unfold the spiritual essence to humanity that he believes to be the driving force of the universe emerge apparent in the very beginning of his epic poem entitled *Jerusalem* (1804)

> ... I rest not from my great task!
> To open the Eternal Worlds, to open the immortal Eyes
> Of Man inwards into the Worlds of Thought, into
> Eternity

Ever expanding in the Bosom of God, the Human Imagination. (Jerusalem, I, lines 2-5)[2]

For Blake Imagination is that potent positive force that enables an inspired individual to illumine the unknown or that lies beyond common human knowledge. He considers Imagination as a power that separates a poet from the rest of humanity. The Imagination holds open before humanity the divine secrets of creation and existence. Hence this responsibility confers upon poets a prophetic role and turns them one of the "unacknowledged legislators of mankind," as Shelley may put it.

Hallam (1831) categorizes poets into two categories, viz. *poets of sensation* and *poets of reflection* in his famous discussion on the Picturesque of the Nineteenth Century English poetry. Poets of sensation responded in a strangely original way to create something of "a sort of magic" through their poetic expressions in the category of which William Blake seems to fall. W.B. Yeats considers this magic to emanate from "disembodied ecsta[sies]" in which the poetic expressions corresponds to "intuited spiritual essences" (Gibson, p. 16). The lines mentioned above epitomize this desire.

Blake is considered by many as a mystic and his mysticism is taken to be the foundation of his art. This mysticism gives rise to his prophetic vision that is expressed through his poetry, painting and engravings. As Ribot observes in his *Essay on the Creative Imagination*

> The root of the mystic imagination consists of a tendency to incarnate the ideal in the sensible-to suppose in things a supra-natural principle that reveals itself to whoever may penetrate to it. Its fundamental character, from which the others are derived, is thus a way of thinking symbolically. (Translated from French by Albert H.N. Baron (Chicago 1906), 221-22.)

What Ribot observes in terms of mystic imagination matches perfectly with what Blake himself thought about the agentive nature of imagination being realized through *vision* to enable the poet to travel beyond the bondage and imprisonment of the real world that they encounter—"The Man, who never in his Mind & Thoughts travel'd to Heaven is No Artist" (Blake, *Annotations to Reynolds*, in Keynes 1969, 458). The current essay will concentrate mainly on his poetry in this light though not in an attempt to provide a decisive interpretation of his aesthetic sensibility.

The impact of "visions" on his use of symbolism can also have a connection with his attachment to the Swedenborgian Society in London. His attachment with the Swedenborgian Society introduced and immersed the poet in the tradition of Swedenborgian Symbolism. His poetry as well as his paintings bear the visible influence of the *Visions of Emmanuel Swedenborg*. However the genius of Blake lies in making what was the "raw material" into an aesthetic object of a heightened spiritual nature. Bloom has rightly pointed out that Blake has been "a system maker, a mythographer who catalogues his meanings" (10). The Swedenborgian symbols of exclusive religious implication upholding the vision of a sage has been elevated to the level of art by the magic touch of the poetic craftsmanship rendered by William Blake. Nevertheless, such symbols proved to be a fertile source of inspiration to ignite the right emotion in the prophet poet who viewed in Swedenborgian representations a replica of his own "visions" of the world which is inherently "symbolic in its whole and in its part" (Katheleen Raine 1969, 4). Raine (1969) notes

> There is no literary value in Swedenborg's symbolism, and nothing could be less poetic that the "visions" of that sage. It is merely raw material. But to a mind naturally gifted, the Swedenborgian doctrines of influx and correspondence present a world symbolic in its whole and in its parts, not by some literary choice but in its very nature, a world informed throughout with imaginative meaning and beauty. (4)

The idea of influx proposed by Swedenborg deems the spiritual life and energy to be manifested in nature via natural forms and appearances (Raine 2002). He espouses a correspondence between the materialistic world of our day to day encounter and the spiritual world in which the "natural world exists and subsists." It is this complementary perception of correspondence between the two apparently exclusive worlds that makes the idea of communion between the spiritual essence and its outward manifestation possible. Blake, too, considers the manifestations of the physical world as symbolic in its very essence though unlike Swedenborg he contends that these forms remain in their *perfect* state in the poet's mind alone as "these are not Abstracted nor Compounded from Nature, but are from Imagination" (Blake 1808, 61). As the sensible representation of the spiritual essence, the reality reflects it and functions as the driving force of ephemeral mortal life. Symbolism of Blake is just a natural extension of these beliefs. In fact the poetry of Blake epitomizes this Swedenborgian theory of influx and correspondence to a great extent. It is to be noted mat Blake's symbolism is by no means sacramental whereas Swedenborg's is heavily so. However, the uniqueness of Blakean symbolism lies in its departure from the traditional symbols and introduction of symbols that is original and bears the mark of Blake's creative genius.

Blake's creative genius finds expression in a blending of forms to represent the aesthetic condensed through symbols created out of "certain propinquity with the beautiful" (Shelley, 1921). Shelley considers poets to be people "who draw into a certain propinquity with the beautiful" (*Defence of Poetry*). In *Defence* he defines a poem as "the very image of life expressed in its eternal truth" and what brings life to poetry is imagery. He considers imagery (images) as one of the most important aspects other than Imagination for poetry as it "acts in a divine and unapprehended manner, beyond and above consciousness." In the art of Blake one may witness a "thousand unapprehended combinations of thought" in order to unfurl thc veiled splendour of the world as Shelley puts it in his *Defence*.

Blake tried to capture this "picture of eternity" as termed by Shelley through such apocalyptic images that owe their origin in the Bible. The picture of apocalypse as we come across in the Book of Revelation forecasts the end of the current *order* and restoration of the perfect order by establishing the Kingdom of God on the Earth. A similar urge can be seen in Yeats in his conceptualizing of the Second Coming. Here the vision of the apocalypse and apocalyptic imagery are strikingly similar. It is the vision of apocalypse in which "[t]he ceremony of innocence is drowned". A Blakean premonition is repeated in portraying the "rough beast" that has "a gaze blank" and is as "pitiless as the sun". This portrayal is reminiscent of the image of Blake's tyger that could only arouse an uncanny fear in observers at its "fearful symmetry." In sharp contrast to the Lamb in *Songs of Innocence*, an image that symbolizes the benevolent Christ figure, the image of the tyger poses an antithesis that can be taken as the predecessor of the Yeatsian antichrist in the *Second Coming*. In Blakean symbolism the brutalized animals signify not only the fallen state of man but the degeneration of Nature as well. His use of brutalized animal images such as the tyger and vulture is intended to denote this unmistakable degeneration that the man and Nature are fallen prey to (Baine and Baine 1975). Blake paints the tyger as cruel and visionless with a retracted nose indicating spiritual insensitivity. Such a portrayal of the tyger to symbolize bloodthirsty cruelty as opposed to the lion image that signify noble attributes runs parallel with the poetic and artistic tradition of the Western World. For example, in *King Lear* William Shakespeare uses the symbol of tiger for Goneril and Regan to signify wickedness in their very nature.

The binary of what the tyger represents is the symbol of the lamb. The lamb signifies innocence and Christ who is consistently represented in the literature as the Lamb of God. The uniqueness of Blake lies in adding a new secular dimension to the symbol of lamb. For Blake the lamb also symbolizes "the quality of divinity which man can attain as well as emulate" apart from its sacrificial and innocent connotation (Wilkinson 1962, 566). Wilkinson (1962) observes that "[i]n his 140 uses of the lamb image Blake consistently utilized the lamb as a symbol of all that is divine in man" (*Ibid.*). Though the tyger is considered to be the binary of the lamb symbol in *Songs of*

Experience, surprisingly Blake never uses the tyger symbol to connote anything either related to Christ or to any other benevolent forces. In this sense Blake uses the tyger symbol in a rather traditional way to represent the vindictive avarice that characterizes the world of experience. The predacious nature of tiger and wolf is placed in sharp contrast with the timid and helpless lamb that is their prey. However, the connotation of the tyger symbol in his prophetic poems differs from the connotation of the symbol in *Experience*.

As Wilkinson (1962) points out that the most comprehensive appearance of the tyger symbol occurs in his major prophesies through a highly developed system of animal imagery. For Blake the blissful "state of visionary, pre-lapsarian Innocence" is turned into a "visionless, post-lapsarian Experience" with the fall of Albion. This is a state when the feeling of love is taken over by terror and hatred completely reversing the pre-lapsarian values; universal principles of amnesty, brotherhood and liberation are replaced by disruptive oppressive powers of culpability and law, repugnance, self-love and violence of which the tyger is a symbol. Wilkinson (1962) notes

> Here Blake clearly implies that reason, degraded and subordinated to wrath, petrifies. When the tigers of wrath assume control of the intellect, the human imagination becomes a spiritual wasteland where no vision can exist. (573)

The visionary poet could see in the symbol of tyger, the ultimate terror in a world of Experience pervaded by the evil. The same poet visualizes the Lamb as the final guarantee of benevolence and benignity of the Creator of the world towards the child of Innocence. This perspective of the animal imagery will enable us to understand the symbolism in several poems in *Innocence* and *Experience* that represents to us the prophetic vision of the painter poet.

References

Baine, R.M. and Baine, M.R. (1975). 'Blake's Other Tigers, and "The Tyger".' Studies in English Literature, 1500-1900, Vol. 15, No. 4, Nineteenth Century (Autumn, 1975), 563-78.

Bentley, G.E. Jr. (2001). *The Stranger from Paradise: A Biography of William Blake*. New Haven: Yale Univ. Press.

Bidney, M. "A Russian Symbolist View of William Blake Author(s)" Comparative Literature, Vol. 39, No. 4 (Autumn, 1987), 327-39.

Bindman, D. (1986). "William Blake and Popular Religious Imagery." *The Burlington Magazine*, Vol. 128, No. 1003, Special Issue Devoted to British Art from 1500 to the Present Day (Oct., 1986), 712-18.

Blake, W. (1808). Annotations to Sir Joshua Reynolds's Discourses. London http://books.google.co.in/books?id=id=H1dersJqUNAC&pg= PA459&lpg=PA459&dq on 12.06.09.

Bruder, H.P. (1997). William Blake and the Daughters of Albion. New York: St. Martin's Press.

Connolly, T.E. (1989). "Little Girl Lost," "Little Girl Found": Blake's Reversal of the Innocence-Experience Pattern.' College Literature, Vol. 16, No. 2 (Spring, 1989), 148-66.

Frye, N. (1951). "Poetry and Design in William Blake." In *The Journal of Aesthetics and Art Criticism*, Vol. 10, No. 1 (Sep., 1951), 35-42.

Frye, N. (1969). Fearful Symmetry: A Study of William Blake. Princeton: Princeton University Press.

Hallam, A.H. (1938). "On Some of the Characteristics of Modern Poetry, and on the Lyrical Poems of Alfred Tennyson." In *The Englishman's Magazine*. http//www. wwnorton.com/college/english/nael/victorian/topic_3/hallam.htm 10.06.09

Hayes, T. (2004). "Willian Blake's Androgynous Ego-ideal." In *ELH* 71, 141-65.

Keynes, G.L. (1957). "Letter to Dr Trusler", 23rd August 1799, in Blake Complete Writings, Oxford, 793-94.

Keynes, G. (1969). Ed. *Complete Writings with Variant Readings by William Blake*. Oxford. OUP.

Partridge, E. (1923). "Inter-Relationships in Blake's Songs." In *Modern Language Notes*, Vol. 38, No. 4 (Apr., 1923), 220-23.

Raine, Kathleen (1969). Blake and Tradition. London: Routledge.

Ribot, Th. *Essay on the Creative Imagination*. Translated from the French by Albert H.N. Baron (Chicago 1906), 221-22). http://www.gutenberg.org/etext/26430 12.06.09

Roberts, J. (2008). *William Blake's Poetry*. London: Continuum.

Shelley, P.B. (1921). A Defence of Poetry, http://www.bartleby.com/27/23.html 12.06.09

Wilkinson, A.M. (1962). Illuminated: Or Not?: A Note on Blake's "Songs of Innocence and of Experience." *The Modern Language Review*, Vol. 57, No. 3 (July, 1962), 387-91.

Notes

1. Though this idea of the androgynous Utopia was considered by some as essentially misogynist, Hayes (2004) revisits this Blakean idea in the light of a paradigm shift in gender and queer studies and refutes the charge of misogyny labeled against Blake in terms of his androgynous utopia. In fact his depiction of the "visionary head" can also be taken as a resistance to code of heterosexual masculinity.
2. http://www.poetry-chaikhana.com/B/Blake William/TremblingIsi.htm 24.06.2009 at 9.00 pm.

Contributors

Bryan Reynolds, Professor of Drama, Claire Trevor School of the Arts, University of California, Irvine, US.

Joseph Fitzpatrick, Andrew W. Mellon Postdoctoral Fellow, Wesleyan University's Center for the Humanities, US.

Bruce Boehrer, Bertram H. Davis Professor, Department of English, Florida State University, Tallahassee, Florida, US.

Esterino Adami, University of Turin, Italy.

Chidananda Bhattacharya, Professor, Ex Head of Department, Rabindra Bharti University, Kolkata, West Bengal.

Kenneth Usongo, University of Denver, USA.

Carole Rozzonelli, Associate Professor in English and ITC, University of Lyon, France.

Sanjay Kumar Sinha, Reader, Department of English, Patna College, Patna University, Patna, Bihar.

N. Sharada Iyer, Head, Department of English, Vasanta College for Women, Rajghat, Varanasi, Uttar Pradesh.

Arpa Ghosh, Senior Lecturer in English, Vivekananda College for Women, Barisha, Kolkata, West Bengal.

Anita Myles, Reader in English, D.D.U. Gorakhpur University, Gorakhpur, Uttar Pradesh.

Purnendu Chatterjee, Research Scholar, Rabindra Bharati University, Kolkata, West Bengal.

Ernest L. Veyu, University of Yaounde 1, English Department, Cameroon, Africa.

Manju Dutta Gupta, Ex-Head of Department, Rabindra Bharati University, Kolkata, West Bengal.

Nandini Sahu, Reader in English (Editing), IGNOU, New Delhi.

Padmini Sahu, Department of English, NGW College, Orissa.

Vinita Singh, Ph.D, Higher Secondary Teacher, Government Higher Secondary School, Patna, Bihar.

Arindam Das, Lecturer of English, Department of Humanities, Heritage Institute of Technology, Kolkata, West Bengal.

Nishi Pulugurtha, Department of English, Brahmananda Keshab Chandra College, (Affiliated to the West Bengal State University), West Bengal.

Bristi Basu, Lecturer, Department of English Rabindra Bharati University, Kolkata, West Bengal.

Reena Mitra, Senior Reader, Department of English, Christ Church P.G. College, Kanpur, Uttar Pradesh.

Vandana Datta, Department of English, College of Commerce, Magadh University, Patna, Bihar.

Sanghita Sen, Senior Lecturer, Presidency College, Kolkata, West Bengal.